GW01418534

VALUING COMPANIES

VALUING COMPANIES

*Analysing Business
Worth*

ALAN GREGORY

WOODHEAD-FAULKNER

NEW YORK   LONDON   TORONTO   SYDNEY   TOKYO   SINGAPORE

First published 1992 by
Woodhead-Faulkner
Campus 400, Maylands Avenue
Hemel Hempstead
Hertfordshire, HP2 7EZ
A division of
Simon & Schuster International Group

Typeset in 10/11½pt Bembo
by Hands Fotoset

Printed in Great Britain by BPCC Wheatons Ltd, Exeter

British Library Cataloguing in Publication Data

A catalogue record for this book is available from the British Library

ISBN 0-85941-756-5

1   2   3   4   5   96   95   94   93   92

To Barbara

CONTENTS

PREFACE AND
ACKNOWLEDGEMENTS

There appears to be an urgent need for a book that discusses valuation in the context of rational economic principles and, in particular, one that shows how such principles may be applied in practice. The objective has been to give practitioners an insight into relevant theoretical developments, explain how these relate to current valuation practice and how such practice might be improved by the application of more sophisticated approaches based on recent developments in the literature. This type of approach to valuation is becoming more common in the United States and forms the basis of some (but not all) of the currently fashionable attempts at assessing the strategic value of businesses sometimes known as 'shareholder value analysis'.

This book should therefore be of interest to all those who wish to attempt to establish a 'rational' value of any business. As is argued later, this should include the managers of any company, as well as actual and potential stakeholders. In this context, stakeholders include investors, lenders, employees, long-standing customers and suppliers. The book should also be useful to MBA and other postgraduate students, together with academics who have an interest in the area. Those who are concerned with topics peripheral to valuation, such as forecasting cash flows, estimating costs of capital and investment appraisal, should also find sections of the book relevant to their needs.

There seems to me to be little point in providing detailed descriptions of 'traditional' practice here. Instead, the focus is on describing recent developments and showing how these may impact upon such practice, as they are beginning to do in some areas. I have also tried to show how, and under what circumstances traditional models work well, and where they do not.

I have kept any use of mathematics to a minimum and have only presented formulae which I believe may be of value in practice. Mindful of the fact that most readers will probably be busy practitioners who may not be interested in the mathematical derivations of any such formulae, I have relegated any such derivations to appendices. The result, I hope, is that no mathematical expertise is necessary; anyone with the equivalent of a Maths 'O' level/GCSE should be able to apply the principles described in the text. In addition, when any formulae are described examples are given to illustrate how they may be applied in practice. Companies that I have invented for this purpose are marked with an asterisk.

The book does not attempt to delve into the intricacies of valuation for taxation and legal purposes, as these matters have been covered adequately elsewhere, and are anyway country-specific. The principles discussed in this text should be applicable in any country with reasonably developed capital markets. The only knowledge assumed is a basic familiarity with financial markets and a working knowledge of company accounting. For readers who feel a little unhappy with the latter, *Understanding Company Financial Statements* by R. H. Parker (Penguin), offers an excellent coverage of the area.

The book has benefited considerably from extensive discussions with practitioners. I should like to express my sincere gratitude to KPMG Peat Marwick, and in particular to Roy Nicholson and Frank Carter, for their practical advice and assistance in compiling this book. I should also like to thank my colleague Dr Terry Cooke, who kindly spent a good deal of his Christmas break reading through a first draft, for his helpful comments on the book. I must add that the only reason it has proved possible to complete the book in its current form is because of the support of my partner, Barbara Merritt. Not only has she tolerated, without complaint, the many hours I have spent in my study and the trial of living with the moodiness of a prospective author but, as a practising accountant and consultant herself, has made many useful suggestions on how the text might be improved; no author could have wished for better support.

Finally, I should like to hear from those working on valuation in practice who would either be willing to participate in a research study on approaches to valuing listed companies or would be prepared to supply case study material that might be included in a future book. In addition, I would welcome the comments of readers on how any future edition of this book might be improved.

Alan Gregory
Department of Economics, University of Exeter
January 1992.

CHAPTER 1

AN INTRODUCTION TO COMPANY VALUATION

We might start with a question – is there any such thing as an objective value? Sidestepping the complexities of the philosophical issues raised by such a question and interpreting it in its most narrow sense, the answer might be 'yes', but only in a strictly limited number of cases. The requirements for this answer include a 'market' composed of a large number of well-informed buyers and sellers, who can trade in a costless and unrestricted manner, and a homogeneous good that can be traded[1]. Although such conditions are not met totally in reality, they are approximated in commodity markets and in some securities markets. Examples of cases where we might establish such an objective value include gold ingots and government loan stocks or bonds. Even then, one might reasonably point out that what we have in fact established is merely a *price*; if, for example, we believed that the market's estimate of future interest rates was wrong we might conclude that a particular government loan stock (generally known as 'gilts' in the United Kingdom, and treasury bonds in the United States) was either over- or under-valued.

However, an important concept in valuation is that of *efficient markets*. This is discussed in more detail in Chapter 3, but for now it is sufficient to approximate the idea by observing that, on average, the market will get it right *based on the current information available to it*.[2] Whilst the natural response of practitioners is to disbelieve in such a notion, the sheer competitive pressure of market participants tends to ensure that at any point in time prices are 'fair'. The paradox is that if market participants actually started to believe in such a concept *en masse*, competitive pressures would ease, making markets less efficient. Research evidence suggests that, on the whole, markets are largely (but not exclusively) price efficient. If we accept this concept, we might conclude that today's price is a fair indication of today's value[3] and this has important implications for would-be valuers.

How does this help us in establishing the value of a company? The answer depends largely upon the purpose of our valuation and the nature of the company. If a private investor (call him Fred Punter) is trying to value Marks and Spencer, the balance of research evidence would suggest that he may as well accept that market efficiency will prevail and that the current share price is the best indicator of the true value of a Marks and Spencer share. This is because Fred faces a market composed of sophisticated investors who are probably much better informed than he is and who, through the balance of their actions, are driving the share price. Fred's best strategy is to buy a balanced portfolio of shares and hold it, rather than trying actively to spot over- or under-valued companies. In fact, there is evidence to suggest that many larger investors may improve their portfolio performance by not attempting to do this and by adopting a strategy similar to that which we have recommended for Fred; indeed, some fund managers do precisely this with at least some of the funds under their control. This investment policy is known as 'passive fund management' and contrasts with the policy adopted by investors who do actively try and pick winners, which is known as 'active fund management'.

The advice we have given Fred is hardly likely to appeal to Samantha Grabbit, the chairperson of Megapredator plc*, who is perhaps interested in taking over the whole of Wombat plc*, a large UK company. Samantha is interested in a whole range of issues, such as alternative business strategies for the company if she acquires it, the realisable value of the company's freehold property, the saleable value of any subsidiaries and any synergistic benefits that may arise from the acquisition. A key difference is that Samantha can actively change the value of the company by her actions, whereas Fred cannot. Furthermore, she will be able to pay advisors to seek out new information on the company and in some cases force the company itself to disclose additional information.

Samantha's case also brings out two other aspects of valuation, which we shall refer to as bargaining strategy and bidder objectives. As regards the former, Samantha will presumably have worked out how much Wombat is worth to her. The key question is how much she will have to pay to win control of the company. Clearly, she will have to pay some sort of premium over the current share price, but the size of that premium will depend upon a number of factors. She somehow has to persuade the current Wombat shareholders to sell their shares; if Wombat has a shareholder profile typical of that of most large companies, this will involve convincing large institutional fund managers of her case. Key factors will be the past performance of Wombat (are the fund managers likely to be happy with the performance of their holding relative to other shares?) and how the acquistion is to be paid for (if cash, what alternative investment possibilities are there? And if the offer is a share-for-share one, how is Megapredator rated by the investment community?).

Bidder objectives are the factor that really drives the valuation process in the context of an acquisition. The value of Wombat to any bidder depends upon what that bidder intends to do with it. If we consider a conglomerate takeover, where the objective is simply to 'improve the running of the company', the value might be similar to a number of different bidders. However, it is quite possible that particular synergistic or strategic benefits make Wombat worth more to one bidder than another.[4] Bidder objectives and bargaining strategies become even richer areas when we consider the case of privately held companies, as we also need to be aware of seller objectives; these topics are discussed in detail in Chapters 9 and 10.

In between the small private investor and the acquisition-hungry predator, there are diverse groups who, for a variety of reasons, will wish to value a non-controlling stake in a company. This will include everyone from analysts, institutional fund managers and venture capitalists to investors considering a minority stake in a private company.

Returning to our opening question, we can see that except in the case of investors who adopt a passive management strategy (and hence implicitly accept that today's price is the best indicator of current value), the value of a company is the subjective judgement of its intrinsic worth to an individual or group of individuals. The central purpose of this book is to enable such people to establish what that intrinsic value might be.

WHO NEEDS TO VALUE A COMPANY AND WHY?

This question may seem a gratuitous one, and indeed many of those who are included in any list we make would fall into the obvious camps of either potential buyer or potential seller. Included as buyers would be acquisitive companies, investment fund managers , management buyout teams and parties interested in taking a stake in a business (in this respect it is important to distinguish between controlling and non-controlling stakes). Fund mangers might also appear as potential sellers, and also in this camp we find individuals and families who have a controlling stake in an enterprise, and companies who want to divest themselves of subsidiaries or business areas.

In addition, there is the investment analyst who is concerned with advising clients on over- or under-valued securities and a range of other advisers who need to perform valuations for various purposes. These include merchant bankers, who may be concerned with activities as diverse as stock market flotations (which in themselves cover everything from small companies entering the Unlisted Securities Market (USM) through to government privatisation issues), appraisal of takeover targets, valuations in takeover defences and valuations in buyouts. Accountancy firms are major advisers in takeover situations and will also be involved in valuations for receivership, regulatory, legal and taxation reasons (as tax valuation is a highly specialist area involving country specific laws; it is not covered in this book). Credit rating agencies (such as Moodys and Standard & Poor) will also have an interest in company valuation.

Lenders should also be concerned with company valuation; even providers of 'straight' loans should have some notion of value, as it is one indicator of loan security. The likely value of the company under various scenarios helps to establish the downside risk of the loan. It is also possible that lenders may find themselves more actively concerned with company value than they originally intended (there have been several recent and interesting examples of forced financial restructuring). Clearly, a particular group that has a keen interest in valuation will be venture capitalists, and the finance provided usually has some equity-like element involved.

All this brings us to the final group, who arguably should be the most interested one *on a continual basis* – the managers of the company. This includes not only the top managers of large public companies, but also the managers of subsidiaries and major business areas, and the managers of even small private companies. Unless these managers have an idea of the value of what they control, they cannot sensibly evaluate alternative business strategies. Neither can they convincingly defend themselves from hostile takeover bids, or indeed perceive whether or not they should feel potentially threatened (if managers really believe that their company is under-valued by the market, they should feel vulnerable to any bidder who realises the same). Without an idea of corporate value they have no means of estimating their past performance, as the objectives of public companies include increasing the wealth of the shareholders.[5] Finally, unless managers are aware of value, they will find it hard to make an objective assessment of whether they should be expanding through acquisitions or 'organic' growth, or whether they should be concentrating the business through closures, divestments or spin-offs.[6] As managers should be taking a long-term view of the business, they should be primarily concerned with the discounted cash flow process described in Chapters 6, 7 and 8.

We can summarise the valuation process into a two-state, four-actor classification. The two states are *ongoing* (or *as is*, which assumes the business continues with its present strategies) and *changed* (which evaluates the effect of different strategies). The actors are *arbitrageurs* (who will principally be involved in short-term investment), *advisors* (who are arguably not full actors in their own right), *controllers* (who are the existing management team or owners) and potential bidders and *stakeholders* (including lenders, who have a degree of influence according to the size of their stake; for these purposes, they are classified as controllers if that stake is more than 50 per cent of the equity). Table 1.1 illustrates this classification and the reasons they may be interested in either valuation state. For the most part, this is self explanatory, but changed state valuation by stakeholders deserves some comment.

In general, small stakeholders dissatisfied with the value of the company with its current managerial strategies have no effective option other than selling, and even that may not be possible in the case of private companies. However, larger stakeholders with influence can attempt to persuade

Table 1.1 Valuation classification

Valuer	State	
	Ongoing (existing strategies)	*Changed (new/revised strategies)*
Arbitrageur	All cases, usually short-term	Value as takeover target
Advisers	All cases	Takeover, spin-off and divestment advice
Stakeholders	All cases	Only where actively involved
Controllers	All cases	All cases – alternative strategy valuation

management to change strategies if they believe such a course of action would add value to the company. 'Persuasion' covers everything from friendly advice through to using voting power to replace directors. In the case where the changed state involves the acquisition of the company (either by take-over, management buyout or the divestment of the business to an outside purchaser), the valuation from the potential purchaser's point of view will include the value of any synergystic benefits he or she hopes to be able to achieve. This, of course, establishes the *maximum* value of the company to the buyer, who will hope to pay something less than this figure.[7]

AN OVERVIEW OF THE VALUATION PROCESS

The valuation process is summarised in Figure 1.1. The first point to be made is that multi-business companies should never be valued as one unit, but should always be valued separately. The reasons for this are, first, that different economic and risk factors affect diverse business areas in different ways; throughout the book we shall keep to this central principle, and refer to separately identifiable business units as *principal lines of business* (PLB). A PLB can be either a geographically distinct activity (such as an overseas subsidiary) or a distinct product or service. For example, a number of UK breweries (such as Vaux) have a hotel operation and a brewing operation.

The second reason for valuing each PLB separately is that it assists corporate management to determine whether or not the best value is being extracted from the operation; it may be that alternative strategies, such as additional investment or the sale of an operation, would produce greater value for the shareholders (this idea of looking at changes in corporate value is sometimes called 'the shareholder value approach'). A possible strategy in question may, of course, be an acquisition, in which case we shall need to value the potential target and attempt to determine whether the firm is worth more with this additional value, less the purchase cost, than it is at present.

Stage 1   Identify separate PLBs and decide upon specific forecast horizons.

Stage 2   Obtain background economic forecasts for specific forecast period.

Stage 3   For each PLB:
           1.   Obtain industry and business specific information.
           2.   Prepare profit and cash flow forecasts for specific forecast period.

Stage 4   Identify a suitable valuation model.

Stage 5   Value each PLB as a 'stand-alone' entity.

Stage 6   Value PLB as above with optimal 'changed state' strategies in place.
              Compare value of company with PLB (plus any relevant acquisition costs) and
           compare to value of company without PLB plus sale proceeds. If the latter is
           greater than the former, sell or acquire PLB in question.

Stage 7   If an acquisition is being analysed, determine financing consideration, bargaining
           area and impact of these on value.

Stage 8   Sum 'best option' PLB values (see Stage 6), (negative) value of head office overheads
           and value of financial assets. (Note that although head office overheads are a cost, the
           services provided should have positive value to the company. Furthermore, the
           services should only be provided by head office if that is the most cost-effective
           and efficient method of provision.)

Stage 9   Consider provision of value-related incentives for management. (Note that some
           reward schemes effectively entail giving up some of the PLB's value to motivate
           management, and this needs to be allowed for in Stages 5–8.)

Figure 1.1   A summary of the valuation process

Once we have determined the value of the individual PLBs after adopting the 'best strategy' alternatives, we can add these up to give the value of the firm's operations as a whole. From this we have to deduct the negative value contributed by head office overheads. Note that we should always attempt to look at alternatives to head office as a source of service provision; PLB managers should be encouraged to look out for other (external or internal within their own PLB) potential sources of service and adopt them if such an alternative is cheaper for the company as a whole.

The last step is always to add in the market value of any marketable financial securities (such as government loan stocks or treasury bills) owned by the firm. What we have at this stage is the value of the entire company with the optimal strategies adopted (in other words, the *changed state* value, which we discussed earlier). It does not follow that this is the same as the ongoing state value (indeed it will not be unless the strategies are already in place), neither will this be the same as the current market value, although in theory if management keeps the market informed of their intentions and the market has similar views on the prospects of the business to management, market value and changed state value should coincide; we explore this point in Chapters 8, 9 and 10.

Note that the approach we have adopted here is to value the *company* rather than the *equity*; to obtain the latter we would need to deduct the long-term liabilities of the firm.

AN OVERVIEW OF THE PRINCIPAL VALUATION MODELS

Essentially, there are three main categories of valuation model. There is the *earnings*-based type of model, which measures value as some multiple of accounting profit; the *asset*-based type of model; which is concerned with the sale or replacement value of the physical and financial assets of a company; and the *discounted cash flow* models, where the factors affecting value are the future cash flow prospects of the company and the opportunity cost of capital. It is sometimes suggested that only the earnings and discounted cash flow models value companies as going concerns or continuing businesses. This is not strictly the case, as asset valuations concerned with the replacement values of assets implicitly assume that the business is to continue in some form; this point is developed in Chapter 2. In addition to these models, which focus upon valuing the entire company, we also need to consider the valuation of minority stakes in unquoted companies, where the holder's only cash flow consists of a dividend stream; this special case is dealt with in Chapter 9.

Earnings valuations

The idea behind the earnings valuation model is to try and estimate the so-called *maintainable profits* of the company and apply a capitalisation factor, known as the *price–earnings multiple* to this profit. This price–earnings multiple reflects the riskiness, cost of capital and growth prospects of the firm. As a simple example, suppose Samantha Grabbit is looking at the profit record of Wombat plc, and believes that the long-term maintainable profit is a simple average of the past five years results. Those results were as follows:

Year ended	Profit (£millions)
December 1991	80
December 1990	110
December 1989	90
December 1988	120
December 1987	100
Average	100

Looking at the *Financial Times*, Samantha sees that companies in the same industry as Wombat have an average price–earnings (PE) ratio of ten, and she believes that since Wombat has industry-average risk and growth prospects, the intrinsic value of the company is 10 × £100 million, or £1 billion.[8]

Fortunately for company valuation professionals and the authors of books on valuation, the real world is a little more complex than implied by this example. In particular, we need to be aware of the accounting techniques used to arrive at the profit figures, the problems of inflation, the definition of 'maintainable profits', the difficulty of forecasting maintainable profit and the question of establishing an appropriate earnings multiple (including the differences between historical and prospective earnings multiples). Lastly, there is the debate about the general validity of using PE-based models; this is a contentious area, but validity would appear to depend upon the context in which the model is used. Earnings-based models are described fully in Chapters 3 and 5.

Asset valuations

To derive the asset value of the company, Samantha would need to discover both the *realisable* value of the assets (what they could be sold for, either piecemeal or as business segments) and the *replacement cost* of those assets (assuming she was interested in the business as a continuing entity). Unfortunately, in respect of fixed assets other than property, she is unlikely to be able to get such information directly from the published accounts. Whilst for many public companies property is shown at current or recent valuation, other fixed assets are shown at historic cost less depreciation. Whether or not these will be useful guides to either realisable value or replacement cost depends upon the type of asset and the relative rates of asset price change (as contrasting examples, consider computers and aircraft). Asset-based valuation models are discussed in Chapter 5.

Discounted cash flow valuations

The discounted cash flow (DCF) valuation model, or present value model, requires the valuer to make an explicit forecast of future cash flow. In theory, that forecast needs to extend over a *very* long time horizon; dependent on the opportunity cost of capital, this might be in excess of 100 years. As few practitioners like forecasting cash flows for the last decade of the 21st century, the approach generally used is to make a specific forecast for a number of years and then to make a general forecast using a base cash flow with some form of constant growth assumption. The valuer will also need to be aware of an appropriate risk adjusted opportunity cost of capital. Returning to our example of Samantha and Wombat plc, let us suppose she has forecast the following cash flows for the next five years as follows:

Year ending	Forecast cash flow (£million)
December 1992	118
December 1993	130
December 1994	50
December 1995	50
December 1996	150

We shall assume that her forecast for 1997 and beyond is a constant cash flow of £100 million per annum and that the estimated opportunity cost of capital is 10 per cent per annum. Applying 10 per cent discount factors to these cash flows gives us a present value, at 1 January 1992, of £1 billion. (Readers unfamiliar with discounted cash flows should put aside any anxieties until they have read Chapter 2, but those familiar with the topic will realise that the problem can be solved by treating the £100m as a perpetuity with a present value of £1 billion in December 1996; discounting this back to January 1992 gives a value of £621m, to which must be added the present value of the five-year forecast cash flows, £379m, resulting in a total present value of £1 billion.)

Fortunately, in this case we arive at the same valuation using both the DCF and PE models. In general, we would expect differences to occur and, although we might hope that these will not be too large, this may be an optimistic view. The reasons for such differences are explored in Chapter 3, and DCF models are explained in detail in Chapters 6, 7 and 8.

A comparison of the alternatives

Assuming that we wish to value companies as going concerns (be that in ongoing or changed states), a key question is whether the DCF or PE valuation should be preferred. From a theoretical viewpoint, DCF has many advantages in that value is calculated in the context of a rational economic framework. It also has the advantage of making all the assumptions made in the valuation process *explicit*. Furthermore, there exist theoretically developed and empirically tested models (albeit imperfect ones) from which we can derive the opportunity cost of capital. By contrast, there is no rational economic model that can be used to derive satisfactory PE ratios, and all the forecast assumptions on risk, cost of capital and growth prospects are *implicit* in the earnings multiple chosen. However, it must be emphasised that a successful valuation depends upon the quality of the sales and cost forecasts made. It is fairly easy to demonstrate that many valuations are more sensitive to accurate forecasting in this area than to the valuation methodology used. If we assume, for example, roughly constant cash flows and profits, a 10 per cent error in the PE ratio or the discount rate will produce a valuation error of around 10 per cent, whereas a 10 per cent error in the sales forecast can produce a much more serious impact, depending upon the relationship between costs and sales; broadly, the higher the proportion of 'fixed' costs (a fixed cost is one that does not vary with output), the greater the impact of any sales change on net cash flow or profit becomes.

None the less, earnings-based valuation models appear to be dominant in the United Kingdom although in the United States DCF-based models seem to be gaining ground rapidly.[9] One reason for this might be habit; another might be the way in which, in this author's experience, DCF models are used in the United Kingdom. A particularly bad example of this is the practice of forecasting cash flows over a short time horizon, and then adding in the discounted value of an assumed 'terminal value' of the business (often derived by taking the profits for the final year of the forecast period and applying a PE multiple based on current industry averages). Such an approach is not generally recommended, and an alternative is presented in Chapter 8. Despite the advantages of the DCF model when properly applied, for as long as market participants use PE-based approaches it will be necessary to calculate both a DCF value and a PE-based value.

Given the fact that many valuations are made in situations that involve some form of bargaining process, and that many people do use PE models, it can be advantageous, for bargaining purposes, to calculate both PE and DCF values. Suppose that Samantha Grabbit is interested in acquiring a private high-technology company from a willing seller. Using reasonable assumptions, she calculates that the DCF value of the firm is £2 million, even though current annual profits are only £80,000 and *public* companies in this type of industry trade on a typical PE multiple of fifteen. It is easy to see that a PE valuation based on current earnings gives her a very useful idea of where to start the bidding for this company even though it appears to be a hopeless indicator of current value.

As a second example, imagine that you are advising members of the beleaguered board of Wombat plc, who are now on the receiving end of a hostile bid from Samantha's company. Based upon your inside knowledge of the company's plans, you believe that the true DCF value is around £1.3 billion, and that next year's profits will be £98 million. Immediately prior to Samantha's bid, the stock market value of the company was £800 million. Although you may be convinced of the validity of the DCF valuation, it is hard to deny that your defence would have to take account of a PE valuation based upon next year's anticipated profit (a solution to the dilemma might be to disclose long-term plans and their long run profit impact).

It would therefore seem that in many valuation cases it is prudent to produce both DCF and PE valuations. To assess alternative strategies it is useful to perform an asset valuation as well. It is for these reasons that subsequent chapters discuss all three valuation methods. In addition, Chapter 9 discusses other aspects of valuation, in particular those relating to takeovers and minority stakes. Chapter 10 discusses the issue of bargaining areas and the financing of acquisitions, whilst Chapter 11 looks at issues relating to management's role, including methods of safeguarding value after acquisition and the important role of the incumbent management at the negotiation stage of the deal.

CHAPTER 2

A FRAMEWORK
FOR VALUATION

Value is always a relative concept, in as much as we can only estimate the value of anything if we are aware of the value of that which we have to give up to acquire it. This is something most of us are familiar with already; it is not the absolute cost of buying a new car that matters, but the cost relative to the value of the alternative item that we have to forgo to buy it. Economists call this concept *opportunity cost*, and it is central in the valuation process. If we refer back to the numerical examples in Chapter 1, we can see that opportunity cost is implicit in the earnings valuation, because the PE ratio was chosen by looking at the multiples found on other similar companies and explicit in the DCF valuation, because the discount rate chosen is the 'opportunity cost of capital'; in other words, the return we would expect to receive on investments of similar risk.

As we have seen in Chapter 1, PE and DCF methods can be used to give us the value of a company as a going concern. However, this does not in itself ensure that we have measured the opportunity value of the business, as we have yet to consider the alternative uses to which the assets might be put; neither does it consider the replacement value of the assets of the business. To illustrate why these matters are of importance, we shall use the simple example of a small chain of fishmongers called Something Fishy Ltd* (or SFL for short), which owns five retail outlets in the Devon and Cornwall area. The business is owned entirely by Mr Sole and his wife, who want to sell it and retire. SFL has the following balance sheet:

Assets	Freehold property, at cost		£200,000
	Shop fittings at cost less depreciation		25,000
	Motor vehicles at cost less depreciation		18,000
	Total fixed assets		243,000
	Stock of frozen fish	2,000	
	Debtors	5,000	

Assets (cont)

Less:		
Creditors	(4,000)	
Bank overdraft	(5,000)	
Net current assets		(2,000)
Net assets		241,000
Financed by: Ordinary shareholder's funds		241,000

SFL is a fairly stable business with predictable cash flows and profits, and you estimate that maintainable profits are around £75,000 per annum. We are advising another firm, National Fishmongers★, which has outlets in most parts of the country except Devon and Cornwall, where it is keen to establish a presence. For now, let us suppose that using both DCF and PE approaches to valuation, we arrive at a going concern value of £600,000 (as in most of our illustrative examples, we shall ignore tax). On investigating further, we discover the following realisable values and replacement costs for the assets (all net of selling costs in the case of realisable values, and including purchasing costs for replacement costs):

Assets	Realisable value	Replacement cost
Freehold property	£480,000	£520,000
Shop fittings	2,000	90,000
Motor vehicles	15,000	25,000
Net current assets (as balance sheet)	(2,000)	(2,000)
Net asset value	495,000	633,000

What is the value of this business to National Fishmongers? If we assume that Mr Sole has no special expertise or relationship with his customers and that the acquiring firm would carry on the business in the same manner the value is £600,000, the going concern value.[1] It is tempting to believe that the value should be the replacement cost of £633,000; the reason that this is incorrect is that a rational management team would not pay £633,000 to acquire assets that were only capable of generating an economic value of £600,000.

Now we shall change the facts a little. Suppose that the National Fishmongers' management team think they can improve SFL's future cash flows by 10 per cent. This means that the going concern value of the business should increase to £660,000. Does it now follow that National Fishmongers should be prepared to pay up to this figure for SFL? The answer has to be 'no', because it can establish an equivalent chain of shops for a figure of £633,000. It therefore follows that the maximum value of any business (or any asset, come to that) is the replacement value of its assets.

A warning is in order at this point. Replacement cost of assets means buying assets *with the same service potential* as the existing assets; for example, it does not imply that the motor vehicles have to be new. They would, in fact, be ones of a similar age and carrying capacity as the existing ones. Furthermore, this idea of service potential extends to the non-financial assets of the business, as well as the financial ones that appear on the balance sheet. We sidestepped this problem above by assuming there was nothing special in the way that Mr Sole ran his business, but in certain companies the main 'assets' may be key managers or employees, as in the case of some design companies and computer software houses. In such cases, it is meaningless to talk about replacement cost of assets unless we take account of the value to the business of such key personnel. Issues relating to asset valuations will be discussed in greater depth in Chapter 5.

Finally, we shall alter the story yet again. Suppose that, since we began valuing SFL, some major health scares relating to fish consumption have arisen, which cause us to believe that future cash flows will fall by 20 per cent from our original estimate, thus depressing the going concern value to £480,000. Clearly, the value of the business under such circumstances must be the realisable value of the assets, as the best available option is termination of the business and the sale of its assets.

All this is summarised diagrammatically in Figure 2.1. The opportunity value of any business can never exceed the full replacement cost of its assets, and cannot be less than the net realisable value of its assets. This opportunity value concept was first applied to accounting problems by Canning (1929) and developed by Bonbright (1937) in the context of insurable values; also in the 1930s, economists such as Coase (1937) applied these ideas in a decision analysis context.

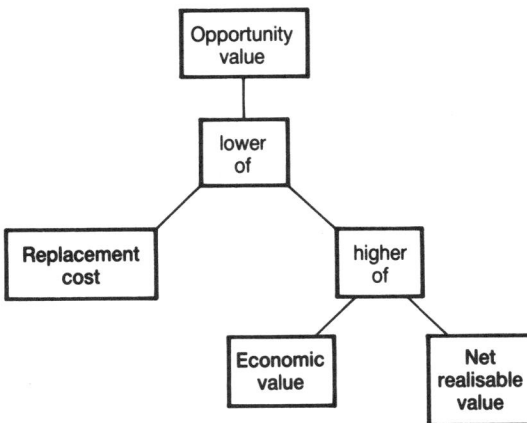

Figure 2.1 Opportunity value or 'value to business'.

Although all this gives us a useful conceptual framework for valuation, it must be acknowledged that the replacement cost of assets will not always be easy to calculate even when there is no 'human asset value' like that discussed above. Take the case of a small electronics company that has just developed and patented the Proustwave Modulator. This little device proves to be extremely useful and looks like being its best selling product. Clearly, this patent might turn out to be its most valuable asset, and there is no replacement cost (although its economic value and its realisable value can be calculated[2]) – in effect, it is infinite. The same type of argument applies in all cases where the company under consideration holds some form of non-replicable asset.

For most practical purposes, given the difficulty of calculating the service potential replication cost of the business, the valuer will be concerned mainly with the going concern or economic value. There will be cases where this is not so, and the realisable or break up value of the business is higher than this going concern value but even then it is likely that economic value will be used to determine the worth of any segments of the business that will continue to exist as separate entities (as, for example, in the case of spin-offs and divestments).

We have already seen that there are two principal methods of estimating economic value, namely the earnings-based method and the discounted cash flow method. In the next chapter, we shall explain the circumstances under which the two are equivalent. As we have noted, the discounted cash flow valuation method is the only one that is derived using a rational economic framework, and is also of central importance in the company valuation framework. Accordingly, we now look at a brief description and revision of DCF principles.

DISCOUNTED CASH FLOW

We start by making some assumptions, which we shall relax later. First, assume that there is no inflation and second, assume that we can predict future cash flows with certainty. Third, we need to assume that interest rates remain constant. Given these assumptions, we can now develop a rational method of assessing the value of future cash flows. Suppose that we are owed £1,000, which is payable exactly one year from now and that we are wealthy individuals with ample funds invested at the current rate of interest of 10 per cent. We are willing to accept an amount to be decided upon in full settlement of the loan today. What should this amount be to make us indifferent as to whether we collect the cash now or wait for one year? Clearly, we would accept something less than £1,000 because if we had the cash now, we could invest it ourselves and earn interest. In fact, we would want an amount that, when invested at 10 per cent pa, gives us £1,000 in a years time. As, at 10 per cent, we receive at the end of the year cash equivalent to 110 per cent of our investment, the answer is found by dividing £1,000 by 1.1, which gives an amount of £909.09. In other words, if the debt was settled by the recepit of this amount today, we would invest it at 10 per cent, obtain interest of £90.91 and have £1,000 at the end of the year. Thus we can say than £909.09 is the *present value* of £1,000 in one years time at 10 per cent.

What if we were owed the £1,000 in three years time rather than one year from now? The principle is the same, except that we have to allow for the fact that we gain interest on the interest that is added to our account each year. If we start with £100 today, and interest rates are 10 per cent per annum (pa), we end up with the following balances at the end of each year:

End of year	Interest for year at 10%	Principal plus interest
1	£10	£110
2	£11	£121
3	£12.10	£133.10

This can be generalised as stating that the *future value* (principal plus interest) is found from the present value by:

Future value = present value $\times (1 + r)^n$

where r is the interest rate per period expressed as a decimal (e.g. 15 per cent gives an r of 0.15) and n is the number of compounding periods. Thus, for our example with £100 invested at 10 per cent pa for three years we get:

Future value = £100 $\times (1.1)^3$ = £133.10

We can also see that, as future values can be calculated from present values, the reverse must be true, and simple rearrangement of our equation gives:

Present value = future value $\div (1 + r)^n$

Thus we can solve our problem of how much we must receive today to settle our debt of £1,000 in three years time; the solution is:

Present value = £1,000 $\div (1.1)^3$ = £751.31

We can thus convert any future cash flow into a present value equivalent in a manner that takes account of opportunity costs, which in the case of capital are related to interest costs. Furthermore, these present values are additive, which means we can handle problems where there are cash flows arising at different points in time. Therefore if we were owed £1,000 in one year and a further £1,000 in three years, the present value of the whole is simply £751.31 + £909.09 = £1,660.40.

As a final, practical, matter, performing the present value calculation (known as *discounting*) becomes rather tedious after a while, and so we usually use tables of *discount factors*. These are calculated as $1 / (1 + r)^n$ and are shown in Appendix A, Table B, at the end of the book. As discount factors are the reciprocal of $(1 + r)$, we *multiply* the future value by the discount factor to obtain the present value; applying this to our example of £1,000 receivable in three years time yields:

Present value = £1,000 $\times$ 0.7513 = £751.30

Application of basic principles

Having established the basic principles behind discounting, we can now see how this can be applied to valuing a business. Suppose that Luciano has offered to sell us his ice cream business (which consists of a fleet of ice cream vans) and that we have the following estimates of annual profits:

Year ended	Ice cream sales less costs	Van running costs	Other costs
December 92	£100,000	£30,000	£20,000
December 93	£110,000	£50,000	£20,000
December 94	£130,000	£50,000	£20,000
December 95	£120,000	£60,000	£20,000
December 96	£100,000	£70,000	£20,000

At the end of this period, we believe that the age of the van fleet and falling demand will mean that it is no longer worth continuing in business, and that the fleet could be sold for a scrap value of £2,000. We have reflected this fact by including £10,000 pa van depreciation in the running costs given above. Other costs includes a figure of £2,000 pa for other equipment depreciation. Luciano has an estimate of 1992 profit similar to ours, and wants a figure of four times earnings (which are £100,000 − 30,000 − 20,000 = £50,000), or £200,000 for the business. So far, we have ignored the question of risk, but let us now suppose that we believe that investments of similar risk normally earn 20 per cent pa (Chapter 6 deals with the question of risk and the discount rate). Should we buy it? The first step is to work on the basis of cash flows, not accounting profits. This is important because opportunity costs of capital relate to cash; in the case of this example, we therefore need to add back depreciation, with the fall in asset values being reflected in the cash flow figure for 1996. For convenience, we shall assume that all cash flows arise on the last day of the year (on page 25 we look at what happens where cash flows arise at other points in time). Having established the cash flows, we can discount these at 20 per cent and obtain a present value of the business at 1 January 1992:

Year end	Accounting profit	Depreciation added back	Cash flow	Discount factor	Present value
December 92	50,000	12,000	62,000	0.8333	51,667
December 93	40,000	12,000	52,000	0.6944	36,111
December 94	60,000	12,000	72,000	0.5787	41,667
December 95	40,000	12,000	52,000	0.4823	25,077
December 96	10,000	12,000	22,000	0.4019	8,841
December 96	*Sale of van fleet*		2,000	0.4019	804
Total present value					164,167

Thus the economic value of the business is only £164,167, considerably less than the sum demanded by Luciano.

One approach to the problem of investigating whether a particular venture is worthwhile is to subtract the purchase price or initial cost from the economic value (also known as the *gross present value*) to give the *net present value* (NPV) of the venture. If this figure is negative, as in this case where the NPV is −£35,833, the investment is rejected, whilst if the NPV is positive, the investment opportunity is accepted. The NPV method is frequently used in appraising capital investment projects in industry and it is worth noting that in informationally efficient markets, a firm adopting a positive NPV project should experience an increase in its market capitalisation equal to the size of the NPV; thus a valuable property of the NPV approach is that it provides a direct measurement of the value of the investment to the shareholders of the company. Generally speaking, our problem in this book is to value companies, rather than to appraise whether investment opportunities are worthwhile, and so we shall make greater use of gross present values than net present values.

A couple of short cuts

In the valuation process, we frequently come across situations where the cash flows are constant for a number of years. Suppose Jeremy wishes to sell his florists business, and the shop is on a five-year lease with no prospect of renewal. Cash flows are very stable, and we think that they will be £20,000 pa for the next five years; on this type of business we believe 12 per cent pa is the opportunity cost of capital. We could multiply each year's flow by its discount factor but a quicker approach is to use the sum of the discount factors (known as an *annuity factor*) and multiply this by the constant cash flow; annuity factors[3] are given in Appendix A, Table D. Applying the five year 12 per cent annuity factor to the cash flows of Jeremy's business gives us:

Present value = £20,000 × 3.6048 = £72,096

A slightly more difficult case is where constant cash flows are expected to arise for a number of years in the future, but not immediately. For example, what would happen if we thought that by good management we could improve the cash flows of Jeremy's business? Specifically, we think we can increase them to £22,000 in year 1, £25,000 in year 2, and that they will then level off at £27,000 pa for years 3–5 inclusive. We now have a three-year annuity of £27,000 pa; the present value of such an annuity (using a three-year 12 per cent annuity factor) is £27,000 × 2.4018, or £64,849. However, this is the value of the annuity assuming the first year of cash flow is year 1; in this case the first year is year 3. We should there-fore discount this annuity by using a year 2 discount factor, because the unadjusted calculation gives us the present value at the beginning of year 3 (or the end of year 2). Jeremy's business therefore has a value to us of:

Year	Item	£	Discount factor	Present value
1	Cash flow	22,000	0.8929	19,643
2	Cash flow	25,000	0.7972	19,930
2	Year 2 PV of annuity	64,849	0.7972	51,698
	Total PV			91,271

This type of calculation can be particularly useful when calculating the economic value of property, a case where the annuity values can be calculated for successive rent reviews and discounted back to give present values.

Finally, we look at the case of perpetuities. This is really just an extreme version of the annuity in that a constant cash flow pattern occurs for ever. The formula for calculating the present value of a perpetuity is simply:

Present value = cash flow ÷ r

As an example, take the case of a shop let on a perpetual basis for a rental of £25,000 pa. If the opportunity cost of capital is expected to be 12.5 per cent for the foreseeable future, the economic value of the shop is £25,000/0.125 = £200,000.[4] Perpetuities are useful tools in the valuation process because we frequently want to know the value of the business once it has reached a 'steady state'. A simple example would be an electronics company, where the last year's cash flow was £100,000 pa. Growth will be 10 per cent pa for the next five years, after which the cash flow will remain constant at £161,000 pa. If an appropriate discount rate is, say, 15 per cent, we can calculate the present value of the first 5 years cash flows as approximately £438,460. We also know that the value of the perpetual £161,000 pa *at the end of year 5* is £161,000/0.15 or £1,073,330. Discounting this back to the present gives us a value of £1,073,330 × 0.4972 = £533,659. We then add this to the present value of the first five years cash flow to give us a total business value of £972,119.

Whilst perpetuities in money terms might be uncommon, perpetuities in real terms might be of more relevance. However, the most useful concept of all is that of constant growth into perpetuity, which is explained below.

A MODEL FOR CONSTANT GROWTH INTO PERPETUITY

In the above example of the electronics company, we made the rather unrealistic assumption of zero growth. In practice, companies in a 'steady state' perhaps might be expected to grow at something like the rate of increase in gross domestic product; in other words, we might expect from them an average rate of growth. We shall now look at the derivation of a formula for calculating the present value of a constant growth business.

Although this is not difficult, those readers with a severe allergy to anything mathematical can skip to the bold formula further down this section without loss.

The generalised form of the present value calculation we used above can be written as:

$$\text{Present value} = \frac{\text{cash year 1}}{(1+r)^1} + \frac{\text{cash year 2}}{(1+r)^2} + \frac{\text{cash year 3}}{(1+r)^3} + \ldots \frac{\text{cash year } n}{(1+r)^n}$$

What happens when cashflow simply increases at some constant rate (expressed as a decimal) over a base year cash flow (cash$_0$)? Our formula above can be rewritten as:

$$\text{Present value} = \frac{\text{cash}_0 (1 + \text{growth})}{(1+r)^1} + \frac{\text{cash}_0 (1 + \text{growth})^2}{(1+r)^2} + \ldots$$
$$\frac{\text{cash}_0 (1 + \text{growth})^n}{(1+r)^n}$$

this carries on into perpetuity when n becomes very large. All the while, the terms on the right hand side are growing at a constant rate; $(1 + \text{growth})/(1 + r)$. What we have is a geometric progression to infinity. Casting our minds back to the days of maths 'O' levels, we shall no doubt instantly recollect that there exists a formula for the sum of such a progression, which is:

Sum = first term ÷ (1 − common ratio)

The common ratio is $(1 + \text{growth})/(1 + r)$, and the first term refers to the right-hand side of the present value equation, which gives us cash$_0$(1 + growth)/(1 + r). Plugging all this into our formula and rearranging it gives us:

$$\text{Present value} = \frac{\text{cash}_0 (1 + \text{growth})}{(r - \text{growth})}$$

As cash$_0$ (1 + growth) is simply the anticipated cash flow in the first year we get:

$$\textbf{Present value} = \frac{\textbf{cash year 1}}{(\textbf{\textit{r}} - \textbf{growth})}$$

Note that this formula requires the discount rate to be greater than the growth rate (if the reverse is true, congratulations are definitely in order; we have just found a company with infinite value).

INFLATION AND VALUATION

There are two basic ways of tackling the problem of inflation in the valuation process. The first is simply to take account of the relevant rate of inflation when estimating the cash flows and express all those at the price levels we expect on the date of the cash flow occurring; this is known as estimating cash flows in *money terms* or *nominal terms*. These cash flows must then be discounted at a money or nominal rate cost of capital, in other words, one that takes account of the effect of anticipated inflation on investors' required rates of return. The alternative approach is to estimate all cash flows on the basis of today's general price levels, which is referred to as stating the cash flows in *real terms*. These figures are then discounted using a *real* discount rate, i.e. a cost of capital that excludes the implicit inflation expectations of investors. In theory (and indeed in practice when done properly) both approaches give the same present value. Note that it is impossible to avoid forecasting inflation for the entire time horizon of the valuation; in the first approach, we have to estimate the effect of inflation upon the different cost and revenue flows of the valuation target, whereas in the second case, given that we generally observe costs of capital from the markets,[5] we need to strip out the impounded inflation rate. This is because any view of opportunity cost of capital obtained from the financial markets is a compounding of the required real rate of return and the consensus anticipated inflation rate for the time horizon of the investment.

We now look at an example to clarify these points; we wish to value Rachmaninov Property Ltd*, which has only one group of properties, a small shopping development in Surrey. The rents on this have recently been reviewed and are now fixed for the next five years at £500,000 pa. The company has staff costs of £50,000 pa, which are expected to increase at the rate of general inflation (as measured by the retail price index – RPI) plus 1 per cent, and other costs of £30,000 pa, which will increase in line with the RPI. We expect the RPI to increase at 5 per cent pa, and believe that the appropriate cost of capital for property firms implied by current stock market prices is 15.5 per cent pa (for now, we shall simply take this figure as given; in Chapter 6 we shall explore the derivation of cost of capital in detail). Finally, it seems highly likely that the town centre in question will be redeveloped in five years' time, in which case the property portfolio will be sold off for around £5 million at current property price levels; we believe such prices will increase by 2 per cent pa in real terms.

To show that the two approaches are equal, we shall value the company in both real and money terms; we can then discuss which is likely to be the more useful in practice. First, we look at the calculation of the various price indices:

Year	RPI calculation	Labour rate index	Property prices index
0	100.0	100.0	100.0
1	105.0	106.0	107.0
2	$105.0 \times 1.05 = 110.2$	$106.0 \times 1.06 = 112.4$	$107.0 \times 1.07 = 114.5$
3	$110.2 \times 1.05 = 115.8$	$112.4 \times 1.06 = 119.1$	$114.5 \times 1.07 = 122.5$
4	$115.8 \times 1.05 = 121.6$	$119.1 \times 1.06 = 126.2$	$122.5 \times 1.07 = 131.1$
5	$127.6 \times 1.05 = 127.6$	$126.2 \times 1.06 = 133.8$	$131.1 \times 1.07 = 140.3$

We are now is a position to calculate the present value in money terms (all figures in £000s):

Year	Rental	Staff costs	Other costs	Property sale	Cash flow	PV @ 15.5%
1	500	53.0	31.5	–	415.5	359.7
2	500	56.2	33.1	–	410.7	307.9
3	500	59.6	34.7	–	405.7	263.3
4	500	63.1	36.5	–	400.4	225.0
5	500	66.9	38.3	7,015	7,409.8	3,604.9
						4,760.8

To obtain a solution in real terms, we must first deflate the cash flows,[6] and then discount at a real cost of capital. To calculate the latter, it must be realised that inflation has a compounding effect, and we cannot simply deduct the 5 per cent inflation rate from the 15.5 per cent. In fact, the realtionship between real and money rates is:

$(1 + real\ rate) = (1 + money\ rate) \div (1 + general\ inflation\ rate)$

Applying this to our example gives:

$(1 + real\ rate) = 1.155 \div 1.05 = 1.10$, i.e. the real rate is 0.1 or 10% pa

Thus the present value calculation in real terms is:

Year	Cash flows calculated in real terms		PV @ 10%
1	415.5 × 100/105.0 =	395.7	359.7
2	410.7 × 100/110.2 =	372.7	307.9
3	405.7 × 100/115.8 =	350.3	263.3
4	400.4 × 100/121.6 =	329.3	225.0
5	7,409.8 × 100/127.6 =	5,805.8	3,604.9
			4,760.8

Although the calculations yield an identical result on paper, in practice it is generally safer and easier to perform the analysis in money terms. This is because there will often be differential rates of price change applying to different types of cost and revenue (obvious examples include labour costs, which historically have risen in real terms, and computers which historically have experienced substantial real reductions); because these have to be estimated anyway, there is little advantage in translating all the money cash flows back into real terms. Perhaps more importantly, taxation is levied on monetary cash flows, and working capital has to be funded in these terms. Attempting to assess taxation (particularly when related to capital allowances) and working capital flows in real terms can be somewhat difficult and is certainly error prone; as there is no advantage to be gained from this, the recommendation must be to use cash flows in money terms discounted by a cost of capital stated in money terms.

ESTIMATING THE FUTURE INFLATION RATE

All of this leaves us with the interesting problem of estimating the future inflation rate. The most obvious source might be published forecasts, such as those provided by economic forecasting services (e.g. London Business School) or stockbrokers. Unfortunately, these all suffer from the weakness of being short term in outlook, typically using a forecast horizon of between one and three years; there is also the usual problem of disagreement between forecasters (two randomly selected examples are given in Table 2.1). Whilst the second problem can be overcome by simply using an average of the various forecasts, which fortuitously tends to be more accurate than individual forecasts anyway,[7] the former problem renders such forecasts virtually useless for the planning horizons we typically need in any serious attempt at valuation. There are two crude solutions available, together with a third, which necessitates employing an economist to make specific forecasts for us; we shall discuss the two crude ones here, both of which use government loan stock market data. Note that by using such data the approach, in principle, is applicable to any country with a liquid government securities market. However, one of the methods uses inflation–linked loan stocks thus requiring a ready and liquid market in these securities. To some degree the United Kingdom has this but this feature is not found in many other countries.

Table 2.1   UK inflation forecasts

London Business School (June 1991)		Philips and Drew (August 1991)	
Year	Inflation rate (%)	Year	Inflation rate (%)
1991	5.5	1991	5.9
1992	3.8	1992	4.9
1993	3.5		
1994	3.7		

The long-term real rate of interest

The problem that both approaches address is the determination of the long–term real rate of interest. The simplest method (in the United Kingdom) is to look at the long–term yield to redemption on index linked gilts; in August 1991, this was around 4.2 per cent. There are several problems with this figure, however. First, the market is much 'thinner' than that for other gilts, meaning that prices are less realistic. Second, these returns may understate anticipated real rates of interest if they reflect the fact that the holder is partly protected from inflation and may therefore accept a lower return for lower inflation risk. Third, these gilts are only *partly* hedged against inflation risk because the RPI for eight months previous to the due date is used in calculating the index adjusted coupon and redemption values;[8] this is why the *Financial Times* (FT) uses two different assumed inflation rates when presenting real yields to redemption. None the less, despite these problems it is an easily accessible view of anticipated real interest rates.

The second method requires us to estimate directly the long-term risk free rate of interest. The generally used approach to this problem is to look at historical rates of return, which raises the interesting difficulty of which piece of history to look at. If we take the United States, Copeland *et al.* (1990) recommend using a real rate of return of between 2 and 3 per cent, based on a twenty-six-year average data published by Ibbotson and Associates. This is of interest elsewhere because a standard economic theory known as the 'International Fisher Effect' predicts that *real* rates of interest should be identical in all countries given frictionless markets. Using UK data obtained from the Barclays de Zoete Wedd (BZW) *Equity–Gilt Study*, we can observe the following real rates of return on gilts:[9]

Period	Actual return (on a gross income reinvested basis)	Real return (%)
1918–1990	NA	1.0
1945–1990	5.29%	−1.2
1965–1990	9.43%	0.36
Successive 25-year holding periods, 1918–43 to 1965–90:		
Average		−0.69
Minimum		−3.9
Maximum		6.8

It seems unlikely that investors would rationally accept negative real returns, and their historical existence is almost certainly due to a failure to foresee experienced rates of inflation. By contrast, in more recent years BZW note that the 4.2 per cent real return on gilts since 1982 'reflects a correct anticipation of the average rate of inflation by investors in the gilt market'. It is also interesting to note that this return is very close to the current yield on index-linked gilts. At the time of writing, concern with funding the restructuring of Eastern Europe might suggest that real rates are unlikely to fall; BZW suggest that real returns on gilts could be as high as 6 per cent to 7.5 per cent in the 1990s *if* government anti-inflationary policies work. The conclusion to all this, based on US and UK data, might be that the real rate of return required on long-term government bond investment is somewhere between 2 and 6 per cent; as the 1982–90 figure and the index-linked gilt yield suggest a real rate of 4.2 per cent, and this falls more or less in the middle of the range given, we shall use 4.2 per cent as our estimate for this chapter.[10]

Using long-term real rates to estimate the future inflation rate

Having established an estimate of real rates of return, we can now use gilt market data to derive anticipated inflation rates. If we assume that the underlying real return that investors require remains constant, we can approximate the market's anticipated inflation[11] by realising that the yield on any gilt is a compound sum of the anticipated inflation rate in each year and the required real rate of return. Thus, if, at the start of 1992, we wish to calculate the implied anticipated inflation rates through to the end of 1994, we need to solve:

$$(1 + yield_3)^3 = (1 + infl_1)(1 + infl_2)(1 + infl_3)(1 + real)^3$$

The way we find the inflation figures for each year is by solving the expression for a one-year gilt, finding the implied inflation rate, using this number to solve for the inflation rate in year 2, and so on. As an example, let us assume we observe the following yields on 10 per cent gilts:

Year of maturity	Yield to redemption (%)
1992	10.33
1993	10.03
1994	10.04

The first step is to calculate the inflation rate implied for 1992. Using our standard relationship between real and money rates of return we have:

$$(1 + infl) = 1.1033 \div 1.042 = 1.0588, \text{ i.e. } 5.88\% \text{ for 1992}$$

Moving ahead to 1993 we have (rearranging our multi-period inflation formula to solve for the inflation rate in 1993):

$$(1 + infl_2) = 1.1003^2 \div (1.0588 \times 1.042^2) = 1.053, \text{ i.e. } 5.3\% \text{ for 1993}$$

Finally, we can solve for the 1994 implied inflation rate:

$$(1 + infl_3) = 1.1004^3 \div (1.0588 \times 1.053 \times 1.042^3) = 1.056 \text{ or } 5.6\% \text{ for 1994}$$

It must be emphasised that this is an approximation, because we have not allowed for coupon and redemption dates. If, for example, we take an estimation date of August 1991 (in fact, the above figures are based upon yields for that month), and a gilt with a redemption date of August 1992, our inflation rate will be the average for the last four months of 1991 and the first eight months of 1992. If we have a forecast horizon of, say, fifteen years we can either continue with the procedure outlined above or we can use a long-term average rate calculated by using the usual real/money relationship. In August 1991, the yield on fifteen-year gilts was approximately 9.9 per cent. If 4.2 per cent is the long-term real rate we have an expected fifteen-year average inflation rate of:

$$(1 + \text{real}) = 1.099 \div 1.042 = 1.055 \text{ or } 5.5\%$$

In general, unless we expect major changes in the rate of inflation, we might settle for estimating specific rates for two to three years (and cross-checking with those supplied by various forecasting agencies) and then using a long-term average rate for the duration of the valuation period.

NON-YEAR-END CASH FLOWS

So far, our DCF calculations have assumed that all cash flows occur at the end of the forecast year. Given the approximations involved in the forecasting process, this is probably adequate except in special cases. Such cases might include large-scale, short-life ventures, or cases where we expect particularly high inflation rates or high levels of risk. Adjusting the DCF calculation to take account of cash flows occurring at periods other than the year-end is not difficult, and merely involves an adjustment to the discount rate. Let us suppose that we wish to value a joint venture in a South American enterprise with cash flows of £1 million per quarter for the next two years. Given the riskiness of the venture, we believe a reasonable rate of return to be 36 per cent pa.[12] Using a conventional year-end assumption, we would value the annual cash flow of £4 million for two years at 36 per cent, giving a present value of £5.1 million. Given the high discount rate and quarterly cash flows, this will considerably under-state the true value of the venture.

The first stage is to calculate the discount rate per quarter; this is *not* 9 per cent, because of the compound nature of interest. If 36 per cent is the required annual return, the quarterly return is found by solving:

$$(1 + \text{period rate}) = n\text{th root of } (1 + \text{annual rate})$$

where n is the number of periods per annum. In this case, we need the fourth root of 1.36, which gives us a figure of 1.0799 for (1 + period rate), in other words a discount rate of 7.99 per cent per quarter. The second stage simply proceeds with a normal DCF analysis, using eight periods with a cash flow of £1 million each, and discount factors calculated at 7.99 per cent per period – all of which produces a present value of £5.75 million. Similar techniques can be used for any number of periods per annum, and some firms use the approach in investment appraisal to calculate discount factors assuming all cash flows arise on a *mid*-year basis.

As a final note on this, some knowledge of capital market conventions is necessary when using yield to redemption data on bonds. In both the United States and the United Kingdom government bond markets, yields are actually calculated on a half-yearly basis, because US treasury bonds and UK gilts bear half-yearly coupons. This means that a *quoted* yield of 10 per cent is *actually* 5 per cent per half year; using the reverse of the above formula, we can calculate that 5 per cent per half year represents an annual percentage rate of 10.25 per cent. By contrast, some eurobonds and most other European government bonds, such as the French *Obligations du Tressor*, have only one coupon payment per annum, so that their quoted yields are annual percentage rates. This does have implications for the calculation of expected inflation rates (see above) and the estimation of risk adjusted discount rates (see Chapter 6).

CHAPTER 3

ESTIMATING
ECONOMIC VALUE

So far, we have concentrated on the essential tools we need to be able to value companies. In this chapter we turn our attention to using these tools in the valuation process; in particular, we look at *how* we can apply the DCF framework, and under what circumstances the DCF and price–earnings ratio approaches give identical answers. We also look at the alternative to estimating value directly – we could simply use the market value if we are trying to value a quoted company. Whilst this is not an option for unquoted firms, its use as a benchmark in the valuation of listed companies should not be lightly dismissed; it is, after all, the market consensus estimate of the worth of the firm we are attempting to value.[1]

To understand why the market capitalisation of the company is of *major* importance, we need to be aware of research into the *efficient markets hypothesis* (EMH), of which there has been a great deal in the past twenty years or so. The seminal reference on the EMH is Fama (1970), who presented three testable versions of the EMH, the *weak form*, the *semi-strong form* and the *strong form*. The theory is concerned with share prices reflecting available information, the varying levels of the hypothesis incorporating different degrees of information. The weak form suggests that current share prices reflect all information contained in past share prices – in other words, it is not possible to make abnormal returns (an abnormal return is a return greater than that expected for a given level of risk) by using trading rules based upon past share price patterns. The semi-strong form states that share prices reflect fully all publicly available information (such as the annual report, press reports and so on), whilst the strong form hypothesises that prices reflect *all* information, no matter whether it is privately or publicly held. The EMH is possibly one of the most misunderstood hypotheses in finance theory; it does not say that the stock market always values shares correctly, neither does it say that future share prices are unpredictable; it is concerned solely with share prices and the currently available information set. It is also widely disbelieved by market professionals – which is just as well, because the paradox is that markets should only be efficient if a sufficient number of people believe they are not. It is the competitive actions of market professionals in searching out and processing new information that ensures that prices do reflect all available information. However, as Grossman and Stiglitz (1980) have pointed out, to establish a true equilibrium there must actually be some optimal level of inefficiency, since our market professionals must make just enough money from their activities to stay in the game.

Clearly all this, particularly the semi-strong and strong forms, has real implications for the valuer; accordingly we now briefly review the evidence on the EMH.

ARE MARKETS PRICE-EFFICIENT?

During the 1970s and early 1980s, a great deal of effort went into testing the EMH, most of it into investigating the semi-strong form.[2] Many of these investigations use what is known as an *event study* methodology, where a particular occurrence is examined across a large number of companies to test reaction of the market. Crudely summarised, the methodology used requires some model of share return behaviour; return is defined as dividend plus capital gain on opening price. Two common models are the *adjusted returns model*, which simply assumes that in the absence of any specific event a share will move in line with the market as a whole, and the more sophisticated *market model*. The market model assumes that share price returns on any individual security, i, are generated by a linear model consisting of an intercept term, α_i, and a market reaction term captured by each security's beta (β_i), so that the expected return reaction is given by $\beta_i Rm$, where Rm is the return on the stock market as a whole. A share that moves roughly in line with the market (such as ICI) would have a β of around 1.0; one that on average moves less than the market (typically utility stocks like British Gas and British Telecom) has a β of less than 1.0 and a share with greater than average reaction to market movements has a β of greater than 1.0. The market model thus makes an attempt to control for the riskiness of individual shares. In a basic version of an event study, the parameters (intercept term and β) are estimated in a period free of contamination by the event in question. We then use these parameters to estimate the predicted returns for the event period, compare these with the actual returns in the period surrounding the event, and employ statistical tests to see if these differences are significant. If we can observe statistically significant abnormal returns in the period following the 'event', then we might conclude that markets are inefficient, because a simple trading rule that 'beats the market' can be followed.

A basic event study

As an example, let us suppose that we wish to test the reaction of the market to share tips given in the city section of the *Daily Digger*★. The first step would be to collect a reasonably sized sample; let us say that the *Digger* gives an average of four 'buys' a week, and that we have five years' worth of data. Using a service such as *Datastream* we obtain share prices for the period of, say, 162 days surrounding the 'announcement date'. We use the period −132 days to −13 days (a 120-day period) as our parameter estimation period and look at the *abnormal returns* (i.e. actual observed returns minus the expected returns) for the period −12 days to +30 days. Given the *Digger*'s tremendous credibility in the city and, more importantly, the fact that tips are always based upon *new* information, we might expect some attention to be paid to its opinions. If there is any leakage of news (such as the tipster's secretary telling his stockbroker girlfriend that Megapredator is to be tipped as a 'buy') on a consistent basis, we might expect abnormal returns to start to accumulate before the date of disclosure in the press. We would expect an almost instantaneous reaction when the market opens on the day of publication, *but no subsequent abnormal returns*. If these were found, it would suggest some level of inefficiency. Suppose, for example, that we found positive abnormal returns continuing to occur for up to five days following publication, and that these were significant. A simple exploitive strategy is to buy the share on publication and sell it at the end of the fifth day − we outperform the market and that is an example of inefficiency. As an alternative, suppose the market over-reacts; on publication, significant abnormal returns of, say, 10 per cent occur, but by the end of the third day the cumulative abnormal return has reduced to 5 per cent; what trading strategy should we employ? The answer is to sell the share short (i.e. sell shares we do not have and buy them for delivery at the end of the third day when prices have fallen)[3] − again, the market would be inefficient.

This is obviously a very crude description of event study methodology, which often incorporates all sorts of statistical refinements; nevertheless, this gives a flavour of the basis of a good deal of the research into semi-strong form efficiency. Examples of such studies include investigations into accounting choices (such as 'last-in, first-out' (LIFO) or 'first-in, first-out' (FIFO) for stock valuation), announcement of takeovers, block trades and stock splits. The better examples of these studies use several models of share price behaviour to measure the relationship between the event and security returns. In general, and with the exceptions of a few anomalies (some of which are mentioned below), the vast majority of the research indicates that the New York and London stock markets during the 1970s and early 1980s were semi-strong form price-efficient. This led Jensen, a leading American academic, to suggest in 1978 that the EMH was the best established empirical fact in economics. At one time perhaps it was, but there is now room for *some* concern over market efficiency.

Before discussing these concerns, we should note that there has not been as much investigation into the strong form of the EMH as there has into the semi-strong form. There are several reasons for this, the first being that those with inside knowledge of companies do not publicly declare themselves. Second, it is difficult even to observe *ex post facto* insider information, and third, it is difficult to formulate enough tests of the hypothesis to draw valid conclusions. None the less, there have been attempts at investigation, several of which involve directors' share dealings. If the share price increased when directors bought, and returns were subsequently normal, it may be taken as evidence of the superiority of insider information. Alternatively, it might just be that investors *perceive* the shares to be a 'buy' simply because the directors have bought; the price reaction described is more or less what happens in the US (but see below). The question of which of these is the correct explanation is still open to debate, with the evidence to date perhaps favouring the 'me too' hypothesis. In general, anecdotal and academic evidence suggests, not surprisingly, that the market is *not* strong form efficient. This rests upon the definition of 'insiders' as those within the company; if we extend our definition to include 'privileged' market participants such as investment analysts we obtain a rather different result. Sadly for the analyst, research in the US and the UK appears to suggest that although there is some information in analysts' forecasts, there isn't much. For example, in the United Kingdom, Dimson and Marsh (1984) found that well under 1 per cent of realised return was explained by analysts' forecasts of returns. Other studies have found similar results in the United States, but, as Elton and Gruber (1991) point out, 'there does not seem to be much, if any, information in acting on the advice of single brokerage firms. However, by aggregating across brokerage firms, there appears to be real information that persists for short periods of time'; in other words, the consensus forecast might be useful.

Anomalies

We now turn our attention to the anomalies in the semi–strong form of the EMH referred to above. It appears that there is persistent evidence of a 'January' effect, at least in the USA; stock market returns seem to be highest in January and lowest in December. It also appears that this is not exploitable after allowing for transactions costs. A second and more puzzling anomaly is the small companies effect. Even allowing for risk (as in the above mentioned market model), it seems that small companies outperform the rest of the market, both in the United Kingdom[4] and the United States. It might be that this is partly due to a misspecification of the risk factor (issues relating to this are discussed in Chapter 6), and partly due to much higher transactions costs and liquidity premia on small firms, but the existence of such an effect has never been explained in a way that is completely satisfactory for proponents of the EMH.

Third, there is evidence that firms with earnings–price ratios (earnings yields) which are high relative to the market as a whole (i.e. the PE ratios are relatively low) have high returns; the debate over this continues, with some writers suggesting that this is another manifestation of the small companies effect – small firms tend to have lower PE ratios. However, there is some evidence of a persistent PE effect even when size is allowed for.[5]

Finally, there is something of a puzzle over the publication of directors' share dealings. We have already discussed the strong form implications of this above, but it appears that simply following directors' trades may be a successful strategy in that the market does not *instantaneously* react to publication of the trade. Studies by Jaffe (1974) and Finnerty (1976) in the USA first drew attention to this, although a later study by Seyhun (1986) suggested that the effect was not significant after allowing for transactions costs. In the United Kingdom, Pope *et al.* (1990) found some significant effect but a study by Gregory *et al.* (1992) found that whilst this does exist it is associated with the small companies effect. Once this is allowed for (by using the Hoare–Govett Smaller Companies Index), the returns from following directors' trades in these firms, whilst positive, are not statistically significant at the 5 per cent level.

Whilst these kinds of anomalies should cause us some concern, a greater challenge for the EMH comes from the so-called 'volatility' studies pioneered by Schiller (1981). Broadly, the problem is that share prices appear to exhibit a far greater degree of volatility than could reasonably be expected given the economic fundamentals. Although the methodology of these studies has been disputed, it does appear that markets might over-react and, furthermore, that trading rules that allow investors to exploit this in a systematic fashion might be derived.[6] Such results are compatible with the idea of 'short-termism' or with 'fads'. Some of the most interesting support for the latter comes from a US paper by DeBondt and Thaler (1985), which found that it was possible to generate abnormal returns over a five-year period by purchasing a portfolio consisting of the worst performing stocks over the previous five years; purchasing a portfolio of the best performing stocks over the previous five years resulted in an under-performance in the following five years. It is important to point out that a five-year horizon gave a better result than shorter ones; for example, no significant over- or under-performance was found using a one-year period.

Implications for valuation

So what messages are there in this research for the practising valuer? The bulk of the evidence still favours market efficiency, in a semi-strong form. This suggests that, on average, the market value will be a reasonable estimate of worth, given current expectations of managerial strategies and any anticipated takeovers. Note that the price reflects the expected value of the latter – if the market consensus is that there is a 50 per cent chance of a successful bid with an expected premium of 30 per cent on the basic value of the share, that share price will reflect a 15 per cent premium already (ignoring time value of money and the probability of other, later bids).

If we wish to value the firm assuming it remains independent, we should therefore strip out the bid premium present in the share price to find out what the market consensus value is under this strategy.[7] Given the fact that markets are largely price efficient, it is sensible to specify exactly why our estimate of value is different from that of the market. Useful questions include the following:

1. Is the difference due to cash flow estimates or discount rate estimates differing from those of the market (the discount rate calculation is covered in Chapter 6)?
2. Are we acting upon privileged information or a different interpretation of existing information? If the latter, when will the market interpret it according to our analysis?
3. Is the difference due to different time horizons? If so, who is being short-term, us or the market? If the latter, when will the 'error' become apparent?
4. Is the difference because of an assumed difference in strategy (such as the fact we intend to take the company over)? If so, do we agree with the market's valuation assuming existing strategies are pursued?
5. Is the problem one of ourselves or the market following 'fashionable' stocks (note that valuers of companies can be guilty of such things; look back with hindsight at many of the acquisitions made during the 1980s)?

In all cases, it is insufficient to conclude simply that the market has 'got it wrong'; the market may *permanently* value the company in this way, no matter how we feel it should do so. The question of *when* the market will come round to our way of thinking and *why* needs to be addressed. So does the blunt fact that while most analysts believe they can spot misvalued shares, the evidence is that very few of them can do this consistently. It probably pays to treat reports of 'under-valued companies' with some scepticism. None the less, there is some evidence that markets might follow 'fads' and that some forecasting methods can help to predict returns,[8] albeit with very poor levels of association. Hopefully, by asking the right questions concerning the valuation process we can spot whether we have identified a misvaluation on the part of the market, or whether we are the victims of over-confidence (in a takeover valuation context, this was referred to as 'hubris' by Roll (1986)) on the part of the analyst or valuer.

An important lesson for managers valuing their own companies and who believe them to be under-valued is that of communication. If they believe the market is overlooking something, or is taking too short-term a view, the company should consider running a presentation, or being more open in its discussions with analysts. Despite some of the criticisms that have been levelled at the City recently, a look at brokers' analyses of firms suggests that the better ones do take a long-term view on at least some occasions. Although the empirical evidence is somewhat lacking in this key area, there have been cases where *companies* are the ones guilty of short-termism, perhaps because they believe analysts only look as far ahead as next year's earnings figure – it is quite possible that they are mistaken in such a belief. Once again, a breakdown of communication may be the problem, although it is hard not to be sympathetic to those finance directors who feel that they spend more time talking to analysts than they do running the company's finances. One solution that some firms adopt is the employment of market specialists to handle relations with the investment community, but it must be emphasised that unless management has a clear idea of corporate value based upon a rational assessment of alternative strategies, it will be hard to argue a convincing case.

An efficient markets approach to valuation

If we are valuing quoted companies for either investment purposes, or for takeover purposes, we have a choice; we can either proceed with a formal DCF and/or PE valuation, or we can simply accept that the market price will be the correct value, on average. Whilst this may be an unpopular thing to do, it is by no means a foolish one. Adopting such a strategy would lead to a 'passive' approach to investment (in other words, buying and holding a well diversified portfolio) and an approach to takeovers that looked at *added* value. This means that we accept the current market capitalisation, net of any bid premium, as the correct value of the firm given the present managerial strategies. To find the value of the target to the bidder, we add in the present value of any efficiency improvements and synergistic benefits.[9] A simple example of this approach is given below.

Suppose that we are advising a large quoted travel business where management is interested in acquiring Biggles' Air Holidays*, a quoted tour operator. Biggles has 10 million shares in issue, and the current market price is £2.50 per share. In the past six months, rumours about a possible takeover have started to emerge, but prior to this the shares were worth £2 per share at a time when the FTA index stood at 1,100. The index has subsequently moved to 1,200, and a 'market model' type analysis has yielded a beta value of 1.4 for the company. An acquisition would yield synergistic benefits with a present value of £6 million and efficiency improvements could result in savings with a present value of £2 million.

Using the 'efficient markets' approach to valuing the target, we would first note that the gain in the FTA was 1,200/1,100, which is equivalent to a 9.1 per cent increase. As Biggles has a β of 1.4, if there had been no bid rumours driving the market price, we would have expected a current share price of £2 × 1.091 × 1.4 = £2.25. Assuming that no other specific news concerning the company had emerged, we would conclude that this was the 'clean' price and that the additional value was attributable to an anticipated takeover premium (note that we have taken no account of dividends; in reality, we would need to do so). The fair value of the company is therefore £2.25 × 10 million shares, or £22.5 million, and the value to the bidder is £30.5 million (£22.5m + £6m + £2m). Even if the reader decides that he or she does not like this approach to valuation, it should always be used as a reference point because it addresses two key issues that are easy to overlook in a more complex valuation. These issues are first the 'hubris' idea discussed above (i.e. why is the market wrong?) and second it forces the valuer to explicitly examine the notions of efficiency gains and synergy and investigate *where* such savings arise.

Having described a method of establishing a reference point valuation, which is obviously appropriate only in the case of listed companies, we now turn our attention to the types of DCF and PE models that are used in valuation and look at the circumstances under which they give equivalent results.

DIVIDEND GROWTH AND FREE CASH FLOW MODELS

If we take a single period perspective of valuation, we can express the value of the company today (ex-dividend) as a function of next year's dividend (assumed to be payable at the end of the year), the year-end value and the required rate of return, r:

$$\text{Value} = \frac{\text{Year-end value} + \text{year-end dividend}}{(1 + r)}$$

In turn, the year-end value will depend upon the year 2 dividend and year 2 estimated closing price, which is itself a function of year 3 dividend and closing value, and so on. If we interpret 'dividends' in the broadest sense (which includes any payment of cash to the shareholders) we have:

$$\text{Value} = \sum_{t=1}^{t=n} \frac{\text{Dividend}_t}{(1 + r)^t} + \frac{\text{Value in year } n}{(1 + r)^n}$$

The Greek letter sigma (Σ) means the 'sum of' and the sub- and superscripts tell us to sum the discounted dividends from year 1 through to year n (the final year of dividend receipt); in other words, the formula just tells us that value is the discounted sum of the future dividends plus the terminal value of the shares. Note that we are concerned with dividends (again in the broadest sense) *not* earnings. If we used earnings we would be double counting because we would be counting the benefits of future investment without taking into account the funds that need to be committed to achieve those benefits. We shall explore this point in more detail in Chapter 8.

Now imagine that n becomes very large, say 100 years. What happens to the last term of our expression? Value in year n is likely to be a big number but, after discounting, the last term becomes insignificant compared to the present value of the dividends. Thus the further we go into the future, the less important the terminal value of the firm becomes. For example, on a share with a current dividend 10 pence, a constant dividend growth rate of 8 per cent pa and a cost of capital of 15 per cent, the current share price would be £1.54, climbing to £72.36 after 50 years and £3,393.91 after 100 years. Although these future values appear very high in current terms, the present value of these prices comprises only 4.3 per cent and 0.2 per cent of today's value, respectively.

A constant dividend growth model

So far, we have a precise formula which is probably unusable. Consider the application of this to any large company that we believe will continue to exist as an independent entity for the foreseeable future; to all intents and purposes, n is infinite. We might just approximate this as 75 to 100 years, because given the discounting process the present value of any future dividend becomes smaller as you head further into the future. Clearly, reality dictates that we need to find some way of making the problem tractable. The simplest solution is to assume that dividends grow at a constant rate. Recall the model for calculating the present value with contant growth to perpetuity from Chapter 2 (the boldened formula on page 19). For 'cash year 1' read dividend in year 1; we now have the standard textbook formula for share valuation, sometimes known as *Gordon's growth model*. Taking a simple example, suppose a company has 20 million shares in issue, and that dividends of 10 pence per share have just been paid. We believe that the historical growth rate of dividends is a good predictor of future growth, and that over the past 10 years dividends have grown from 3.5 pence per share to the current level. Finally, 16 per cent pa represents a reasonable cost of capital for this type of investment.

First, we calculate the historical growth rate; as we have 10 years of growth, 1 + growth can be found by solving for the tenth root of 10 pence divided by 3.5 pence; this gives us a growth factor of 11.1 per cent. We now plug this into the formula, remembering that the relevant dividend figure is the year 1 value, which by assumption is 10 pence × 1.111 or 11.1 pence per share. Given 20 million shares in issue, this gives us a total dividend of £2.22 million and a value of:

$$\text{Value} = \frac{2.22}{(0.16 - 0.111)} = \text{£45.3 million}$$

Allowing for a changing rate of growth

Obviously, the assumption of constant growth will be unrealistic in the majority of cases, particularly where historical growth has been unusually high or low. Analysts who use this type of approach usually make specific dividend forecasts for a number of years, and then resort to general growth patterns. An example of a US adaptation has the investment analyst making a specific forecast for years 1–5, an industry average forecast for years 6–10, and a general growth forecast for year 11 onwards. To illustrate how this type of model works, we shall use a simplified version and apply it to Stravinsky Spring Manufacturing plc*, an engineering company. We have the following estimate of dividends per share (the company has 10 million in issue) for the next five years:

Year	Dividend per share (pence)
1	10
2	14
3	20
4	24
5	27

For years 6–10 inclusive, we believe that the company's dividend growth will decline to the industry norm of 5 per cent pa in real terms; beyond year 10, we think that the growth in the electronics sector will fall to the average growth in GDP, which we forecast at 2 per cent in real terms. Our assumed inflation rate is 5 per cent pa throughout, which gives us growth levels of 10.25 per cent and 7.1 per cent in money terms for industry and general growth, respectively. Finally, we shall assume a discount rate of 18 per cent pa. We start by continuing the forecast dividend for years 6–10, using the industry growth factor:

Year	Dividend per share
6	29.8
7	32.8
8	36.2
9	39.9
10	44.0

We are now in a position to calculate the value of the company. To start, we value the implied closing price of the shares in year 10, using Gordon's model and a growth factor of 7.1 per cent:

$$\text{Value year 10} = \frac{44.0 \times 1.071}{(0.18 - 0.071)} = 432.14 \text{ pence per share}$$

Discounting this back to present day values using a ten-year discount factor at 18 per cent gives us 82.57 pence per share. To this figure we need to add the present value of the dividends for years 1–10; again using 18 per cent discount factors we obtain a value of 103.25 pence. Thus the value of a share is £1.0325 + £0.8257 = £1.8582, and the value of the company is £18,582 million. Notice that some 44.4 per cent of the value is contributed by the terminal value we have arrived at by using very general assumptions. We shall pay more attention to this issue in Chapter 8, but for now it is sufficient to note that we should have some disquiet about cases where this figure is a high percentage of total value. Generally, this is more of a problem with high growth companies – the answer is that the valuation of such firms requires a longer investment horizon, and this can be more than 20 years in some cases. In case this seems like nonsense, imagine that we had been trying to value Boeing at an early stage in the development of the 747 airliner. How far would we have got with a ten-year horizon? The point is that a crude forecast beyond year 10 is probably better than no forecast. Using techniques like assumed average growth imply that the company will be average – if there are good reasons to believe it will not be, our model should incorporate the fact but we must guard against undue optimism. If we believe that a company will continue to grow at a faster rate than GDP *ad infinitum*, we are implicitly forecasting that at some point in the future the company will be bigger than the rest of the economy. On the whole, this seems an unlikely scenario for any major European country.[10]

The relationship between dividend growth and retention policy

Interesting questions arise here concerning dividend payout ratios. What happens to firms that simply do not pay dividends? First, we need to establish the reason; if the company is quoted, zero or low dividends are normally associated with good growth prospects. Some firms take the view that there is little point in paying out dividends if the money can be invested internally in positive NPV projects (there are doubtless other reasons, such as 'managerialism' but a discussion of this is beyond the scope of this book, except to note that firms that retain cash to invest in negative NPV projects should experience a fall in value). If they are correct in this view, the effect of increased retention should be to increase the future growth rate in dividends; at *some* point in the future higher dividends will be paid, presumably when the marginal return on new investment projects starts to decline. This must happen eventually, as no firm manages to keep a profitable market entirely to itself forever. It should also be noted that the UK tax system does not cause high payout firms to be at a disadvantage; higher rate taxpayers generally prefer capital gain to income, but pension funds actually prefer dividends from a taxation perspective. Transactions costs, for companies and for individuals who adopt a buy and hold strategy, favour retention policies although the 'discipline' value of new issues has to be set against this; companies who follow high payout policies need to obtain new shareholders' funds from the market, and this necessitates the release of a prospectus that broadly informs investors of the intended use of the funds.

We can also establish a formula for the growth in dividends based upon the retention policy. This is of conceptual value only, as the formula neatly assumes that all investment earns a constant rate of return, and that this starts to occur one year after the investment takes place. Given these rather restrictive assumptions, we can see that earnings next year must be the same as earnings this year if no further investment takes place; in this case all the earnings are paid out as dividends. If we retain a proportion (call it RE for retained earnings) of these earnings, we reinvest this at a constant return on new investment (RONI)[11] and this increases our earnings next year by RONI × RE = g. Thus we have a formula for calculating g, and a decision rule − only retain funds for new investment if RONI is greater than or equal to r, the return required by shareholders.

With unquoted companies, the position is somewhat more confused, as many closely held companies do not pay dividends, and either plough back all earnings into new investment or release positive cash flows through benefits of one form or another (conversely, salaries in such firms are sometimes artificially low, with higher dividends paid to avoid national insurance contributions). In this situation, it is important to ascribe fair relative values to the remuneration and dividend components, the guiding principle being that all salaries must be based upon going rates for the job. This helps to establish the prospective dividend payable if the firm was quoted; it is also essential to bear in mind that this may well occur in the future, as the company may be planning a listing on the USM or the main market.

The free cash flow model

The alternative to the dividend growth model is the free cash flow model. Although it amounts to the same thing in a different form, it can be intuitively more appealing for small firms and can also help in situations where cash is being generated but not paid out as dividends − this is not uncommon with several leading companies having so-called 'cash mountains'. Another advantage of this model is that it allows us to cope with non−equity financing in a variety of ways. To be able to develop our free cash flow model, which is the one we shall concentrate on for the remainder of the book, we now break down a company's profit and loss account and cash flow statement into their principal components:

	Cash flow	Profit and loss
Total revenue	TR	TR
Cash operating expenses		
variable	VC	VC
fixed	FC	FC
Operating cash flow	OCF	OCF
Depreciation	−	DEP
Operating cash flow/profit before tax	OCF	PBT
Cash taxes	CT	CT

	Cash flow	Profit and loss
Changes in deferred and other tax provisions	–	ΔT
Operating cash flow/profit after tax	CFAT	OPAT
Working capital investment	WCAP	–
Investment in fixed assets	INV	–
Free cash flow	**FCF**	
Interest income net of tax	INT	INT
Interest net of tax	NI	NI
Cash flow/profit attributable to shareholders	CFS	PATS

Note that cash flow attributable to shareholders is *net* of investment, and is therefore equal to dividends plus the change in cash deposits. It is also possible to look at the free cash flow (FCF) figure in terms of its financing (the above looks at its operational creation):[12]

Interest income net of tax	INT (+ve)
Interest payments net of tax	NI (−ve)
Dividends paid	DIV (−ve)
Change in cash deposits and investments	ΔCDI (+ve/−ve)
New borrowings	D+ (+ve)
Loan repayments	D− (−ve)
New share issues	E (+ve)
Free cash flow	**FCF**

We can now see the comparability of this with the dividend discount model; if there are no borrowings or cash deposits, DIV = FCF and the two models are equivalent. However, when cash deposits are involved (which in reality they will be, given the lumpy nature of investment), the two models can give different results if care is not exercised. It happens that the FCF model is simpler to use, as the following naive example illustrates. Suppose that Constant plc* has a constant net cash flow of £100 pa with no growth opportunities; given this absence of any alternative use for the cash, management pay all this out as dividends each year. One day, when management are preparing their three year plan (which given the boring nature of Constant's activity, is not a long process), along comes an investment opportunity that will require an investment of £315.25 at the end of year 3 and produce cash flows of £35 pa in perpetuity with effect from year 4. Given that Constant's cost of capital is 10 per cent pa, they realise that they have stumbled upon a positive NPV project (in fact, the NPV is +£34.75).

Overcome with excitement at having at last found a positive NPV growth opportunity, Constant's finance director intends to finance the investment by witholding the dividends for the next three years and placing the money in risk-free investments, which earn the fair risk-free rate of 5 per cent pa; this will yield a terminal value exactly equal to the necessary £315.25. We shall now see how our two alternatives measure up, but first we shall try and logically assess the value of the firm.

First, the value of the *continuing* business is not altered in any way by the retention of dividends; it therefore follows that no change in shareholder wealth results from this so we have a present value of this existing business of 100/0.1 = £1,000. To this we add the NPV of the new investment, £34.75 in year 3, discounted back to present value terms, which is £26.11, giving us a total value of the firm of £1,026.11. Following the outline given above, this is exactly the result we get from the FCF model:

Item	Year 1	Year 2	Year 3	Terminal value (year 3)
CFAT	100.00	100.00	100.00	135 ÷ 0.1 = 1350
INV	0.00	0.00	315.25	
FCF	100.00	100.00	−215.25	1350.00
Discounted value @ 10%	90.91	82.64	−161.72	1014.28

Adding up the discounted cash flows gives us £1,026.11, which agrees with our 'logical' answer. Unfortunately, the dividend discount model does not. The discounted value of the future dividends is simply £1,350 in year 3, discounted back to year 0 (today), which gives us the £1,014.28 shown as the PV of the terminal value above. Essentially, the dividend discount model has taken the view that those cash deposits were invested in a negative NPV project, as they were earning 5 per cent and not 10 per cent. This is not the case, because the company *could* have paid out those dividends and gone for a rights issue in year 3; clearly, if the shareholders had put that money into risk-free investments themselves, they would be in the position suggested by our 'logical' calculation and FCF formula. The only way of rescuing the dividend model is to recognise that the risk of the business is changing consistently between year 1 and year 3, and the appropriate discount rate therefore changes (essentially, in year 1 it is 1/11 risk-free and 10/11 'risky', in year 2 2.05/12.05 risk-free, and so on); it almost goes without saying that this is not a recommended approach, and we shall therefore stay with the FCF valuation.

There are other reasons why, in practical terms, the free cash flow formula is simpler. First, the exact sources of cash flow creation/consumption are broken down in a form comparable with the familiar profit and loss account; this is useful because we will probably want to look at earnings multiple valuations anyway. Second, once we introduce debt financing, problems can arise with the dividend discount model if we do not allow for the impact of changing payout ratios on the gearing levels of the firm. Whilst we explore the exact relationship in Chapter 6, we can note for now that increasing gearing leads to an increase in the cost of equity capital, thus *ceteris paribus* increasing the payout ratio means increasing the discount rate. In fairness, however, we should realise that exactly the same type of logical error can beset the FCF method because, via the same argument, if gearing changes then so might the weighted average cost of capital.[13]

In general, there are two principal ways of applying the FCF model to value the firm. The first method involves discounting the FCF at the opportunity cost of capital, which reflects the business risk of the company, and adding in the present value of the tax relief on future debt interest (see Chapters 6 and 7). The second method discounts the FCF at the weighted average cost of capital (WACC), which gives the value of the entire firm, and then deducts the value of the debt claims, which results in the value of the equity. Properly applied, with consistency of assumptions, we should get identical results; these models are discussed in Chapters 6 and 7.

PRICE EARNINGS MODELS AND THEIR RELATIONSHIP WITH FCF AND DIVIDEND DISCOUNT MODELS

It must have crossed your mind by now that FCF valuation seems to be a reasonably complex methodology, and that perhaps a good old fashioned PE valuation based upon next year's earnings might do just as well; the answer is that, on occasions, it can. Knowing when the PE method is likely to work, and why, is useful because it avoids some computational complexity. It is also important to note that *the forecasting skills necessary to make a successful PE valuation are identical to those required for FCF valuation*. This point deserves heavy emphasis; of vital importance is the forecasting of sales and costs, which we shall deal with in Chapter 4. The PE multiple, which will be discussed in Chapter 5, is a complex function of future growth rates, risk, payout ratios, inflation rates and opportunity cost of capital. In the FCF method, risk and the cost of capital are reflected in the discount rate, with growth rates and payout ratios appearing in the cash flow forecasts. The FCF method explicitly models the complex relationships involved between these variables. When these relationships can be simplified, as in the case of constant growth models, the PE approach can be a useful time saver; however, when this is not the case, calculating a sensible PE ratio without going through the cash flow modelling process is a hazardous task.

To explain the relationship that exists between the PE ratio and FCF methods, we shall use the example of Standard plc*, which has a policy of steady expansion and also has predictable and constant growth rates. Standard is all equity financed, and has a cost of capital of 15 per cent pa;

the year 0 asset base consists of £4,000 fixed assets and £1,000 working capital. Forecast cash flows and profits look like this:

	Year 1	Year 2	Year 3	Relationship
Operating cash flow (OCF)	1650	1815	1996.5	33% opening assets
Depreciation (DEP)	400	440	484.0	10% fixed assets
Taxes (paid as cash) (CT)	500	550	605.0	★
Investment in:				
working capital (WCAP)	100	110	121.0	increases in line with expansion
fixed assets (INV)	800	880	968.0	†
Cash flow (= OCF−CT− WCAP−INV) (FCF)	250	275	302.5	
Profit (PATS)	750	825	907.5	

★For simplicity, depreciation is assumed to be tax allowable and a 40 per cent tax rate is assumed.

†Investment is a replacement of existing assets (note implicit assumption of no inflation) and expansion of existing base by 10 per cent.

We can see that the two valuation approaches are equivalent, and that the PE ratio is related to the required rate of return. First, notice that the growth rate in FCF is 10 per cent pa. We already know that any cash flow increasing at a constant rate can be solved via the boldened formula on page 19. In this case, 'year 1 cash' is the FCF and r is the required return of 15 per cent pa, so we have a value of:

$$\text{Value} = \frac{250}{(0.15 - 0.10)} = £5,000$$

If the PE approach is to give the same result, the prospective PE ratio must be £5,000 ÷ 750 = 6.67×. Notice that this PE ratio remains constant each year. In year 2, with a PE of 6.67 the firm is worth 825 × 6.67 = £5,500. Our shareholders have just received a dividend of £275, and a capital gain of £500 since year 1, which gives a return of 15 per cent; the PE ratio and FCF formula are compatible. Notice also that the prospective PE ratio is simply the reciprocal of 0.15, the required rate of return. This relationship only holds when the return on new investment (RONI) is exactly equal to the return required by shareholders. In cases where this is not so, the general relationship is given by:

$$\text{PE} = \frac{1 - g/\text{RONI}}{(R - g)}$$

The derivation is given in the appendix to this chapter (see page 48). To illustrate the application of this formula, return to the example of Standard plc but imagine that management have come up with some efficiency improvements, so that all investment will now generate a cash flow of 38 per cent pa, rather than the 33 per cent we previously assumed. Taking years 1 and 2 only, the following cash flow pattern arises:

Item	Year 1	Year 2
OCF	1900	2090
DEP	400	440
CT	600	660
WCAP	100	110
INV	800	880
FCF	400	440
PATS	900	990

Using the normal growth formula gives:

$$\text{Value} = \frac{400}{(0.15 - 0.1)} = 8,000$$

The return on new investment is £900/5,000 = 0.18 or 18 per cent, so, using our formula for the PE ratio gives us:

$$PE = \frac{1 - 0.10/0.18}{(0.15 - 0.10)} = 8.89\times$$

Checking our valuation on a PE basis yields 8.89 × £900 = £8,000. Whilst this works wonderfully with constant rates of investment and growth, sadly, it does not work with lumpy investment patterns. Look back at the example of Constant plc above. The initial prospective PE ratio is 10.92, and this begins to rise in years 1 and 2 in anticipation of increased profitability, but by year 3 the *prospective* PE has fallen back to 10, as there are no further growth prospects in the offing. In theory, it is possible to derive a formula for the PE under all types of scenario, but in practice it is easier to use the FCF formula whenever investment patterns are lumpy and growth is erratic. None the less, we have shown that the two approaches are equivalent in the type of situation we frequently assume when calculating the terminal or horizon value of a company. Strangely enough, despite our earlier misgivings, it turns out that it can be valid to use PE ratios to calculate these horizon values, provided the PE is calculated using assumptions about cost of capital, growth and returns on new investment compatible with those used in the rest of the forecast. These issues are discussed in more detail in Chapter 8.

VALUATION OF GROWTH OPPORTUNITIES

In the above analysis, we have concentrated on a direct valuation of the business in terms of the cash flows and profits it is expected to produce.

In practice, some valuers prefer to work out what they think the maintainable profits are from the existing business, and then add in a value for the growth opportunities, sometimes called the 'hope for' value, or similar. It is perfectly possible to apply this type of approach to our above examples. First, let us take the first case where the firm was reinvesting at just the rate of return required by the shareholders. With no growth opportunities, the firm would only reinvest sufficient funds to replace the existing assets and, in our simplistic scenario described above, where there was no inflation, this amounts to paying out all its earnings. We therefore have a free cash flow identical to accounting earnings and, since this cash flow is maintainable in perpetuity, a value of:

$$\text{Value} = \frac{750}{0.15} = £5,000$$

Alternatively, we already know that in this situation the PE ratio would be 6.67 times (the reciprocal of the cost of capital), so that the earnings multiple approach gives us the same result as the DCF valuation. We can now add the net present value of the growth opportunities. By assumption, the return on these projects is just equal to that required by the shareholders, the NPV on these is zero, and thus there is no value to these opportunities.

We shall now look at the more complicated case where reinvestment was possible at a higher rate than that required by shareholders. The base value if no reinvestment takes place is the distributable cash flow (earnings) discounted into perpetuity at 15 per cent, giving a present value of £6,000. Now consider what happens when the company invests in growth opportunities. In effect, the shareholders are being asked to give up £500 of dividends in order to invest in 'growth'. This £500 generates free cash flows in perpetuity (given the required reinvestment of £40 per annum) of £90, which discounted at 15 per cent gives us a gross present value of £600. As it required the investment of £500 to achieve this result, the *net* present value is £100. This little exercise takes place every year; furthermore, the incoming cash flows on each of these 'projects' themselves can be analysed in a similar fashion. We thus can treat these NPVs in the same way as dividends in the dividend growth model; in this case the year 1 NPV is £100 and the growth rate in these NPVs is 10 per cent per annum. All this gives us a value for the growth opportunities of:

$$\text{Value}_{\text{growth}} = \frac{100}{0.15 - 0.10} = £2,000$$

Thus we can explain the value of the firm as the present value of the earnings from current investment (always assuming that the rate of inflation is zero), plus the present value of the growth opportunities. In the presence of inflation, we can no longer assume that accounting depreciation is equal to the replacement cost of assets. In fact, such a model will not work unless the rate of asset replacement is constant in money terms.[14]

This method of analysing value draws our attention to two important factors. The first is that a PE multiple derived from looking at stock market averages cannot be applied directly to a *maintainable* earnings figure, because the multiple will reflect average growth expectations; we discuss this in more detail in Chapter 5. Second, pulling out separate growth opportunities draws our attention to an important assumption that is being made in our example. This is the continued availablity of positive NPV projects into perpetuity. There is every reason to suppose that this will not be the case for many companies. Economic theory suggests that positive NPV opportunities will eventually be competed away; straightforward business logic might produce a similar conclusion, because profitable market niches tend to attract competition. It is very easy to inadvertently over-value a company by ignoring this fact, and this must be borne in mind when preparing forecasts of revenues and margins.

THE FCF MODEL AND 'LUMPY' INVESTMENT FLOWS

So far, we have assumed a situation where future investment takes place on a continuous basis. However, in reality investment in fixed assets tends to follow a 'lumpy' or discontinuous pattern. The FCF model is capable of dealing with this, by simply taking the free cash flows described as before, and discounting these at an appropriate rate. Unfortunately, the consequence of this type of cash flow pattern is that we cannot use the growth-based models we described above because they assumed a constant rate of cash flow growth. None the less, we can use some short cuts to arrive at a value of the firm in such situations, and the methodology we employ is based on the concept of 'annual equivalent cash flows'. In principle, any net present value can be turned into an annual equivalent cash flow; the cash flow is found by dividing the NPV by an annuity factor for the required life of the cash flow. Suppose that Saunders plc* is a single project company that has just been set up to manufacture 'strikers', a product apparently in great demand in Europe. The shareholders have just invested £1 million in the company, and this money has been used to purchase the necessary capital equipment, which will have a life of ten years. We shall assume (initially) that there is no inflation, that the equipment will have a scrap value of zero at the end of its life, that the annual net cash inflows (after tax) will be £0.17 million for the next ten years and that the required rate of return on this type of investment is 10 per cent pa. Calculating the NPV in the usual manner gives us a positive value of £44,576. In terms of annual equivalence, having this much positive NPV today (year 0) in exchange for a £1 million outlay is the same as receiving, for the next ten years, an amount of £44,576 divided by a ten–year annuity factor @ 10 per cent pa (6.145) or £7,254.5 pa with no investment in year 0. This is because the NPV of these two cash flow streams (the outlay of £1 million and ten years inflow of £0.17 million, compared with £7,254.5 pa for ten years) are identical. This turns out to be a very useful concept in valuing companies where projects are repeated on a cyclical basis.

In the case of our example, if Saunders is successful in its manufacture of strikers and the market remains stable, in year 10 it will reinvest in the necessary equipment and repeat the whole cycle all over again. Now this gives us a free cash flow pattern of (all figures in £000s):

	Year1	Year2	...	Year10	Year11	...	Year20	Year21	...
Cash inflows	170	170		170	170		170	170	
Investment				1000			1000		
Free cash flow	170	170		−830	170		−830	170	

We could continue estimating these cash flows over a very long period (say, 100 years) and discount them, which would give us a net present value of £72,545 after taking off the year 0 investment cost. In rational markets, the value of Saunders would therefore be £1,072.5 million (NPV plus initial cost). However, this is hardly a time-efficient way of calculating the value of the firm. A faster method is to recognise that the annual equivalent cash flow can be viewed as occuring every year of the ten–year cycle; as this cycle is continuously repeated, we have the equivalent of a perpetual cash flow of £7,254.5 pa. At a discount rate of 10 per cent, this gives a NPV of £72,545 (£7,254.5 ÷ 0.1), which is the same solution as that given by the conventional NPV calculation but much faster.

This approach is also very useful when it comes to calculating the value of a company part way through the life of one of its investments. Suppose we wish to value Saunders plc at the end of year 6. Before we can do this, we need to make an assumption about the dividend payout policy followed by the company; broadly, we can either assume that this is to pay out all surplus cash flows as dividends, and then make a rights issue for the necessary proceeds, or we can assume that the company has retained enough cash (and invested it at a fair rate of return) to finance the equipment replacement when it falls due. We shall assume the latter, and further assume that the cash retained has been invested in financial assets yielding a return of 10 per cent pa. The necessary retention must be sufficient to produce £1 million at the end of ten years; in other words, £1 million is the *future* value of an annuity of an unknown amount at 10 per cent pa. Using tables for the future value of such an annuity indicates an annual retention of £62,745; the balance of each year's cash flow is assumed to be distributed by way of dividends.

We can now value the company at the end of year 6 as follows (all figures in £000s):

PV of annual cash flow of £170 for years 7 to 10 @ 10%	538.9
PV of year 10 perpetual NPV; £72.545 discounted back to year 6 @ 10%	49.5
Value of operating activities	588.4
Value of financial assets (interest reinvested)	484.1
Present value of company	1,072.5

Note that the value of the company has remained constant because of the assumption that retentions are just sufficient to finance the new equipment needed in year 10. If we assume a more generous distribution policy, market value will fall until the necessary finance is raised in year 10, when it returns to £1,072.5 million; however, the *returns* to shareholders remain unaffected (at 10.725 per cent of their initial (year 0) investment, or 10 per cent of market value) because there is a direct trade-off between the fall in market value and the higher dividend.

Adapting the model for inflation

All this offers a useful insight into the valuation of steady-state companies with lumpy investment patterns but to make it practically applicable, we need to be able to adapt the basic analysis to cope with inflation. Fortunately, this is not difficult because the annual equivalent cash flow can be expressed in real terms and indexed up each year as appropriate. Let us stay with the example of Saunders plc, but modify our analysis to incorporate an expected inflation rate of 10 per cent pa. Our money (or nominal) cost of capital will now be 21 per cent pa. Given our previous discussion on real and money terms evaluation of companies and projects, we can readily see that the year 0 value of Saunders remains unaffected, at £1,072.5 million. We can also see that the replacement cost of our equipment in year 10 will become £1 million × 1.1^{10} = £2.5937 million. The necessary annual retention to fund this replacement will now be £62,745 in year 0 terms, which must be indexed up each year in line with inflation, and invested at 21 per cent pa. The balance of the cash flows (which of course will also be increasing in line with inflation) can be distributed in dividends. Under such assumptions the value of Saunders in year 6 will now be (figures in £000s):

PV of annual cash flow of £170 × 1.1^6 (i.e. £170 in year 6 price levels) for years 7 to 10 @ 10 per cent*	954.7
PV of year 10 perpetual NPV; £72.545 × 1.1^{10} discounted back to year 6 @ 21 per cent	87.8
Value of operating activities	1,042.5
Value of financial assets (interest reinvested)**	857.6
Present value of company	1,900.1

*NB We can also use money cash flows discounted at 21 per cent pa to give the same result.

**This can be found by realising that the first year's cash investment is £62,745 × 1.1; this is invested for five years (to end of year 6) at 21 per cent. Repeating this process for each year's investment yields the value of financial assets given.

Note that this value of £1.9 million is the same as that found by indexing up the starting value by six years inflation. In practice, this use of real annual equivalents will prove a very useful valuation device because for many companies, this 'steady-state' of replacing old equipment at regular intervals can be used to estimate the terminal value of the company at the end of the specific forecast period, which in the case of Saunders was year 10. This point is further developed in Chapter 8.

SUMMARY

In general, we have seen that by far the most flexible approach to estimating economic value is the use of free cash flow discounted by the business's cost of capital. Free cash flow was defined as the cash flow from operations, less cash taxes and investment in fixed and working capital.

In the case of constant rates of growth in all cash flows, and constant relationships between all the variables, this approach can be shown to be equivalent to the use of the familiar price–earnings multiple. However, where the investment flows are lumpy, or where the relationships between the variables are in any way not constant, this turns out not to be the case.

APPENDIX

From the dividend discount model we know that:

$$\text{Value} = \frac{\text{DIV}}{(R - g)}$$

Now dividends are simply earnings (ENGS) multiplied by 1 minus the proportion retained, i.e.:

$$\text{DIV} = \text{ENGS}(1 - \text{RE})$$

We also know that $g = \text{RONI} \times \text{RE}$, and therefore that:

$$\text{RE} = \frac{g}{\text{RONI}}$$

It therefore follows that:

$$\text{Value} = \frac{\text{ENGS}(1 - g/\text{RONI})}{(R - g)}$$

Dividing both sides by ENGS gives us:

$$\frac{\text{Value}}{\text{ENGS}} = \frac{(1 - g/\text{RONI})}{(R - g)}$$

and Value/ENGS is the *prospective* PE ratio, QED.

CHAPTER 4

FORECASTING COSTS
AND REVENUES

A key factor in performing successful valuations is an understanding of the relationships between the forecast variables, as this allows an appreciation of which variables are likely to have the greatest impact on business value. All forecasts should be analysed to show the effect of a change in each of the variables, a process known as *sensitivity analysis*. It is also a good idea to set up the forecast on a spreadsheet model in such a way as to allow several variables to be changed simultaneously, so that we can ask 'what if' type questions about the valuation. This is sometimes called *scenario modelling*. In terms of valuation sensitivity, the most critical variable in the forecast is usually the sales revenue. In general, as the ratio of fixed costs to variable costs increases, any given change in the sales revenue has a greater impact. This phenomenon is sometimes known as *operational gearing or leverage*. To illustrate the relative impact of changes in revenues, variable costs and fixed costs, we shall take the original case of Standard plc used in Chapter 3 (see page 41). Let us suppose that the breakdown of the operating cash flow comes from the following cost and revenue structure:

		Year 1	Year 2	Year 3
Total revenue	TR	16,500	18,150	19,965.0
Cash operating expenses				
variable (80% sales)	VC	13,200	14,520	15,972.0
fixed	FC	1,650	1,815	1,996.5
Operating cash flow	OCF	1,650	1,815	1,996.5
Depreciation	DEP	400	440	484.0
Taxes (paid as cash)	CT	500	550	605.0
Investment in:				
working capital	WCAP	100	110	121.0
fixed assets	INV	800	880	968.0
Cash flow (= OCF − CT−WCAP−INV)	FCF	250	275	302.5
Profit	PATS	750	825	907.5

Note that this assumes that the fixed costs are in fact driven by fixed asset investment, but are invariate with respect to sales changes in any one year.

Our original value, on a DCF basis, was calculated by noting that growth was 10 per cent pa and cost of capital 15 per cent, giving us a value of:

$$\text{Value} = \frac{250}{0.15 - 0.1} = £5,000$$

Now suppose we were wrong about the cost of capital (if we were using a DCF methodology) or the PE ratio (if we were using an earnings multiple approach). Let us assume that the error in the estimated cost of capital was 5 per cent adverse. The correct value of Standard should therefore have been calculated using a 15.75 per cent discount rate, which gives us:

$$\text{Value} = \frac{250}{0.1575 - 0.1} = £4,347.80$$

The original solution represents a valuation error of 15 per cent compared to the correct value above. If 15.75 per cent was the correct cost of capital, then given the relationship we derived in the previous chapter, the PE ratio used should have been:

$$\text{PE} = \frac{1 - 0.10/0.15}{0.1575 - 0.1} = 5.797\times$$

Note that we cannot simply change the PE ratio by 5 per cent, because this would imply that all the variables that make up the earnings multiple (growth, cost of capital and return on new investment) had changed, whereas we are assuming here that only the cost of capital has changed. The PE valuation is therefore $5.797 \times 750 = £4,347.80$. Naturally, we could have misspecified the PE ratio with an error margin of 5 per cent, in which case the value of the firm simply changes by this amount. Note that as the growth factor, g, increases the *relative* impact of a change in cost of capital, compared to a change in the price–earnings ratio, becomes greater.

However, when we examine the effect of a change in the sales revenue figure, we find a far greater impact for our 5 per cent change than we obtained by changing the cost of capital. If the sales had been over-estimated by 5 per cent, it follows that the correct figures in year one are:

		Year 1
Total revenue	TR	15,675
Cash operating expenses		
variable (80% sales)	VC	12,540
fixed	FC	1,650
Operating cash flow	OCF	1,485

		Year 1
Depreciation	DEP	400
Taxes (paid as cash)	CT	434
Investment in:		
working capital	WCAP	100
fixed assets	INV	800
Cash flow (= OCF − CT − WCAP − INV)	FCF	151
Profit	PATS	651

Now, assuming that our original cost of capital is correct (at 15 per cent) we can see that even with the assumption that 80 per cent of the costs are variable, the valuation changes dramatically to:

$$Value = \frac{151}{0.15 - 0.10} = £3,020$$

Thus, our original valuation was an over-estimate of no less than 65.6 per cent; a similar change results from altering the contribution margin (sales less variable costs as a percentage of sales) by the same amount. Finally, if we change the cost structure so that of the original estimate of £14,850 costs, £3,300 are fixed and £11,550 (70 per cent of sales) are variable, we get a year 1 cash flow of:

		Year 1
Total revenue	TR	15,675.0
Cash operating expenses		
variable (70% sales)	VC	10,972.5
fixed	FC	3,300.0
Operating cash flow	OCF	1,402.5
Depreciation	DEP	400.0
Taxes (paid as cash)	CT	401.0
Investment in:		
working capital	WCAP	100.0
fixed assets	INV	800.0
Cash flow (= OCF − CT − WCAP − INV)	FCF	101.5
Profit	PATS	601.5

Which, discounting in the usual fashion,[1] gives us a valuation of £2,030, implying that the original valuation was an over-estimate of 146 per cent. Whilst this is a rather simplistic example (in particular, such sensitivity analysis implies that *every* year's sales revenue has been over-estimated by

5 per cent), it does illustrate that, ultimately, we need to worry most about the revenue estimates. This is not to imply that the other variables are unimportant factors, but it does help to give an idea of the relative impact of each of the variables. If we continued our analysis, we would find that a 5 per cent error in fixed costs based on the original analysis produced a 19.3 per cent valuation error, whilst on the revised cost structure the effect is to give a 65.6 per cent error. Finally, if we had been wrong about the growth rate by 5 per cent (i.e. the correct rate was 9.5 per cent not the 10 per cent we assumed), the valuation error would have been 10 per cent.

Having noted that changes in costs, contribution margins and revenues can have a far greater impact than the cost of capital, we now turn our attention to the estimation of these variables; a summary checklist of the forecasting process is given in Appendix I of this chapter (see page 74).

FORECASTING: GENERAL PRINCIPLES

Before starting the valuation itself, background information on the economy, the industry and the company itself needs to be obtained. A crucial factor here is the standpoint of the valuer. In many cases, such as management's own valuation, the acquisition of a privately held company, consultant's valuations and so forth, we have access to internal information, which will cover areas such as strategic plans, contract details, cost structure and management's own forecasts (be they good or bad); in this situation, we would also be able to obtain management's feedback on the valuation, and be able to question managers on the critical factors affecting the valuation. Equally, there are cases, such as independent investment analysis and hostile takeover attempts, where this information is not available and the valuer has to rely upon information available in the public domain, plus that which can be gained through personal contacts, rumour and other sources (for example, it is possible to get an approximate idea of the value of a company's property by inspecting land registry documents and viewing buildings externally). Clearly, the degree of information forthcoming from these other sources will depend upon the context of the exercise; investment analysts are likely to have some sort of access to managers, whereas a hostile potential bidder is unlikely to be offered the option of tea and biscuits with the finance director. However, from a predator's perspective, it is possible to tease out more information by actually bidding for the company (the extent of the information gained will depend upon whether any details have been disclosed to a third party; the City Code requires information symmetry between rival bidders).

Economic background

A vital input to the valuation process is the forecast of economic indicators. We have already discussed inflation forecasts in Chapter 2;

other macro–economic variables that will need to be estimated include interest rates (again see Chapter 2), exchange rates, growth in gross domestic product (GDP), unemployment and taxation rates. GDP growth, unemployment and interest rates are all indicators of the general health of the economy, and therefore have an important influence on our sales and cost forecasts. In particular, interest rates have had a substantial effect on most companies, as recent governments have used interest rates as a central plank of economic policy. Given this importance in policies for controlling inflation and growth, interest rates have had a 'double hit' effect on companies because they have influenced both demand for products and financing costs. In the case of exchange rates, it may be obvious why we need a forecast for those companies that export, buy imported raw materials or have overseas subsidiaries, but perhaps not so obvious why we need a forecast for companies that do not indulge in any of these activities. The first point that needs to be considered here is the influence of exchange rates on demand in remote, but none the less important ways; these are discussed below. The second point is that exchange rates interact with both interest rates and inflation rates.

In theory, interest, inflation and exchange rates should all be inter-related, at least in the long run, so that we should always check that our long-term forecasts for each of these variables are consistent with one another. In the absence of exchange controls, the required risk–free rate of return should be equal in all countries, so that the difference in interest rates should be explained by differences in the expected inflation rates. Futhermore, this difference in interest rates is what drives the difference between spot and forward rates of exchange (in fact, this is precisely how market participants set the forward premium or discount; if they did not take these interest rate differences into account it would be possible for arbitragists to make risk–free gains). Finally, the difference between forward and spot rates should equal the expected change in the spot rate,[2] which in turn should equal the difference in expected inflation rates; this, of course, is where we came in.

An example may help to illustrate these relationships; we shall assume that our problem is to forecast future exchange and inflation rates for Rush–Hughes Malt Distilleries plc★, a company that operates in the Welsh whisky industry and exports its products to Japan. Suppose that the spot rate between sterling and Japanese yen is ¥222.5 = £1, and that the Japanese risk–free rate of interest is 6.1 per cent pa whilst the sterling rate is 10.2 per cent pa. Looking at the forward rate premium on the yen gives us an annual premium of 3.9 per cent (all these figures can be found in the *Financial Times* on a daily basis); let us further assume that our estimate of inflation in the United Kingdom is 5 per cent per annum. Using the relationships described above, we can see that the forward rate is related to the spot rate through the differential risk-free interest rate; formally, $(1 + RF_£) \div (1 + RF_¥) = (1 + \text{forward rate premium})$, so:

1.102/1.061 = 1.039

which agrees with our forward rate above (insomniacs can repeat this exercise themselves using euro–deposit rates and forward premia from the *FT*). As the forward rate is the market's expected future spot rate, the implied spot rate in one year's time is found from $(1 + RF_¥) \div (1 + RF_£) =$ expected spot rate $\div$ current spot rate, thus by rearranging we have an implied exchange rate in one years time of:

(1.061/1.102) × 222.5 = 214.2

or ¥214.2 = £1. Finally, given that the expected change in the spot rate (i.e. the forward rate compared to the spot rate) reflects the expected differential inflation rate, we have:

Expected spot rate $\div$ current spot rate = $(1 + infl_{JAPAN}) \div (1 + infl_{UK})$

which, by rearranging, gives an implied Japanese expected inflation rate of:

[(214.2/222.5) × 1.05] − 1 = 0.011 or 1.1%.

Whilst a knowledge of these theoretical relationships is useful, it must be emphasised that these equilibria do not necessarily hold in the short-term.

Turning to the issue of obtaining forecasts for all our required economic variables, obvious sources are stockbrokers and the various economic forecasting agencies but, as with the inflation predictions discussed in Chapter 2, an average of these forecasts tends to give better results than any individual forecast. Again, we have the problem that forecasts are often available for a period perhaps shorter than we would wish; depending on the country we need the information for, we might be able to obtain forecasts for up to five years ahead, but often we will not be able to achieve such a horizon. If all else fails, for the longer term we simply have to fall back upon long-term averages, so that for example we might forecast the long-term rate of growth in GDP for the United Kingdom to be around 2 per cent pa.

Industry background

Whenever we attempt to value a firm, all aspects of the forecasting process should be considered in terms of principal lines of business (PLBs); for single business companies, this will not present any difficulty. Neither will it do so in the case of a valuation of a multi-business company using inside information. However, when valuing from an external perspective, this can cause problems where companies are diverse conglomerates, which report their results under general segment groupings. It is often very difficult to obtain a clear idea of where sales and margins are coming from in such situations; it is to be hoped that investor pressures (such as is now being exercised by UK pension funds) and accounting standard changes will result in the position becoming better.

This brings us to the industry factors that need to be considered for each PLB. First, there are the questions concerning the market itself; these include asking the following:

1. Do we expect any fashion changes, and if so how will these impact upon demand for particular products?
2. Do we expect changes in competition?
3. What is the impact of changing technology on the types of products the industry produces (compare, for example, the drinks industry to the computer industry)?
4. What is the likely growth in the market, and where is this likely to occur?

We also need to be aware of the way in which market changes compare in different areas or countries. The other critical factors concerning the market are its maturity and expected life, and the market shares of competing firms in the industry.

Then there are issues relating to the production technology of the industry. Forecasting here is a difficult process, but an awareness of changes occuring in other countries or other industries would be helpful. Such changes will also have an impact on the supply of labour and the skills required of employees. It can even have profound implications for both suppliers and customers (for example, the use of just-in-time stock control in the motor industry has had a marked effect on component suppliers). In addition to these factors, there is the importance of regulatory changes and political awareness; the most obvious example at the moment is the effect of environmental legislation and concern on industry. It might have been reasonably forseeable some years ago that industrial processes giving rise to pollution may have been required to clean up their emissions within the near future.

Company background

Having established the contextual factors, we can now move on to consider the company-specific items. Necessary background information on the company includes the following:

1. Group structure and management.
2. List of susidiary and associated companies in the group, including country of incorporation, date of acquisition, and proportion and class of capital held.
3. Names of senior managers and directors, together with profiles of experience, where possible.
4. Full accounting information, including interim results, all published accounts for the last three to five years, and results of subsidiaries and associates where possible.
5. An outline of the accounting policies used, with particular reference

to any changes in policies and any exceptional features of such policies.

If the valuation has access to inside information, independent company advisers (such as stockbrokers, bankers and auditors) can also be approached, with permission. Other key pieces of information that will be available in such cases include the corporate plan, minutes of board meetings, and the management's own longer-term forecasts and assumptions used in the preparation of those forecasts. Should there simply not be a corporate plan or long-term forecast or budget, we might reasonably start off with a slightly wary view of the organisation. When such forecasts are available, it can be very instructive to look at historical forecasts versus actual outcomes, to see if the management consistently over- or under-estimates costs and revenues. In this context, it is important to establish that we are dealing with forecasts that estimate expected outcomes, rather than budgets that contain a 'behavioural' element designed to motivate enthusiastic managers (or frighten timid ones). With inside information, it should also be possible to identify:

1. Activities that are large relative to the PLB as a whole.
2. Major limiting factors on output (e.g. demand, skilled labour, capital investment, supplies).
3. Unusual operating conditions (e.g. strikes, temporary shortage of supplies).

Finally, when using accounting information we need to bear in mind the quality of the system itself and the reporting conventions being used. The internal accounting systems of some companies leave a great deal to be desired, and this is of particular importance when unaudited information is being used. In addition, the nature of some businesses means that sales revenue and costs may be difficult to confirm; building contractors are notable examples, because of the long-term nature of the contracts.

In addition, we need to perform what is sometimes referred to in the management literature as a 'SWOT' analysis for each PLB. This consists of identifying the major strengths, weaknesses, opportunities and threats to the PLB. Whilst we need to be wary of being misled by what one might refer to as 'company propaganda', properly carried out this exercise can provide a useful checklist when reviewing the realism of the assumptions made when preparing the forecast. Furthermore, it also helps when applying scenario modelling to the forecast. Company visits play a vital role in the SWOT analysis because they allow the valuer to make intuitive judgements about issues such as the quality of the management team, the nature of the workplace (for example, if it is a factory does it have a 'Dickensian' appearance, or is the impression one of a modern and efficient manufacturing environment?), and the 'feel' of the business unit in general. It is important to note that this requires visits to the shop floor, not just the boardroom. If it is not possible to gain access to the firm itself, it may be possible to make use of any contacts with suppliers, customers or financiers and obtain their impressions of the valuation target.

Related to the SWOT analysis, we need to perform an analysis of risk factors. One type of risk is what might be called economic risk exposure; finance theorists capture this type of risk through a risk index known as (β) beta, which measures the relationship between returns on the company's equity and returns on the stock market as a whole. As 'the market' is driven by economic prospects, this relative measure gives us an idea of how the company reacts to changes in these economic prospects. All this is discussed in detail in Chapter 6, but for now we can note that this type of risk can be incorporated into the discount rate. All of this leaves us with other risk factors to consider. First, let us assume that our PLB is located within the United Kingdom. What specific risk factors do we need to consider? Whilst exposure to general economic factors can be incorporated through our β measure,[3] it can still be useful to specify the effect of such factors on the PLB. For example, a leveraged buyout of a luxury car dealership can run into severe problems in the face of sustained high real levels of interest rates.

This leaves a whole host of other risk factors, which might include failure to renew major contracts for existing work, failure of new products to win anticipated market share, loss of key personnel, industrial relations problems and even political risks. It should be apparent that political risks do not just affect companies trading overseas; for example, the Gulf War had a fairly dramatic impact upon some London hotels, whilst government policy and regulatory decisions can have a profound impact on some firms. We might feel that the one thing we do not have to worry about is exchange rate risk; sadly, we would be wrong. Apparently remote factors can affect company value; for example, any leisure activity that depends upon overseas tourists is subject to some degree of exchange rate risk, as is any manufacturer who depends upon imported raw materials or components. Less obviously, a firm that manufactures entirely from domestically sourced material and sells in domestic markets might also be at risk in the longer term from currency movements, as a manufacturer in a country undergoing exchange rate appreciation will face an increasing threat from imports by foreign manufacturers who find that their competitive position has improved.[4]

Clearly, if the PLB is a foreign subsidiary, a whole range of other environmental and risk factors come into play. Some of the major factors will be an analysis of political risk (which covers regulatory controls, threat of nationalisation, problems connected with the repatriation of cash flows, cultural factors, government stability and relationship with neighbouring countries), exchange rate risk, exchange controls, transfer pricing legislation, infrastructure development, availability of investment incentives and subsidies and labour availability, amongst others.[5]

The final consideration on risk should be to what extent these risks can be hedged, and at what cost. Whilst a detailed discussion of hedging is beyond the scope of this book, we should note that it is by no means clear that a quoted company should hedge such risks.[6] To start with, investors can diversify away many of these risk factors by simply holding a balanced portfolio; furthermore, they may actually want to take on currency and foriegn economic risks as a way of limiting their exposure to the UK economy. Second, it is notoriously difficult to hedge uncertain long-term cash flows,[7] and attempts to do so have sometimes met with spectacular failure (there have been some notable recent UK experiences). Third, we have the alternative of relying upon the type of long-term economic equilibria described above. Finally, the most effective method of limiting such risk may be to finance expansion in foreign countries with local borrowing, although this will not always be possible (for example, at the time of writing it would be difficult to adopt this approach to investing in Eastern European countries).

Having described the background factors that need to be considered, we can now move on to the forecast of sales revenues.

SALES REVENUE FORECASTING

Not only is the sales forecast the most sensitive variable in the valuation, it is also the most difficult to estimate. One of the reasons for this is that the forecast relies on a lot of external factors, which are partly economically driven (hence our need for forecasts of the relevant variables), and partly driven by the opportunities and threats that have, hopefully, been picked up in our SWOT analysis. The only way that these can be accommodated is via sensitivity and scenario analysis, which are discussed below.

Once the environmental background has been investigated, the first step in the sales forecasting process is the identification of any limiting factors on output; in most PLBs, this will normally be demand but occasionally other factors can restrict output in the short to medium term. The key issues here are the production capacity and the efficiency of production. It is also important to analyse the timescales and risk involved in increasing productive capacity; this can range from simply buying the necessary new equipment through training of skilled labour to the complete construction of new plant.

The most helpful way of proceeding with the forecast is then to analyse exterior and interior factors governing demand. Exterior factors are those beyond the immediate control of the PLB and include:

1. The state of the market itself, in terms of expansion or contraction.
2. The volatility of demand attributable to non-economic factors (for example, demand for skiing equipment varies with weather conditions, whereas demand for squash racquets tends not to).
3. The current environment; is this one of discounting to gain market share, or are quality and market positioning more important?
4. The pricing strategies pursued by competitors.

5. The likely response of competitors to any change in pricing or marketing policy and the likelihood of pre-emptive moves by competitors.
6. The possibility of new competition entering the market.
7. The relative market shares enjoyed by the valuation target and its competitors (in general, the market leader will have a much greater ability to decide upon strategy changes).
8. The relationship between price and demand.
9. Any seasonal demand patterns.

Interior factors are those over which the company has some immediate control and include:

1. Existing and proposed product ranges.
2. Where these products are in terms of their life-cycles, and how this contrasts with the situation of competing products (this also has implications for research and development costs, which we discuss below).
3. Product mix.
4. Product specification and quality.
5. Market positioning.
6. Advertising and marketing policy (see page 62).
7. Royalty or licence payments receivable.

The historic pattern of sales growth and the historic pattern of competitors' positions is always a useful input to the forecasting process, especially when these trends are monitored against economic variables such as GDP growth. Industries respond to economic growth changes in different ways; for example, the major food retailers tend to be relatively recession-proof, whereas some analysts believe that advertising agencies tend to follow a 'J' curve-type pattern when emerging from a recession, because revenues pick up slowly at first, and then accelerate rapidly as advertisers spend to build market share in the upturn. When projecting any historic trends into the future, it is as well to remember that rapid growth is unlikely to continue for ever; sooner or later, competitive resistance is likely to be met. In the long term, it is worth contemplating why the valuation target's revenues should change at a different rate from GDP growth; they clearly cannot do so for ever.

Nature of sale and customers

As a start in our analysis here, it can be useful to dichotomise the form, purchase frequency and type of customer in the following manner:

Form of sales:	Contract	Non-contract
Type of purchase:	Continuous	One-off
Customer:	Trade	Individual

It is quite possible that different combinations may arise within a PLB.

If we take the example of a car manufacturer, we would typically have private buyers, where the nature of the sale is non-contract/one-off/individual, and the supply of fleet vehicles where the nature might be contract/one-off *or* continuous/trade. We can also add to our list the unit value of a sale (i.e. high or low) and, where the purchase is of a continous and non-contract nature (such as consumable products), the degree of customer loyalty.

In conjunction with the nature of the sale, we need to consider the customer base of the business, in particular the dependency of the PLB on key customers. All other things being equal, the businesses that are most exposed to sudden changes in demand are those where there is a reliance upon a few major customers, especially if there is some critical mass in the market for the product. A good example of this was the trading stamps phenomenon; the decision of a major customer to cease giving trading stamps with its retail sales led to a fall in the interest of consumers in the stamps, and the rapid demise of the product. When there is a dependency on key customers, the relationship between the two parties is of great importance, as is the financial health of the customer and the relative size of the supplying firm and the customer. The risk of loss of business will also depend on competition, relative quality and security of supply (customers may well be prepared to pay higher prices for a more reliable service) and the degree of substitutability of the product. Additionally, in the case of a valuation where there is access to inside information, an examination of the current state of the order book, relative to its past state, will assist in the prediction of revenues in the short to medium term. In contract-type businesses, this is probably the best indicator of likely demand in the current year. However, a reasonably sceptical view can be taken of orders where management (who are usually great optimists in such situations) insist that 'there's every chance we'll win this one', or similar.

Export sales

In the case of export sales, the factors we outlined above concerning overseas PLBs will need to be considered, and of principal interest are exchange rates and political and local economic factors. In addition, import duties and quotas will be important; in fact, the presence of these is one motivation for companies to establish a local manufacturing base, (as in the case of Japanese car firms building manufacturing plants in the United Kingdom), and this alternative may be relevant to the valuation if local demand is strong enough, especially if transportation costs are high. Once again, the past export record of the business will be an input to the forecasting process.

Problems of new ventures

In the case of new ventures, without historical sales records, revenue estimation becomes a much more difficult process. Valuations of this type are quite likely to be linked to venture capital proposals, so that managerial forecasts will be available; however, without a past trading record, the analysis is bound to be more judgemental and rely heavily upon issues like quality and experience of the management team, together with the proportion of their personal wealth they have committed to the venture. In terms of 'hard' forecasting data, we would hope to see good market research, including an analysis of market size, competitors' positions, propensity to purchase the proposed product at various price levels and so on, together with a clear statement of the assumptions made in arriving at the final demand forecasts. A sensitivity analysis to determine the critical success factors is particularly important in valuing this type of situation.

Marketing expenditure

The final area concerned with sales that must be investigated is the marketing and distribution of the products. Marketing includes a review of the advertising policy, advertising and marketing plans and expend-itures, their projected impact upon sales revenue and the success in this respect of past promotional campaigns, competitive response and any changes in sales outlets or selling method planned. Selling method can be by direct selling, dealership or agent distribution, or franchise-type arrangements. We would also want to check upon the effectiveness of the sales organisation, and the method by which any sales force was remunerated. Sales terms, credit arrangements and customer satisfaction also need to be monitored, as do any special sales financing arrangements, such as hire-purchase agreements. If it is possible to obtain information on the number of defective products returned from customers, this can help to identify any quality control problems and the likely level of customer dissatisfaction. In our investigation of the distribution network, we need to ensure that the revenue forecasts are compatible with the capacity of the system, and that there are arrangements to cope with any disruption to the network.

PRODUCTION COST FACTORS

The production environment

Before we can start to forecast production costs (and in this sense 'production cost' includes the direct cost of supplying services as well as manufactured goods), we need to review the production environment. This means, first, understanding the process of production, the technologies involved, the number of production stages and sites required and so on. In the case of a 'nuts and bolts' manufacturing organisation, this might well involve a standard factory layout, whereas the production arrangements of the water supply side of the recently privatised water companies are obviously a little different.

Assuming that we are dealing with a manufacturing operation, we must be aware of:

1. The capacity and suitability of the premises themselves.
2. The proximity to sources of supply and access to distribution networks.
3. The likelihood of future rental increases and the possibilities for expansion or sub-letting if production rises or falls.
4. The age and condition of the premises and the importance of this in predicting maintenance, capital expenditure and running costs.

These considerations also apply to the plant and machinery; again we are concerned with:

1. Capacity, maintenance and running costs.
2. The replacement cost of the equipment and the likely timing of any replacement (past replacement policies may be of some help in predicting the optimal replacement interval).
3. Flexibility with respect to changes in product design or manufacture.
4. The efficiency and quality of production compared to that of competitors.

Given the pace of technological change in many industries, together with the impact of such change on both product marketing and production cost, Appendix II (see page 76) discusses this topic.

Supply of materials and labour

Having discussed the fixed asset side of production, we next turn to the supply of materials and labour. The key issues regarding the former are availability and sources of supply, the number of suppliers, future price increases, the likelihood of disruption of supply, whether the source is domestic or foriegn (if the latter, the possibility of disruption is greater and there is a direct exposure to exchange risk), the financial stability of the supplier and the existence of, and renewal arrangements on, supply contracts. Also to be considered under this heading are the extent to which supplies are, or incorporate, basic commodities that are subject to price fluctuation. It must be borne in mind that some industries (such as airlines) are particularly exposed to such changes, although in the short-term commodity price changes can be hedged against.

In respect of materials, we also need to consider the stock-holding patterns, any changes in these (in particular, see Appendix II on production technology changes), the implications of any such changes and the timing of the payment for the supplies.

Turning to labour, the required skills of the labour force will be a critical factor in determining the ability of the company to increase or reduce its capacity at short notice. Demographic trends, educational and skill standards of the labour supply, local competition for that supply and the past industrial relations will all affect the availability of labour and the local cost of that labour. Furthermore, security of employment, remuneration (both level and structure) and skill factors will impact upon the capacity, efficiency and quality of the manufacturing process. It should also be borne in mind that any organisation is likely to need a wide variety of skills (e.g. managerial, administrative, craft, unskilled) and that even in areas with high unemployment, shortages can occur in key areas. Finally, pension and other employment costs need to be incorporated into the analysis, as do redundancy costs (where necessary) and training costs. It should also be noted that technology changes have tended to increase the demand for skilled labour, reduce the demand for unskilled labour and overall have led to labour costs becoming a declining proportion of total costs.

Indirect production costs

Besides the direct factors of the production process, we also need to examine the indirect factors, such as the efficiency of the administration system, the stock control system, production planning and scheduling, warehousing and distribution (including the efficiency, capacity and age profile of any vehicle fleets), whether any necessary patents are owned for products made (or the production processes used), whether licence or royalty fees must be paid and the cost control system.

An analysis of the latter is especially useful because, if we are carrying out an inside valuation, we shall normally be making use of management's own information, as reported and analysed by the management accounting system. Although we might expect such information to be reliable, we may find ourselves disappointed. It must be realised that in a large number of cases the management accounting system does not have the sole objective of supplying 'truthful' information. Indeed, the very word 'truthful' is misleading, because 'truth' is contextual; a 'cost' for one purpose may be totally misleading when used for a different purpose.

The cost of a unit of finished goods stock reported in the annual accounts of a company is the *average* cost, arrived at by dividing the production overheads of the firm over the number of units produced and adding this figure to the direct cost of producing a unit (traditionally, materials plus labour plus any directly observable overhead cost, such as machine power). In the case of multi-product, multi-department firms this process of dividing up the overhead will involve all manner of arbitrary cost allocations, so that any two sober, sensible and normal accountants can easily produce equally defensible but different figures for the 'cost' per unit. Clearly, such an arbitrary cost is of little use for decision-making,[8] for which we typically need the *marginal* cost, which may be better approximated by the direct cost. Not only can the management accounting system easily mislead the unwary by producing numbers that are valid for one purpose but not for another, but it can also produce budgets that are targets rather than forecasts, and may even report numbers in a certain fashion because of internal politics rather than business logic.

All this means that we need to be very wary when using internally generated accounting information. For valuation purposes, our need is to determine the relevant *cost drivers* in the production process, and the cost changes associated with each cost driver. A cost driver is anything that causes costs to vary; whilst the most obvious cost driver is volume, others may include the relative size of the production run, the number of different product specifications, the number of customers and their proximity to the factory, the degree of standardisation of components across product ranges and so on. Given the nature of valuations, we shall be interested in long-term as well as short-term cost changes so that relatively few costs will be 'fixed' in the traditional management accounting sense of the word. As far as possible, the aim is to model the PLB's cost structure so that we can see the effect of capacity changes (which will follow from our revenue forecasts) and can also perform a sensitivity analysis or ask 'what if' type questions (scenario modelling). If we are performing a 'changed state' type valuation, we shall also want to consider the effects of efficiency improvements, cost reduction programmes and synergystic benefits here.

A relevant issue here is the PLB as a 'stand-alone' business versus the PLB as part of a company. Given that many businesses will consist of more than one PLB, the question of centrally supplied services arises. Accounting practices vary, but these centrally provided services are often charged out on some sort of basis, which can be usage-determined but is frequently determined by some other method, such as equal distribution or pro-rata to sale (alternatively, these overheads are sometimes not recharged to the PLBs at all). In general, central services are not charged on a basis that reflects the cost of service provision on a 'stand-alone' basis; yet if we wish to value such PLBs as independent units this is the cost we need. Such a valuation is required in the case of a PLB being valued for the purpose of divestment and we therefore need to eliminate centrally allocated costs from the PLBs forecast costs and cash flows, replacing them with the costs and cash flows that would be incurred by an independently operated PLB.

However, in these cases we must be aware that the costs then borne by the remaining businesses will *not* be the original cost less this calculated stand-alone cost, because issues like economies of scale in the provision of services arise. In general, the overhead cost data we require are the 'stand-alone' cost of the PLB, the overhead costs incurred by other internal services users without the PLB and the incremental cost of the PLB joining a coalition of other users. In fact, it is often a good idea to compute such figures in any valuation conducted by the company's management (or by any predator) to ensure whether or not central provision is the optimal method of providing such services.[9]

Valuation without access to internal records

If we are attempting to value the firm from an outsider's perspective, arriving at an idea of the cost structure at business unit level is extremely difficult. A potential acquirer in the same industry will have an idea of likely cost structures, and indeed may be practising what is sometimes known as 'strategic management accounting' (see Bromwich and Bhimani, 1989), whereby firms attempt to identify and monitor competitors' costs and marketing, but an independent valuer will have greater difficulty. Possible routes to identifying such cost structures include company visits, talking to past employees, discussions with equipment suppliers, press (including trade press) reports and a careful look through the annual report. For example, companies frequently make reference to major modernisation programmes and are often unable to resist the inclusion of a glossy photograph of one of the directors leaning against the new piece of plant that has just been purchased. An informed analyst may be able to identify this as a MkIII Widgetbanger and form some idea of productive output and running cost.

RESEARCH AND DEVELOPMENT COSTS

Research and development (R&D) costs are of central importance in some industries (e.g. pharmaceuticals, aerospace), and we would obviously have some reservations about firms that had a record of spending below the market average; given the international nature of the markets for many of these types of product, we also need to make comparisons with foreign, as well as domestic, companies. Where possible, these costs should be identified between pure research, product/process applied research and product/process development. The link between pure research and 'bottom line' benefit is notoriously difficult to predict, but the link between development cost and benefit is more tangible. In particular, we need to be wary of companies that forecast above industry-average sales growth with below industry-average R&D expenditure. We should, logically, expect some link between development and revenues (or cost reductions/changes in the case of process development expenditure). Analysis of past performance can give some idea of the lead times between development cash flows and benefits, but changing technologies in some industries mean that there may be a reduction in such lead times. For example, the use of computer-aided design/computer-aided engineering technologies in the motor industry has resulted in a considerable reduction in the lead time on new models.

Other important factors here are the relative product advantages or disadvantages the company enjoys at present (does it need to spend more in order to catch up?) and the possibilities of externally sourced R&D, for example joint ventures with other companies or universities, or the use of outside design or engineering consultancies.

MARGINS AND PROFITS

We have already discussed the identification of costs and revenues and so, implicitly, we will already have forecast the gross profit margins on each product line. Therefore, we shall focus here upon the reasonableness of our forecast assumptions and scope for changing profitability.

First, margins should be checked against those that have been achieved in the past, and those being achieved by competitors. In particular, a forecast of increasing margins relative to historical patterns and competitors' positions needs to be viewed with some caution. Clearly, such patterns can emerge (an example is the recent trend in 'quality' supermarket margins) but they are unlikely to continue in the long-term because price competition to gain market share will take place or new firms will enter the market place. The ability to achieve higher margins will also depend upon relative product quality (do the cost forecasts reflect this?), market share and marketing expenditure (again, check the compatibility of the cost forecasts). An idea of currently achievable margins can also be obtained by looking at the margins on current tenders and the percentage of these resulting in firm orders. We would also expect the margins forecast to reflect the health of the economy as measured by factors such as the rate of GDP growth and interest rates present in our economic forecasts. We also need to identify whether or not margins are seasonal.[10] Naturally, margin forecasting is easiest when the firm produces many similar products, and most difficult where the products are one-offs or where the firm operates in the contracting industry.

It may also be possible to improve margins by changing the product mix, although we do need to be aware of the fact that changing the mix may mean changes in achievable product prices or changes in production efficiency.

CASH FLOWS

Depending on the valuation methodology used, the cash flow forecast will either be prepared to value the PLB directly (as in the case of a DCF valuation) or to check on the financing needs, liquidity and gearing of the business, and forecast financing charges (in the case of an earnings valuation). As we have already estimated many of the basic components of cash flows, in forecasting the costs and revenues of the business, we shall concentrate here on the additional issues that need to be addressed when preparing the cash flow forecast.

The first of these is timing, which is not only important in terms of time value of money, but is vital when looking at the potential liquidity of the business. In general, those companies with the most seasonal businesses will tend to be the most cash-hungry in terms of working capital funding. This is a particular trap for the unwary, who might be tempted to focus on year-end accounts and earnings forecasts. Take the extreme example of a toy manufacturer who sells the vast majority of its output before Christmas through retailers who receive two months' credit. These retailers will have needed to buy all their stock by the 1 December, so will presumably have paid in full by 31 January. Suppose the toy manufacturer chooses this date as the accounting year-end; a casual glance at the balance sheet will show low stock levels, low debtor and creditor levels, and high cash levels. This is, of course, in total contrast to the position around October and November, when high stock and debtor levels will need to be financed.

Ideally, forecasts should be prepared on a monthly basis, at least for the first year; thereafter a quarterly forecast is desirable, unless the business exhibits little or no seasonality. When forecasting receipt and payment patterns, past experience will generally be a good guide, except where the credit terms offered are being changed as part of the marketing package, or where sales are forecast to increase rapidly, in which case receipts from new customers may follow a different pattern from past experience. Note also that bad debts and credit period taken by customers will tend to be a function of the state of the economy; our forecast for these cash flow variables should therefore take into account our economic forecasts, which form the backbone of our whole forecasting process. When a long period of credit taken is forecast, we should always investigate whether this is the result of successful creditor manipulation, or whether it suggests that the company is in some trouble with its suppliers. In general, large suppliers (particularly those with a large market share) can and do use the sanction of discontinuing supply if purchasers stretch the credit period beyond that permitted in the agreed terms of business.

Besides these working capital considerations, we also need to concern ourselves with fixed asset formation and financing. First, when considering our sales and cost forecasts, we noted the need to increase, change or simply replace the asset base. The pattern of these investment flows will typically be lumpy, and accounting depreciation will usually be an extremely poor proxy for the reinvestment needed, partly because of this unevenness of investment flows and partly because of inflation. Even with inflation at quite modest levels, the accumulated sum of accounting depreciation is a hopelessly inadequate measure of the amount needed to replace an asset; for example, with inflation running at 5 per cent pa, prices double every fourteen years. This is not the only fact to be borne in mind when assessing the cash flows necessary for future investment; specific price changes (an example is the relative rate of price increase on cars and computers) and technological changes must also be taken into account.

Financing flows

Having forecast asset acquisition patterns, we need to forecast the necessary financing flows. The key consideration will be whether the assets can be funded by cash held within the company, or whether external financing of some form is necessary. The relative costs of these forms of finance are discussed in Chapter 6, and here we concern ourselves solely with the cash flow elements. Equity issues will need to be 'serviced' in terms of dividends and capital gains, but only the former impose a direct cash drain on the firm. By contrast, debt-like financing can impose a variety of cash flow patterns on the firm ranging from leasing (where the payment patterns are negotiable), to straight debt (variable or fixed interest) and 'low coupon' type arrangements, such as zero-coupon bonds (the extreme case), deep discount loan stocks and convertible loan stocks. Clearly, companies with onerous short-term cash flow commitments will tend to prefer the latter types of borrowing (note that there is a tax shield trade-off, discussed in Chapter 6) but it is very important for the valuer to investigate the reasonableness of the financing assumptions; for example, it is unlikely that Joe Blogg's Bargain Package Tours plc*, which has a somewhat chequered history, is going to be able to raise money via a zero-coupon debt issue, whereas it may well be able to secure a variable interest secured loan with a major bank, or leasing finance on any aircraft it may wish to buy. Care is also needed when reviewing the assumptions implicit in convertible loan stock financing arrangements. In general, these loan stocks are issued with the assumption that they will be converted into ordinary shares in the issuing company. However, the valuer should always look at the potential downside; if conversion does not take place, many current convertibles require the issuer to redeem at a premium, and this has caused severe problems for firms such as Saatchi and Saatchi. Finally, issue costs, which can be substantial, must be allowed for when looking at financing flows.

Having forecast the financing flows, we are now in a position to estimate the interest or servicing flows on this financing. In the case of fixed interest debt, there is nothing to be done other than simply recording the necessary outflow on the due date; variable interest debt involves the prediction of future interest rates, which is one of our economic variable inputs discussed above. Usually, variable interest payments will be set according to some base, such as LIBOR (London Inter-Bank Offered Rate) on a specified date (quarterly or semi-annual fixings are common) plus so many basis points;[11] in the case of smaller company borrowings the base is usually the lending bank's own published base rate.

Lease arrangements can be either short-term operating leases, or longer term financing leases, in which case the implied interest rate can be either variable or, more usually, fixed. In the case of convertible debt (or convertible preference shares), we are left with the interesting problem of forecasting the conversion date. Unfortunately, dealing with convertibles requires an understanding of option pricing techniques; this topic is covered in Chapter 7. For now, we can make some preliminary observations. The first is that a convertible loan stock is really a combination of an option-like instrument (a warrant) on the issuing company's equity, plus a 'straight' unsecured loan stock. To the holder, an option is normally worth more 'alive' (i.e. unexercised) than 'dead' (exercised). Although this is explored in detail in Chapter 7, by intuition we can probably conclude that this must be the case. For example, suppose we own an option to buy shares in Hanson plc for £1.50 each, which is exercisable at any time between now and five years time. Assume that the current share price is £2.20; why convert today, and pay £1.50 when we can benefit from any upside movement, and still hold on to our cash for another five years? From the issuer's point of view, the opposite is true – it would much prefer to have the £1.50 today than five years from now.[12] Because of this, many convertibles have conditions attached to them which allow the issuer to force the holder to convert provided the share price is greater than the exercise price embedded in the convertible. We thus have a general rule for forecasting conversion dates; if there is a 'forced conversion' condition, assume the company will use it as soon as the forecast share price exceeds the exercise price (see Chapters 5 and 8 for share price forecasting) and if there is no such condition then assume conversion will take place at the end of the exercise window.

The final consideration in forecasting financing service costs is, of course, the need to estimate the future dividend payments of the company. Note that this has implications for the value of the shares (see Chapters 2 and 3) and possibly for the cost of equity capital (see Chapter 6); it also has a direct impact on financing requirements and interest income.

Other cash flow considerations

To complete our cash flow forecast, we need to build in *cash* tax payments, which will comprise advance corporation tax and mainstream corporation tax liabilities, as well as value added tax payments (made quarterly). We are now in a position to calculate the periodic cash surplus or deficit of the business; once this has been done the short-term financing strategy, together with interest earned or paid, can be derived.

Before leaving the subject of cash flow forecasts we should highlight the differences between a PLB and the whole company; depending on the context of our valuation, we may be valuing the PLB on a 'stand-alone' basis, or as an integral part of a company. There is often a substantial difference in the cash requirement between these two alternatives, because the holding company typically acts as a 'banker' for the group, skimming off any cash surpluses and funding any deficits. This is of particular importance where the various PLBs are involved in activities with different seasonal sales patterns and can mean that a 'spun-off' subsidiary has much greater financing requirements than it has as a member of a group (cash-generating businesses, such as food retailers, may have substantially reduced financing needs).

PROFIT FORECASTS

Finally, we come to the forecast of net profit. If the valuation methodology in use is the earnings multiple approach, this will be the objective of the forecast. In Chapter 5, we discuss the concept of maintainable earnings; here we are concerned with the key points that need to be borne in mind when preparing the net profit forecast for each year of the forecast period. We will have already arrived at forecasts of sales revenues, production costs, gross margins and administration costs; we have also considered the forecasting of distribution, marketing and research and development costs. We thus have forecast all the components of operating profit for each PLB; in addition, we will have forecast financing charges and interest receipts in preparing a cash flow forecast. The profit before tax forecast therefore follows axiomatically. Forecasting the tax charge is rather more problematic, as the accounting treatment involves an attempt to smooth out lumpy *cash* tax flows by using the mechanism of deferred tax. Arguably, it is the tax provision after due allowance has been made for deferred tax that is of most use when estimating the long-term maintainable profit of a business. A simple example of deferred tax is given in Appendix III (see page 80).

Whilst the profits after deferred tax adjustment are useful for estimating maintainable profits, they should not be used when a discounted cash flow valuation is being made because the opportunity cost of capital should be applied to the *actual* cash flow, not a smoothed version thereof. A simple *full provision* model (such as that presented in Appendix III) has intuitive appeal, and can be defended on theoretical grounds (see Edwards et al., 1987). Unfortunately, there are complications, which mean that it is very difficult to unravel the treatment of deferred tax in practice. Accounting for deferred tax has been, perhaps surprisingly, a contentious issue involving the withdrawal of an accounting standard and its subsequent reissue (SSAP 15). The reason is that expanding firms, are continually purchasing new assets, giving rise in themselves to new writing down allowances; as a result, many firms would not expect their tax charge to rise through time (as was the case in our Appendix III example). The accounting standard therefore only requires firms to provide for deferred taxation when there is a probability that a liability will crystallise in the forseeable future (known as a *partial provision* approach). Whether such a liability will arise is, of course, dependent upon the future capital expenditure plans of the company; as these are a necessary part of the forecast, it may be possible to check that the accounting treatment of deferred tax is compatible with the capital expenditure plans. Another source of deferred tax liability is the future sale of property that has been revalued in the accounts; if the company intend to sell such property at some future date, a provision for deferred tax must be created.

From the perspective of an outside valuer, it is only possible to monitor changes in the accounting treatment of deferred tax to try and establish the reasonableness of the tax provision in the profit and loss account, and to gain some sort of clue about the capital expenditure plans of the company. If, for example, a company suddenly starts providing for substantial deferred tax liabilities, it may be an indicator that future capital expenditure plans are being revised downwards.

BALANCE SHEET FORECAST

Except where the valuation is on an asset basis, the forecast balance sheet is not a central aim of the forecasting process. Instead, its purpose is to provide a check on the profit and cash flow forecasts, from both arithmetic and logical consistency perspectives. As such, it is vitally important that a forecast balance sheet is always prepared. Fixed asset changes should agree with new purchases given in the cash forecast, less any depreciation expenses through the profit and loss account; the same holds for intangible assets, such as any goodwill arising on the planned purchase of any subsidiaries, or the capitalisation (and subsequent write-off) of any development expenditure. Working capital (stock, debtors and creditors) should be checked by reconciling closing balances with the opening balances plus assumed purchases/additions/sales incorporated into the profit forecast, less asssumed payments/receipts from the cash flow forecast. Taxation has already been dealt with above, and dividend provisions should reflect any final dividends forecast in the profit and loss account (this assumes that the interim dividend has already been paid). Finally, the financing side of the balance sheet should reflect additional capital injections from the cash flow forecast, changes in *retained profits* and any movements in the reserves occasioned by asset revaluations, direct write-offs, and so on. Where applicable, any changes in minority interests must also be accounted for.

When the balance sheet is that of a group, the normal principles of consolidated accounts need to be followed; in particular, profits on intra-group sales need to be eliminated and any share of associated companies' profits or losses and net assets need to be included (in accordance with SSAP 1).

Finally, as part of the process of ensuring logical consistency, it may be helpful to construct trend statements (i.e. changes in assets/liabilities over the forecast period expressed in index form, with the base being the most recent *actual* balance sheet of the company), common size statements (all assets and liabilities expressed as a percentage of net assets) and to perform a quick check on key ratios such as return on capital employed, asset turnover, liquidity and gearing. We should be rather wary of forecasts that seem to imply dramatic improvements in such ratios, particularly in companies with fairly indifferent past performances; we should be equally suspicious of forecasts suggesting that spectacular past improvements in such ratios will continue indefinitely.

THE EFFECT OF CHANGES
IN FORECAST VARIABLES

Any good valuation should include an analysis of the effects on that valuation of changes in the key variables such as sales, margins, capital expenditure plans, growth rates and so on. There are three principal ways in which this can be done, which are not mutually exclusive. To perform these analyses, it helps enormously if the forecast is prepared using a spreadsheet model. The first of our risk analysis methodologies is sensitivity analysis; essentially, this is an extremely simple (but none the less effective) approach to the problem. Sensitivity analysis involves changing each of the forecast variables indepently by pre-set percentages (say, 5 per cent, 10 per cent and 15 per cent) and recalculating the valuation accordingly. Whilst the approach has its merits, its weaknesses are that a uniform change in one variable is assumed to occur in each and every year of the forecast, whilst all other factors are held constant. This can be a problem when variables are related to one another; for example, selling price and demand are related, whilst inflation usually has some impact on all the forecast variables.

Because of these weaknesses, many forecasters prefer to set up the valuation model in a format that allows 'scenario modelling'. This is really nothing more than a deluxe version of sensitivity analysis, in that we can now change several variables simultaneously and ask questions of the model, such as 'what if interest rates stay high for the next three years, inflation remains at 5 per cent and sales growth is only 2 per cent pa instead of the expected 5 per cent?' This approach is frequently used in conjunction with sensitivity analysis.

The last of our approaches to this problem involves the specification of event probabilities for each of our forecast variables; this is a very complex process because not only do we need to specify a probability factor for each point estimate for each variable, but we also need to specify links between the variables themselves. To give a simple example of this, let us suppose that we are trying to forecast sales for the years 10 and 11 of the Welsh whisky venture referred to on page 54; it takes ten years to mature the product, so supply cannot be readily increased, although stock not sold can be carried forward. The maximum number of cases available for sale in each year is 10,000, plus any stock carried forward. Furthermore, the more successful the sales are in year 10, the more likely it is that sales will be successful in year 11. Putting all this together with our market research might give us the following:

Year 10 sales	Probability	Year 11 sales	Probability	Combined probability
8,000	0.3	6,000	0.2	0.2 × 0.3 = 0.06
		8,000	0.4	0.4 × 0.3 = 0.12
		10,000	0.3	0.3 × 0.3 = 0.09
		12,000(max)	0.1	0.1 × 0.3 = 0.03
10,000	0.7	8,000	0.2	0.2 × 0.7 = 0.14
		10,000(max)	0.8	0.8 × 0.7 = 0.56
				1.00

This process would then need to be repeated for all the other factors affecting cash flow and profit. At the end of all this, we should be able to perform what is sometimes called a *Monte Carlo simulation* exercise, which would produce a probability distribution of all the possible cash flow patterns; we could even go further and produce distributions of the valuation. However, we need to be a little cautious of the meaning of such distributions; if the valuation is done on a DCF basis, the discount rate chosen will already have reflected the risk of the PLB (see Chapter 6). Using a probability distribution of the valuation to assess riskiness therefore effectively double-counts risk; it might seem that one way around this problem is to use the risk-free rate as the discount rate, but Brealey and Myers (1991) refer to such valuation distributions as 'bastard NPVs', which reflects the lack of economic meaning in such numbers rather than being a judgemental statement about discounted cash flows in general. Whilst all this may sound like an impossible task, there exist computerised packages (such as *Risk*) which allow various types of distribution to be specified for each variable, and also allow the specification of correlation co-efficients between such variables.

Because of the complications caused by the interpretation of NPV distributions, the most easily applied approach is probably to use unbiased estimates of the cash flows, discount these at a risk-adjusted rate (see Chapter 6; valuers preferring an earnings multiple approach should see Chapter 5), and conduct both a sensitivity analysis and a scenario-modelling-type exercise to see the effect of changes in the variables on the valuation. It can be hard to justify the additional effort involved in going for a full Monte Carlo simulation model, although an idea of the probability of certain events occuring is clearly helpful in interpreting the results of the sensitivity analysis/scenario modelling exercise.

APPENDIX I: PROFIT, CASH AND BALANCE SHEET FORECAST SUMMARY CHECKLIST

Context   Internal/external perspective?

Economic factors: GDP growth
Inflation
Exchange rates
Interest rates
Unemployment rates
Tax rates

Industry factors: Market changes (fashion, growth, maturity)
Market shares of leading companies
Technological changes
Political/regulatory changes

Company factors:
Background   SWOT analysis, risk exposure and risk hedging
Sales   Limiting factors
Markets (share, positioning and strategy)
Marketing (prices, demand, advertising and
   promotion, economic factors)
Sales growth (historic, competitors, economic
   factors)
Nature of sales (contract, non-contract, etc.)
Dependence on key customers
Market research
Distribution
Seasonality

Costs   Technology and structure of
   processes
Capacity
Plant and equipment (type, age and replacement
   cycle)
Technological change
Materials (price, supplies, stock-holding
   requirements)
Labour (skills, costs, availability, training,
   redundancy, pension and other employment
   costs)
Other costs (administration, overheads, stock
   control, distribution, quality control)
Cost drivers
Cost structure (fixed, variable, etc.)
Allocated costs versus stand-alone costs versus
   economies of scale
Research and development costs (relationship with
   sales, lead times, current state of products/
   production technologies)

Margins   Historical
                   Competitors'
                   Product quality
                   Product type
                   Seasonality

Cash flows   Timing
                   Seasonality
                   Credit allowed/taken
                   Asset purchases (timing, inflation, relationship
                      with sales)
                   Financing (debt, leasing, convertibles, equity)
                   Servicing flows (interest, lease payments, dividends)
                   Interest paid/earned

Profit forecast   Implicit tax charge
                   Deferred tax
                   Distribution policy

Balance sheet   Arithmetic check
                   Check for logical consistency (ratios, common size
                      and trend statements)

Variable changes: Sensitivity analysis
                   Scenario modelling
                   Probabilistic modelling

APPENDIX II: NEW TECHNOLOGY AND ITS IMPLICATIONS

Many firms are now confronted by new production technologies and a considerable number of these will have either installed some of these technologies, or are likely to consider such an installation in the near future. In particular increased automation in manufacturing has been facilitated but perhaps of most importance is the fact that greater integration of industrial and commercial processes has become possible. For some time, firms have used computers for various aspects of their control and planning activities; for example, in performing engineering calculations required for product design, control of stock levels and production scheduling. Gradually, these systems have become more complex and comprehensive with perhaps the ultimate, but so far unachieved, objective of computer integrated manufacturing (CIM). However, considerable progress has been made in establishing the complete computerisation of some aspects of the design, manufacturing and product/service supply processes. Typically, many firms now operate computer-aided design (CAD), computer-aided engineeering (CAE), and computer-aided manufacturing (CAM) systems. For example, Coulthurst (1989) describes the succesful development and use of CAD systems in Austin–Rover, Jaguar and Ford. CAE systems can be used to assess alternative production technologies and feed off the CAD system; thus the Ford system has computer links with component suppliers, so that they can use Ford specifications to design and test the feasibility of their own component products. In principle, the CAE system could transmit information direct to the CAM system, which could control electronic work stations directly, facilitating a completely automated process of manufacturing with no human intervention. In practice, this has yet to be achieved and instead we have what Lee (1987) describes as 'islands of automation'.

However, extant technology has progressed as far as the flexible manufacturing system (FMS) which is a computer-controlled production line linking computer-controlled machines in such a way that product specifications can be altered quickly and efficiently. Japanese companies appear to have made extensive use of this type of technology, which is also being adopted by US and European firms; Lee offers the example of a General Electric plant in the United States, which is, 'capable of producing deisel engines of substantially different sizes on the same automated production line, without substantial retooling and setups'. The benefits of all this can be dramatic; Coulthurst quotes the case of the Yamazaki Machinery Co (Japan), which reduced the number of machines from 68 to 18, employees from 215 to 12, floorspace to around 30 per cent of former requirements and cut the average processing time from 35 to 1.5 days. However, he also warns that the expected benefits are not always realised, as in the case of General Motors, which invested $60 billion in advanced manufacturing technology (AMT).

Perhaps examples such as the latter help to draw attention to the fact that simply buying the latest 'high-tech' equipment and bolting it to the factory floor is not sufficient. The process of change has to be managed, the optimal investment decisions need to be made and the planning and control systems have to be set up in a manner compatible with the production technology employed (it is worth noting Coulthurst (1989) who observes that, 'Management style and labour relations appear to be at least as important in raising efficiency as is technology'). In particular, each organisational function must have access to an integrated database, which allows the control of the production schedules, stock levels, distribution and financing. One approach to this area is that of manufacturing resource planning (MRP II, so called to distinguish it from a partial stage of the process, material requirements planning (MRP)). Starting from a product demand forecast, MRP II uses computer-based models to generate a manufacturing plan and production schedule, which 'spins off' stock level requirements, material purchase requirements (allowing the automatic generation of orders) and capacity requirements. Advanced versions are also capable of generating accounting information; in essence, MRP II represents the automated version of the classic textbook 'master budget'. In addition, some MRP II systems allow actual results to be monitored against the original plan; appropriate amendments can then be made. However, from a valuations point of view this is not quite the good news that it might seem, as budgets produced by such systems are usually short-term.

A logical outcome to this type of process is the just-in-time (JIT) system, a step made possible by the production scheduling possibilities offered by MRPII and the integration of databases allowed by advances in computing technology. The idea behind JIT is that stock levels can be eliminated by producing parts and sub-assemblies only when they are actually required for production. If the manufacturer's computer is linked to the supplier's (an example of electronic data interchange, EDI), then component deliveries can take place exactly when required on a flow basis rather than a stock delivery one. Perhaps the most frequently quoted example is that of Toyota (see Lee (1987) pp. 19–22). Note that whilst AMT is not necessary for the successful operation of MRPII, which can be applied to any manufacturing technology, it is a requirement for JIT, which requires an FMS to eliminate or drastically reduce set up times; in the absence of this, optimal batch quantities will exist, necessitating the maintenance of stocks.

Kaplan and Atkinson (1989) point out that the use of JIT to reduce stock levels saves factory space previously required for inter-process buffer stocks (WIP), and allows work stations to be moved closer together, thus reducing conveyance time and distance. A related technique, OPT seeks to optimise factory throughput by eliminating bottlenecks rather than stock levels. Kaplan and Atkinson quote Goldratt as observing that, 'cost accounting is the number one enemy of productivity', because managers are not penalised for stock build-up in most accounting performance measures. Furthermore, traditional standard absorption costing actively encourages this by generating positive overhead volume variances when production is greater than budget, no matter what the final product demand looks like. A further point is that the use of JIT and OPT is not confined to manufacturing industry; for example, the use of electronic point of sale (EPOS) technology allows improvements in delivery scheduling and stockholding in the retail industry.

A few general observations can be made on the effect of all this on forecast cost and revenues. First, AMT and other information technologies require large initial investments, which generally tend to produce benefits that are of a long-term nature (typically spanning over several product life-cycles) and include substantial real but intangible benefits (e.g. greater product quality). Second, when appraising the impact of such investments, we need to make the comparison not against the status quo, but against the position that will result if the investment is not made. Third, investment of this nature tends to change the cost structure of the firm; many costs become sunk once the investment is made, and in general 'fixed' costs tend to be substituted for 'variable' costs (but see the comments on *production costs* on page 62).

Perhaps the most difficult practical aspect that will confront the valuer is the quantification of some of the 'intangible' benefits of the investment. These will include increased quality, greater flexibility and reduction of raw material and WIP stocks through the use of JIT techniques. Attempts to quantify these factors might include, *inter alia*, consideration of increased sales, lower material and labour costs, and smoother production flows. Increased sales may arise from several sources, such as improved customer satisfaction, reduced lead times and greater flexibility in product specification, whilst lower costs might be attributable to faster set up times, less reworking of defective items and greater productivity. Smoother production flows mean less expenditure on warehousing and storage space, and saving on working capital investment.

When considering the change in the cost structure associated with investment in new technology, the following issues are of importance. First, direct labour costs are a declining percentage of total costs (the CAM-i (1988) survey of UK companies in advanced manufacturing environments find that the average has declined to 12 per cent), whereas materials are a more significant percentage (CAM-i suggest a figure of just over 50 per cent). It may well be the case that materials are now the only significant volume-driven cost for many companies, with direct labour being virtually a fixed cost in the shorter term. Set up costs may also have been reduced by investment in FMS, whilst design costs may also be cut through the use of CAD and CAE. Product specification changes and product design changes may thus be more frequent and feasible than was previously the case; the product-costing implications are that some of the traditional academic marginal and opportunity cost prescriptions for decision-making may actually be of increasing relevance and, because of the existence of computerised databases containing information on cost structure, may be more easily applied. (For a detailed discussion of this point, see Gregory, 1991.) This could fulfil a very useful function in the managerial process, as the changing competitive environment may well require a series of short-term tactical decisions to be made on such product changes.

It also seems increasingly unlikely that firms will be able to succesfully employ a naive cost-plus pricing policy. It is notable that many Japanese companies view the whole product production and pricing decision from the starting point of attempting to establish what the market price of a product under development is likely to be, and then working down to specifying a target cost necessary to make production of the product worthwhile. Part of the design and production process is then the search for necessary productivity and technology changes.

APPENDIX III: ACCOUNTING FOR DEFERRED TAX

To illustrate the basic mechanics of deferred tax accounting, we shall look at a highly simplified model, which uses the UK system of capital allowances.

Suppose that the rate of mainstream corporation tax is 35 per cent, the rate of writing down allowance (WDA) on all assets owned by the firm is 25 per cent pa, and that the tax payment lag is one year. For simplicity, we shall ignore advance corporation tax (ACT) in our analysis. Now imagine that our firm has stable sales, costs and cash flows, and replaces its machinery every four years. Each set of plant and equipment costs £1 million, and is sold for £300,000 at the end of its four-year life. The capital allowances and written down values (WDV) for the period of ownership will therefore be:

Year	WDV brought forward £	WDA (25%) £	Tax saving @ 35% £
1	1,000,000	250,000	87,500
2	750,000	187,500	65,625
3	562,500	140,625	49,219
4	421,875	121,875*	42,656

*In the year of sale, any difference between WDV and sale proceeds is tax allowable. The tax allowance is therefore based upon £421,875 brought forward, less the £300,000 sale proceeds.

Now if we assume that the costs (excluding depreciation) are £500,000 per annum, and that sales revenues are £1 million per annum, the tax charge in any year will be 35 per cent multiplied by the gross margin of £500,000, less the tax saving calculated above. We therefore end up with the following after tax profits (assuming depreciation is calculated on a straight line basis) if we fail to adjust for deferred taxation (all figures in £000s):

Item	Year 1	Year 2	Year 3	Year 4
Revenue	1,000.0	1,000.0	1,000.0	1,000.0
Costs (including depreciation of £175,000 pa)	675.0	675.0	675.0	675.0
Profit before tax	325.0	325.0	325.0	325.0
Actual tax charge	87.5	109.4	125.8	132.3
Profit after tax	237.5	215.6	199.2	192.7

An accounting treatment like this could not only mislead investors, but looking at the first years profit forecast would give a misleading impression of maintainable earnings. What deferred tax accounting does is to equalise the tax charge over the life of the investment. We have a total tax allowable depreciation charge of £1 million less £300,000, or £700,000; this averages out to £175,000, which is, of course, the same as the accounting depreciation figure. The equalised tax allowance per annum is therefore £175,000 × 35 per cent, which gives a figure of £61,250. The accounting treatment entails making the following entries to the profit and loss account and balance sheet accounts:

Year 1: Actual writing down allowance received:	87,500
Equalised allowance:	61,250
Credit deferred tax account (debit profit and loss a/c)	26,250

The credit side of the balance sheet will therefore show:

Deferred tax account	26,250
Current taxation payable	87,500

Year 2: Actual writing down allowance received:	65,625
Equalised allowance:	61,250
Credit deferred tax account (debit profit and loss a/c)	4,375

The credit side of the balance sheet will therefore show:

Deferred tax account	30,625
Current taxation payable	109,375

Year 3: Actual writing down allowance received:	49,219
Equalised allowance:	61,250
Debit deferred tax account (credit profit and loss a/c)	12,031

The credit side of the balance sheet will therefore show:

Deferred tax account	18,594
Current taxation payable	125,781

Year 4: Actual writing down allowance received:	42,656
Equalised allowance:	61,250
Debit deferred tax account (credit profit and loss a/c)	18,594

The credit side of the balance sheet will therefore show:

Deferred tax account	nil
Current taxation payable	125,781

The effect of all these entries is to produce a constant profit figure (apart from roundings) each year as follows (all figures in £000s):

Item	Year 1	Year 2	Year 3	Year 4
Revenue	1,000.0	1,000.0	1,000.0	1,000.0
Costs (including depreciation of £175,000 pa)	675.0	675.0	675.0	675.0
Profit before tax	325.0	325.0	325.0	325.0
Actual tax charge	87.5	109.4	125.8	132.3
Deferred tax adjustment	26.3	4.4	−12.0	−18.6
Profit after tax	211.2	211.2	211.2	211.3

CHAPTER 5

ACCOUNTING-BASED
VALUATION MODELS

As we have already seen, there are three basic alternative methods available for the valuation of companies; (i) the discounted cash flow model; (ii) the earnings multiple (or price–earnings) model; and (iii) asset valuations. In the last two of these, accounting data is central to the valuation, although, as we noted in Chapter 2, replacement values and realisable values of all the assets are important additional pieces of information for an asset valuation. In this chapter, we shall examine these two alternative accounting-based models, and one other model that falls into this category, known as the 'super-profits' valuation. In practice, the most commonly used approach to valuation appears to be that of the earnings multiple model, whether the valuation is of unlisted or listed companies, or for acquisitions or general analysts' recommendations on investing (see, for example, Arnold and Moizer (1984) and Day (1986)). The appeal of such an approach doubtless owes much to the combination of simplicity and the ready availability of forecast earnings (at least for one year ahead), price–earnings multiples for all listed companies and industry sectors, and price–earnings multiples on completed acquisitions.

Before investigating these accounting-based models in detail, it is important to understand the limitations of current accounting practice, as in all cases our valuation will be reliant upon the validity of the accounting numbers themselves. We shall therefore take a look at the problems caused by what are sometimes called 'generally accepted accounting principles' (GAAP)[1] and their practical application and manipulation. In some cases these problems are caused by accounting conventions (the best example is probably that caused by the historical cost accounting convention in times of inflation), in some cases by different GAAP applying in different countries and often by the fact that companies report results, within the confines of GAAP, in a manner (often highly innovative) that best suits their own purposes. This whole area is sometimes termed 'creative accounting' and, until recently, has been something of a growth industry in the United Kingdom. We shall look at some of these problems first, and then move on to consider the application of earnings multiple and asset valuation approaches in the light of some of these problems.

PROBLEMS CAUSED BY GAAP

In an ideal world, comparability would be assured not only between the results of the same company across different years (the position that exists largely in the United Kingdom because of SSAP 2 and SSAP 6) but also between companies, something that clearly does not happen at the moment in the UK. Different policies can be pursued with respect to asset valuation, rates of asset depreciation, the capitalisation and amortisation of such intangibles as goodwill, development expenditure and brand values, stock valuation (although it must be acknowledged that the United Kingdom permits less flexibilty here than is found in most other countries), the treatment of certain types of financing, deferred taxation,[2] interest capitalisation on new asset construction, and the classification of extraordinary items to name but some of the options. The basic problem caused by such flexibility is that in practice, valuers tend to use *analogue* or *proxy* companies to determine either a reasonable PE multiple in the case of an earnings valuation, or a price-book value ratio in the case of asset driven valuations (the latter is far less common than the earnings multiple approach); clearly, such a process is likely to be more reasonable when all companies follow the same accounting practices than when they do not.

It therefore follows that the first step in an accounting-based valuation is a thorough analysis of the accounting practices used by the object of the valuation and any other companies used as proxies for earnings multiples. The second step is then to restate the accounts of proxy and object companies on a common basis, wherever possible. Unfortunately, this is sometimes an extremely difficult task, because of a shortage of some of the necessary information, although the requirements of SSAP 2 (which requires the disclosure of accounting policies) provides some help. None the less, serious problems can arise, particularly in the case of 'off-balance-sheet financing' (discussed below), where the estimation of the true debt obligations of the company can be a daunting (if not impossible) task. By contrast, some changes are easily made. For example, if the company we wish to value has capitalised development expenditure whilst comparable companies have not, the adjustment would consist of reducing the asset value of our company, writing off the actual expenditure in the year to the profit figure and adding back the amortisation of previous years' expenditure (both of these figures must be disclosed in the notes to the balance sheet referring to changes in assets). Note that it does not matter which accounting basis is adopted when making such changes; the aim is to ensure comparability, not to present an ideologically 'correct' version of the accounts.

The off-balance-sheet financing problem

At the time of writing, it would probably be fair to say that the greatest problem in terms of establishing what accountants like to refer to as a 'true and fair' view of any business is the existence of off-balance-sheet financing arrangements. This is of particular concern to the valuer, because it affects valuation in two respects; first, it causes problems in picking suitable analogue or proxy companies because, by its very nature, off-balance-sheet financing does not exist in a financial accounting sense. To a large extent, the 1989 Companies Act has brought about a considerable improvement over the position that existed prior to accounting periods beginning on or after 23 December 1989; the definition of a subsidiary undertaking is now extended to cover unincorporated businesses and defines subsidiaries by any of a majority of voting rights, control of voting rights at board meetings or the ability to exercise a 'dominant influence' over the subsidiary.[3]

However, Pimm (1990) has drawn attention to the fact that the Act allows off-balance-sheet financing to persist in cases where the 'parent' (or, strictly, the 'investing') company retains the benefits from any transactions, but is prepared to relinquish control on either a permanent or temporary basis. Such structures can include the situation where the investing company receives the majority of the benefits in exchange for relinquishing control to a third party – say a 'financier'. As our financier's interests coincide with that of the investing company, there may well be no problem for the latter in surrendering control. However, the Act would require the financier to consolidate the subsidiary (always assuming, of course, that the financier is a UK company). Another possibility is some form of ownership where the investing company owns an intermediate subsidiary jointly with the financier, which in turn jointly owns a subsidiary with the investing company; in this case neither company actually owns the final subsidiary, although the investing company clearly obtains the majority of the economic benefits (Figure 5.1).

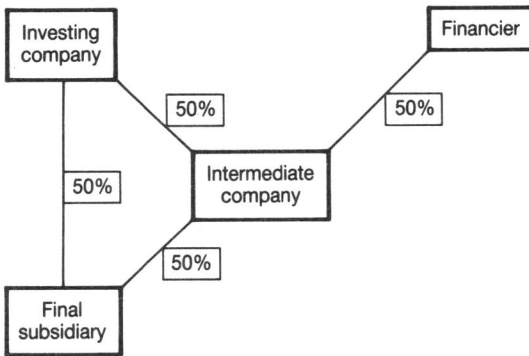

Figure 5.1 Off-balance-sheet financing using an intermediate company.

Also, whilst options to acquire control are included in the calculation of 'participating interest' in any subsidiary, it seems that this is only so if the options are *currently* exercisable; it would therefore appear that if the options are exercisable at some time in the future, the 'subsidiary' is not legally defined as such until the options are actually exercisable (irrespective of whether exercise actually takes place).

To give an example of all this, suppose that Superclothes plc★, a retailer, has entered into a property development venture, which has dramatically increased its gearing levels because the venture has been backed by Graspitt Bank Holdings plc★ (GBH). Without the assistance of a little massaging, let us say that the balance sheet of Superclothes for the coming year will end up looking like this:

	£m	£m
Fixed assets:		
retail	10	
development	10	
Total fixed assets		20
Other assets		10
Total assets		30
Financed by		
shareholders' funds		15
debt		15
Total		30

All this will, of course, come as something of a shock to Superclothes' shareholders, who on the basis of past results are expecting far more modest gearing levels. At this point, the Superclothes finance director, believing that the first rule of finance is that merchant bankers will do anything for a large enough fee, proposes the setting up of a development subsidiary, Devsub★, which is 40 per cent owned by Superclothes and 60 per cent by GBH; this subsidiary would have a nominal equity element (say, 1 per cent of assets), with the assets being financed almost entirely by GBH's loan. Superclothes would have an option to buy back the remaining equity two years from now, when the development should be sold, at a price that covers GBH's fee and interest charges. GBH will also insist that they have a put option exercisable against Superclothes for a similar amount, just to cover themselves against falling property prices and so on. Now until the option is actually exercisable, in two years' time, Superclothes does not have control over Devsub, although to fulfil the requirements of the Act it would also need to be demonstrated that the management of that company were not under the *dominant* influence of Superclothes. The latter's balance sheet would now look more reasonable, showing only the *retail* assets financed by £15 million equity and £5 million debt.

We need to be aware that there are two pitfalls here for the naive valuer; first, if he or she is conducting a valuation for investment analysis purposes, or for a hostile takeover, there will be no access to internal information so that gearing may be substantially under-estimated. Second, our naive valuer may be using Superclothes as a proxy company to estimate a suitable earnings multiple.[4] Now, if the investment community has picked up rumours concerning Superclothes' financing deals (as they may well have done), a natural response is to mark down the share price, which has the effect of lowering the PE multiple; our naive valuer may therefore end up under-valuing his or her valuation target because he or she is unaware of Superclothes' funny financing arrangements. Unfortunately, there will be no easy solution to this sort of problem unless and until the Accounting Standards Board (ASB) take some positive action; an attempt has been made by the ASB's predecessor, the ASC, in exposure drafts 42 and 46, but at present these do not constitute legal or professional practice requirements in the United Kingdom.

There are other areas where accounting practice remains unsatisfactory (for example, in the treatment of convertibles and deep-discount loan stocks), but probably the area of off-balance-sheet financing is the one of greatest concern at the moment. The main message to the valuer here is to scan the notes to the accounts very carefully, to try and determine exactly how the company reports its state of affairs; it is naive to expect anything other than that the company will select the allowed accounting treatment, which is expected to show its position in the best possible light in the long-term, bearing in mind the limitation that SSAPs 2 and 6 effectively prevent companies from changing policies from one year to the next unless prior year results are restated to show the effects of any changes. Clearly, such a situation represents less of a problem to anyone valuing the company with access to internal information, provided that person asks the right questions (which generally start with 'Can you tell me how you have treated . . .') but still causes difficulties in the selection of proxy company earnings multiples.

The problem of historical cost accounting

Even in a world where everyone was pure and innocent, and accounted for everything in the best possible way (from a 'true and fair' perspective), we would still have a problem with a central principle of accounting, that of historical cost. To illustrate the problem, let us take the simple example of two companies, in the same industry, which have bought their equipment at different points in time. To simplify matters further, we shall assume that there is no change in productivity associated with older equipment, that all such equipment has a ten-year life, that inflation rates of 10 per cent have affected all asset prices, costs and selling prices, and that the required return on all investment is 10 per cent pa in *real* terms. We shall further assume that the equipment is worthless at the end of its ten-year life and that accounting depreciation is charged on a straight line basis. The base year for our analysis is year 0, and on that date real cash flows were estimated at £170,000 pa for each of years 1 to 10, and the investment cost in year 0 was £1 million. Incredibly alert readers will be getting a distinct sense of déjà vu at this point; in fact, this is the situation we used to explain annual equivalent cash flows using the example of Saunders plc in Chapter 3 (see page 45). In such an environment, imagine that there are two companies, Saunders and Toshack*, which are identical in all respects except that Saunders bought its assets five years before Toshack, the latter having bought its assets at the beginning of the current year, which is year 6. Starting with the position of Saunders: £1 million was paid for its assets in year 0; so far, the expected net *real* cash flow of £0.17 million pa has been generated, and this is expected to continue for the forseeable future (duly replacing its assets in year 10), thus we would expect the market value at the end of year 6 to be the £1.9 million we have already calculated in Chapter 3 (see page 47). In a rational market, given that these investments in fixed assets are positive NPV ones, if we assume that all cash flows necessary to replace the existing equipment are reinvested in financial assets, which yield a 10 per cent real rate of return (i.e. a 21 per cent money rate) both firms should have an identical value of £1.9 million. The position of Toshack can now be analysed in the same way that we have used to value Saunders. First, the cash flows for year 6 will be £170,000 × 1.1^6 = £301,165. Following the same approach used to calculate the value of Saunders we have (all figures in £000s):

PV of annual cash flow of £301.165 for years 7 to 15 @ 10%	1,734.4
PV of year 15 perpetual NPV; £72.545 × 1.1^{15} discounted back to year 6 @ 21%	54.5
Value of operating activities	1,788.9
Value of financial assets (year 6 portion of cash flow retained)	111.2
Present value of company	1,900.1

In both cases, net cash flow for the current year will be identical at £301,165 and, as we have seen, the market value of the companies should be identical; however, the reported accounting profits will be (again, all figures in £000s):

	Saunders	Toshack
Cash flow	301,165	301,165
Depreciation	100,000	161,051
Operating profit	201,165	140,114
Interest on opening financial assets*	129,554	0
Reported net profit	330,720	140,114
Price multiple of current earnings	5.75	13.56

*The opening balance on these (calculated in a similar manner to the calculation of the closing balance explained in Chapter 3) is £616,927. Interest is received at 21 per cent of this amount at the end of the year.

Clearly, the PE multiples are not comparable because of the differences in depreciation that occur; even if we omit the interest income element, we are still left with a vast difference between the quoted PEs.[5] One way around this problem is the use of a *cash* earnings multiple. Cash earnings are simply operating profits with depreciation added back (in fact, they are the same as the 'funds from operations' shown in the funds flow statement of UK companies), and so the cash earnings multiple (P : CE) is simply market price divided by the cash earnings. This gives us an identical P : CE of 6.31 for both companies. The use of P : CE ratios should be considered as an alternative to PE ratios whenever the age structure of the assets differs between companies used in any comparative analysis. It is also worth noting that a current cost accounting operating profit, calculated according to SSAP 16 (now withdrawn), would yield an identical price–current cost earnings ratio for both companies. Unfortunately, in the absence of any accounting standard requiring the production of current cost accounts, it is all too easy to forget the distorting effect that inflation has on accounts prepared using the historical cost convention.

International comparisons

So far, we have noted that the use of proxy or analogue companies in the valuation process is hindered by accounting choices exercised by individual companies, and by the presence of inflation. These difficulties are encountered in a domestic setting; when we attempt to extend comparisons to different countries, as is currently being done in the area of cross-border acquisitions and in the valuation of companies in countries that do not have developed capital markets (e.g. privatisations in Eastern Europe), we encounter further difficulties because of differences in GAAP between countries. Nobes and Parker (1991) suggest that financial reporting differences can be attributed to differences in legal systems, the providers of finance, taxation, the accounting profession, inflation, theory and accidents of history. Western legal systems can be classified according to whether they are based on common law (e.g. England and Wales, United States) or codified Roman law (e.g. France, Italy and Germany), providers of finance classified according to whether there is a reliance on a stock market for new finance (e.g. United Kingdom and United States), or whether there is a strong reliance on banks (e.g. Germany) and classifications based on taxation can be made according to whether the published accounts form the basis of taxation (e.g. France and Germany) or whether taxation is separately calculated (e.g. United Kingdom or the United States). In the case of countries where the former is true, there will be an incentive to declare the lowest possible profit, which is a phenomenon that will not occur in countries where the latter is true.

As regards the other factors affecting financial reporting, Nobes and Parker (1991) note that in high inflation countries (e.g. some in South America) there is a tendency to use general price-adjusted accounts, whilst theoretical developments have led some countries to use different GAAP (e.g. the use of replacement cost accounting in the Netherlands); finally, historical accidents explain factors like the SEC requirements in the United States, and the presence of UK-based practices in many ex-colonial countries.

In terms of the practical impact of such international differences in GAAP, Weetman and Gray (1991) conducted a comparison of US, UK, Dutch and Swedish accounts reported in the United States and noted that UK GAAPs are significantly less conservative than US GAAPs in terms of their impact on reported profit. They go on to comment that, 'the overall quantitative impact of differences in accounting principles on profits in the US, UK, Sweden and the Netherlands is often significant and, in individual company cases, may be dramatic'.

All this would not matter very much if all valuers only valued domestic companies. However, the trend appears to be towards a globalisation of capital markets, a growth in cross-border merger and acquisition activity (see Cooke, 1988) and the opening up of new financial markets, particularly in Eastern Europe. Confronted with these new requirements to appraise investment opportunities, valuers naturally tend to fall back upon tried and tested methodologies, which include earnings multiple based valuations and discounted cash flow approaches. Now if we are attempting, say, to value an acquisition target in a country with a developed capital market such as the United States, there are plenty of proxy US companies that we can use to derive an expected PE multiple or cost of capital. However, if our task is to value a Hungarian hotel group, there are no such proxies available. Our valuer will almost certainly have to fall back on other European proxies. When our valuer does so (and realistically, there is very little alternative), he or she must have a strong awareness of the country differences in financial reporting and their likely effect.

To give an example, German companies tend to use much higher depreciation rates than UK companies because the rates are specified for tax purposes; German legislation requires that these same rates must be used in the preparation of the financial accounts. As Nobes and Parker (1991) note, these depreciation rates are unlikely to be thought of as 'fair' in the financial reporting sense. Now throw into this situation the fact that, over the past few decades, the United Kingdom has had a higher inflation rate than Germany, together with the tendency for German companies to replace their assets more frequently than UK companies, and we have a real chance of making misleading comparisons between UK and German firms. Weetman and Gray (1991) point out that it is not easy for analysts to develop quantitative rules of thumb to deal with these inter-country differences. One partial way out of this problem may be the use of cash earnings multiples; many investment analysts involved in pan-European equity analysis use precisely such an approach. Table 5.1 gives comparative PE and P : CE multiples for major equity markets.

Table 5.1   PE and P : CE multiples for major equity markets, January 1992

Country	January 1992 PE ratio	P:CE ratio
UK	15.7	8.7
USA	23.2	10.1
France	13.9	6.0
Germany	15.4	4.8
Japan	33.8	9.7

Source: Morgan Stanley Capital International.

The most interesting feature of this table is the tighter grouping of P : CE ratios compared to PE ratios; it does not, of course, explain all of the diversity in PE ratios across countries. As Cooke (1991) notes, concerning Japan, not all differences in PE ratios can be explained by accounting factors; other issues such as economic confidence, savings ratios, etc., have an important impact. Allowing for this means that we should not expect cash earnings ratios to be identical across countries; none the less, when making international comparisons P : CE ratios would appear to offer more insights than simple PE ratios. Perhaps the best solution of all in this type of situation would be the use of discounted cash flow models, as economic logic would suggest that we can reasonably expect some sort of comparability between required rates of return in different countries (see Chapter 6). Having discussed some of the difficulties posed by accounting practices, we can now take a more detailed look at the earnings multiple approach.

THE EARNINGS-MULTIPLE-BASED APPROACH TO VALUATION

The basic idea behind this approach is to estimate the future earnings figure for the PLB or company, and apply to this figure an estimated price earnings multiple. This process begs two key questions, namely which earnings figure should be used? and which PE multiple should be used? If we have been following the methodology used in Chapter 4, we shall have forecasts for a number of years into the future. The question of precisely how many years forecasts are needed depends upon the nature of the business and its cyclicity, together with the maturity of the firm, its products and the industry. Generally speaking, the less the cyclicity and the greater the maturity, the less far into the future we need to forecast.

However, it is hard to imagine that even in the most stable of situations we would need a forecast with a horizon of less than three years, and more usually we should expect to need a forecast that extends at least five years into the future. Going further into the future gives us the problem of balancing the real information content of the further forecasts against their diminishing accuracy. Ideally, it is desirable to have forecasts going out to ten years if possible, but in certain industries with long product development lead times (e.g. the aircraft industry) the horizon has to be considerably longer.

Unfortunately, the dilemma is that we have observed that we have need of shorter forecast horizons in stable industries, and longer ones in cyclical or immature industries, yet the ease of forecasting is inversely related to this need for forecasting. Industries like electronics, where the pace of change is rapid and products have short lives, are those that need the longest forecast horizons; implicitly, this involves forecasting sales and cash flows for products that have not yet been invented – an interesting example of the valuer as science fiction writer and a whole new meaning to the term 'creative accounting'. In this type of situation, it is hard to give the practical analyst any easy answers. Clearly, access to internal information on research and development plans, strategies and so on are likely to help considerably, as is an analysis of the company's strengths and weaknesses (see Chapter 4). It is also vital to obtain the opinions of industry specialists, who should be able to provide some useful insights into likely product development. However, we shall still be left with the inevitability of a great deal of the value of the company resting upon earnings that have not been explicitly forecast; the only helpful suggestion we can make is that a crude specific forecast is likely to be better than the alternative of falling back on 'let's assume the PE ratio is the same as the industry average'. Finally, we should note that the situation described above is the most pessimistic scenario; in many industries we should be able to make specific forecasts up to five years out, and reasonable estimates anything up to ten years out. As a general rule, five years should be regarded as the minimum forecast horizon.

A note of caution should be injected here, because many analysts apparently believe that it is enough simply to forecast next year's earnings, or at most earnings two years ahead (see Day, 1986) and apply an assumed PE multiple. Indeed, some have argued that analysts do not really need to do much in the way of forecasting at all because the current UK practice of companies holding analysts' briefings effectively supplies the analysts with an accurate picture of the likely profits for the current year. The problem with this is that the analysts may well fail to conduct a longer term analysis of the company and simply accept what they are told. As an interesting article in *Accountancy* (November 1991, p.23) notes, 'At present, the market seems to operate on the basis of winks, hints and nudges given by manipulative directors to complaisant analysts. This is an unhealthy situation.' Whilst many analysts may not be so easily misled, the same article quotes Pen Kent, associate director of the Bank of England, as observing that company directors often felt that analysts' knowledge of their companies is, 'to put it bluntly, poor . . . At results presentations, for example, analysts often fail to ask intelligent or penetrating questions. To put it another way, the analysts have to be spoon-fed.' This seems to echo the findings of academic researchers; both Day (1986) and Lee and Tweedie (1981) have noted that the understanding of accounting exhibited by many analysts leaves more than a little to be desired.

Returning to our desired situation of a forecast with a minimum horizon of five years, we should also note that 'extraordinary items' should not be included in any earnings figure to which a PE multiple is applied, because the effect of such items is 'one-off'; to the extent that they represent good or bad news to the company, their effect on value should be allowed for, but such an effect is not of a recurring nature and should not therefore be priced through the application of an earnings multiple. We should also exclude items such as interest income, or indeed any income from financial assets. The reason for this is that the income from such assets has a materially different risk from that of the business we are attempting to value (for example, the risk on most bank deposits (BCCI notwithstanding) is virtually zero); as such, the correct approach is to value the business on its profits from operations, and then to add in the market value of any financial assets at the end.

Factors determining the PE ratio

So far, we have forecast earnings for at least the next five years; the question is, to which one should we apply the chosen PE ratio? To answer this, we need to consider the factors driving the price–earnings ratio; as we have seen in Chapter 3, these factors should be the required return (cost of capital) on investments of a given risk (as we shall see in Chapter 6, this can be expressed in terms of a risk index, a market risk premium and the risk-free rate of return), the return that the company is able to earn on new investment, the dividend payout ratio and the dividend growth rate. In fact, provided that all these factors are constant into perpetuity, the relationship is:

$$PE = \frac{1 - (\text{growth} \div \text{return on new investment})}{\text{Cost of capital} - \text{growth}}$$

See Chapter 3, Appendix, for the derivation of this formula.

When these factors change from year to year, so does the price–earnings ratio. Now the problem is that the reason we make specific forecasts of earnings over five years or more in the first place is that we expect such changes in these components of the PE ratio. If we did not, there would be no point in forecasting five years out, as it would be sufficient to forecast next year's earnings and specify constant growth, cost of capital and return factors. Clearly this is not a situation we should expect to encounter outside the realms of textbook examples because demand is usually cyclical and investment cash flows are lumpy in nature, amongst other reasons. Let us take the more realistic example of Pastoral Ltd★, a company which is in the engineering industry; Pastoral is a subsidiary of Beethoven plc★, whose management is considering a divestment programme. Demand follows a cyclical pattern, but the company is growing in terms of sales trends and investment. The forecast earnings and free cash flows for the next five years are as follows (all figures are £000s):

	Year 1	Year 2	Year 3	Year 4	Year 5
Operating cash flow (OCF)	3300	3267	3993	4832	4832
Projected long-term trend +10% pa (forecast average 10%)					
Depreciation (DEP)	800	820	1000	1430	1450
Taxes (paid as cash) (CT)	1085	490	0	1480	547
Investment in:					
working capital (WCAP)	0	220	710	0	290
fixed assets (INV)	200	1800	4300	200	3270
Cash flow (= OCF − CT−WCAP−INV) (FCF)	2015	757	−1017	3152	725
Projected long-term trend +10% pa					
Profit (PATS)	1415	1957	2993	1872	2835
Projected long-term trend +10% pa (forecast average 19%)					

For the financial year just ended, Pastoral had a free cash flow of £455,000 and a profit after tax of £1,364,000. At the time of forecast preparation, the average industry PE is 7.2, and this reflects growth expectations of only 5 per cent pa, with long-term returns on new investment of 14 per cent; our valuation target is expected to achieve a long run target of 15 per cent. Two things should be apparent; first, that the higher return and growth expectations associated with Pastoral should be reflected in a higher PE ratio and second, that even if we could observe the PE ratios of companies in the industry with similar prospects to Pastoral, it is by no means clear which year's profit figure they should be applied to. Strictly speaking, a historic PE multiple can only be applied to historical earnings, whilst prospective PE ratios can only be applied to prospective earnings. Unfortunately, it is not the case that we can take the prospective PE for companies with similar long-term prospects to Pastoral, because it does not follow that the *pattern* of earnings changes is the same (i.e. is Pastoral outperforming them in the short term, given its five-year average profit growth of 19 per cent pa?).

A discounted cash flow approach does not have such difficulties because it can make a more flexible use of proxy companies in determining a suitable cost of capital (see Chapter 6) and considers every year's cash flow in the analysis (see Chapter 7). For this reason, we are left with the conclusion that DCF methods may actually be easier to apply in valuations, although current practice in the United Kingdom still favours the PE approach. However, the use of DCF methods appears to be gaining ground, particularly in the United States, and this author expects it to do so in the United Kingdom and other European countries. None the less, because many practitioners still use earnings multiple methodologies, and doubtless will continue to do so for some time to come (in part, this may be driven by issues like legal precedence[6] for both taxation and other cases, and understandability by the client for the valuation), we shall see if we can make the PE method yield a useful result. As was discussed at the beginning of Chapter 4, it must always be remembered that the quality of the forecasts for costs and revenues will normally have a bigger impact on the valuation than the choice between a PE or DCF approach in any case.

PE multiples and earnings growth

The first issue that would need to be investigated is which year is representative of the maintainable profit margin on sales, because presumably it is this margin that will grow in line with sales. The choice of the appropriate year is critical; if we assume that the *prospective* PE ratios of companies with similar long-term growth prospects to Pastoral is 8.33, our range of values are between a low of £11.787 million (based on year 1 profits), and a value at the end of year 2 (based on the prospective earnings for year 3) of £24.931 million. This latter figure would, of course, need to be discounted back to give a value in today's terms. If we assume that the cost of capital is, say, 14 per cent[7], this would give us a current value of £19.184 million (in this example, note the importance of realising that the PE ratio from proxies is a prospective one, and that therefore the value at the beginning of the year is given by applying the multiple to the earnings one year ahead). Finally, we are assuming that the PE multiple of proxy companies remains constant throughout the five-year forecast period; in so far as these companies experience constant profit growth and the market's expected return on such investments remains constant, this is a reasonable assumption; if we expect either non-constant profits growth or non-constant discount rates, we should also expect the PE multiple to change.

One point that needs to be emphasised here is that we can speak meaningfully of maintainable margins, but the oft-mentioned 'maintainable profits' is an altogether more elusive concept. In a company where there is no long-term growth, but simply year to year fluctuations in activity in line with economic cycles, its meaning is fairly clear. Under such circumstances, 'maintainable profit' really means average profit. Even here, however, we have the problem of the impact of inflation on the reported profit figures. When the business is growing, it is difficult to pin down the meaning of the term; does maintainable simply mean current year's profit, or does it mean the profit that can be generated from the existing asset base (if this is currently being used to capacity, the two will be the same)? The real difficulty arises with the application of an earnings multiple, because the multiples of proxy companies reflect their future expected earnings, not their maintainable earnings. If we are going to attempt to split future earnings into that coming from existing business and asset bases and that coming from projected future activities (sometimes called 'hoped for' earnings), we need to be very careful in our choice of a suitable earnings multiple.

As we have noted, the chosen earnings multiple is usually based on observations of other companies' PE ratios. Typically, the process involves finding companies in a similar line of business to that which we wish to value, and then adjusting the PE to take account of size differences, whether or not the valuation object is quoted (see Chapter 8 for a discussion of the valuation of unquoted companies) and whether the valuation is being prepared for a possible acquisition, with the attendant need to include a control premium (for a discussion of bid premia, see Chapters 9 and 10). In the case of the latter, a typical approach involves assembling a list of recent bid PE multiples from *Acquisitions Monthly* or a similar source; alternatively, we might take the average industry bid premium observed from deals reported in the recent past, and apply this to the valuation arrived at by the use of proxy PE ratios observed from the market to give a *maximum* bid price. We might feel that an altogether more rational approach in this type of situation is to value the company in both its 'as is' state, and in its post-acquisition state, including the value of any synergystic benefits. Unfortunately, this latter value is not a simple thing to calculate when using the PE approach because the PE ratio must alter as growth prospects change, so that if the improvement results in progressive changes over a number of years, it is by no means obvious what the PE ratio should be. By contrast, no such problems arise when using a discounted cash flow approach, because the discount rate alters only when economic risk changes; efficiency changes merely alter both short- and long-term projected cash flows (the latter via the assumed growth rate).

Another point that must be emphasised, which has already been illustrated in the above example, is the need for the proxies' earnings multiple to reflect similar patterns of growth, and not have just the same long-term growth prospects as the valuation target. It should be evident that the implication of this is the need to forecast (at least in broad terms) the likely earnings growth of all those companies used as proxies; we also need to discard those companies that do not exhibit similar growth patterns to the company we wish to value. Thus, if we are to use the PE approach to valuation in a rigorous manner, the data collection and analysis implications become rather onerous, to say the least. Perhaps surprisingly, the discounted cash flow approach outlined in Chapters 6, 7 and 8 turns out to be *less* demanding in terms of this data collection and analysis, and additionally allows the use of a larger sample of proxy companies; this is because there is no requirement for proxy and valuation target companies to have similar growth rates.

We have already drawn attention to the difficulty of finding a suitable PE multiple to apply to a maintainable earnings figure; the discussion in the previous paragraph should serve to underline why a market-derived PE cannot be applied directly to maintainable earnings, except in the case where the proxy companies themselves show no growth. The effect of applying such a multiple is somewhat indeterminate, but as it will usually be the case that anticipated future earnings exceed maintainable earnings (defined here as earnings from existing assets), we shall usually expect that such a valuation tends to under-state the 'true' value of the business in question. The cynical might argue that as, in the case of acquisitions, there is some evidence of a tendency to over-pay for companies (see Chapters 8 and 9 for a discussion of this evidence), perhaps this element of conservatism might have a useful role to play. The counter-argument is that it is not the role of the valuer to supply downward-biased forecasts[8] (especially if the valuation is for a bid defence or divestment decision) but that this role should be the preparation of an unbiased estimate of value. However, to some degree this argument is a little academic because in general a range of values is presented, partly from sensitising the earnings forecasts and partly from sensitising the PE multiple; none the less, typically there will be pressure on the valuer to settle on one specific value as opposed to a range of values, despite the fact that the former may be a more honest assessment of reality.

PE ratios and gearing

Another point relating to the comparability of PE ratios is relative riskiness of the proxy companies and the business being valued. If appropriate proxies are chosen from the industry, then it might be reasonable to assume that the underlying business risk is similar. However, if the companies chosen as proxies have different gearing (leverage) levels, then the risk of the companies' shares will change because higher gearing increases the 'bottom line' variability of the earnings. It is reasonable to expect that shareholders in those highly geared companies will demand higher returns in exchange for that increased risk, which will have the effect of placing such companies on a lower earnings multiple. This can be allowed for in two ways; either by further eliminating from the sample of proxies those companies with different gearing levels from the object of our valuation, or by specifically recalculating the PE ratio to allow for the change in gearing. In principle, this can be done by following a similar route to that used in Chapter 6 to adjust the discount rate, but under such circumstances it is hard to see the advantage of a PE methodology compared to a DCF one. It is also difficult, if not impossible, to adjust sensibly a PE multiple to take account of the risk implications of recent complex capital issues, such as swaps and convertibles; we show how the discount rate can be adjusted for such factors in Chapter 7.

PE multiples and loss-making businesses

So far, we have assumed that we have a figure called 'earnings', to which we can apply a multiple. An interesting case is that of the loss-making firm; clearly, there must be a lower bound to its value, which is basically the saleable value of the company's assets, by either business unit disposal or liquidation. If we wish to value the company as a going concern, we need to be aware of what the profit potential might be. It might be thought that this is not a problem at all, as we can simply forecast each year's results far enough out to allow any necessary changes to take effect so that the company is (hopefully) restored to profitability, establish a suitable base year and long-term profit growth forecast, and apply our chosen PE multiple accordingly. Unfortunately, we encounter the usual problems with establishing a suitable proxy earnings multiple. In addition, because this value will be the earnings multiple valuation at some point in the future, we somehow need to translate this back into a present-day value. As we need to establish a suitable discount rate to do this (note that this rate must allow for the risk of such investments), it becomes impossible to use a 'pure' PE approach in this type of situation. We should also note that on some occasions an added complication will be the availability of tax shields resulting from past losses. As proxy companies will not normally be in this position themselves, the problems of selecting an appropriate multiple become even greater.

PE ratios and the trade cycle

The final point we need to be aware of is the relationship between the PE ratio and the trade cycle. In general, any PE ratios observed in the market will reflect, *inter alia*, the market's expectation of changes in the economy. Suppose for the moment that the market correctly anticipates such cycles; shortly ahead of any down-turn, company accounts, which are published on an annual basis and several months after the year end, will still be showing profits earned under favourable trading conditions. Meanwhile, back at the market, analysts and investors will be attaching a lower value to these companies in anticipation of the down-turn, and PE ratios will therefore start to fall. As we start to head out of the recession, share values pick up, but the published earnings figures are now reflecting unfavourable trading conditions. PE ratios will therefore tend to look rather high; as accounting earnings start to reflect these improvements so the observed PE multiple will fall back. A simple graphical summary of this is shown in Figure 5.2. It should also be obvious from this analysis that it is invalid to take a PE ratio derived from proxies in *current* market conditions and apply

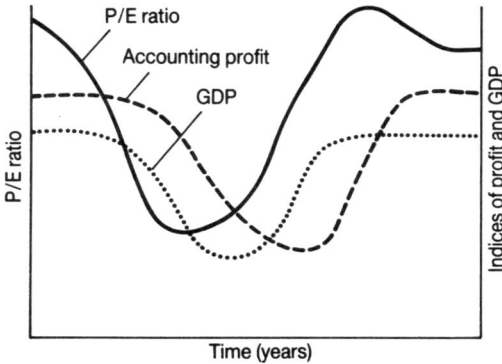

Figure 5.2   PE ratios and the trade cycle.

this to an *average* of the historical earnings figures whenever cyclical factors have influenced such a figure.

Conclusions on the use of PE multiples

Our conclusion on earnings multiples must therefore be that they are rather in the nature of what language students sometimes call 'false friends'. At first sight, the application of a market-derived PE to estimated future earnings seems reasonable, but on closer investigation we find that it must be used with some caution. First, there are problems relating to the comparative calculation of the earnings numbers themselves, which are partly attributable to differing accounting practices and partly to the problems caused by the historical cost accounting convention; as we noted, the use of cash earnings multiples can help to overcome the latter. In a cross-border context these difficulties are exacerbated. Second, there are real difficulties encountered in attempting to derive a suitable earnings multiple; differing growth patterns, risks and the cyclicity of PE ratios all contribute to these difficulties. This is not to say that the approach cannot reasonably be used; it can be, provided these problems are recognised and overcome. However, this is by no means a trivial task and it is hard to see why we should positively recommend the earnings multiple approach compared to the DCF alternative, which has the advantage of making many of these assumptions explicit rather than implicit (it should be noted that the assumptions necessary to use market-based earnings multiples are, in their way, just as onerous as those needed to use the market-based discount rates discussed in the Chapter 6; it might be just that in the former case the assumptions are 'in the closet', and therefore not discussed as often as they perhaps should be). None the less, there is some good news for keen supporters of the earnings-based approach – because many market participants use an earnings-based valuation methodology, in the case of a valuation prepared for the sale or purchase of a business it is a useful and necessary negotiating tactic to have prepared such a valuation irrespective of any views one may have of its validity. Furthermore, given the inevitably subjective nature of any valuation, it is always a good idea to prepare an earnings-based valuation to check against the result of the DCF analysis for reasonableness of the assumptions being made in *both* valuations.

Before leaving the topic of earnings multiple based valuations, we should note there are special cases where market practitioners regard PE multiples as irrelevant in determining values, because other factors (usually asset-based) drive market value. Examples include banks, investment trusts, insurance companies and property companies.

ASSET VALUES

In the strictest sense of the phrase, we cannot talk about asset-based valuations because, as we have seen in Chapter 2, the worth of any business is driven by the concept of opportunity value. Under certain circumstances (essentially, when the company is not viable as a going concern), the lower bound to opportunity value is the net realisable value of the assets; on other occasions, the upper bound to value will be the replacement cost of the assets, although as we noted in Chapter 2, we must be very careful with our definition of replacement cost because this must reflect the replacement of assets with the same service potential and must also reflect the value of all the assets, including those that are not normally valued in financial terms, such as personnel, market share, geographical location and so on. In short, what we are trying to value is really the *replication cost* of the business. Note that such a cost would also need to reflect any timing disadvantage that resulted from replicating the firm; given the time involved in setting up an enterprise from scratch, such costs may be substantial.

The need to look at asset values, then, is partly to check that the business cannot be replicated more cheaply than it can be bought; whilst this is of most relevance in a takeover situation, it might also serve as an indicator of a possible over-valuation in other cases, because the implication of market value exceeding replication cost may be that there is some scope for competing firms to enter the market. Realistically, however, such a value will be very difficult to arrive at, and will probably include a great deal of subjectivity. It is probably of most relevance to the valuation of small, unlisted companies, where replication might be relatively straightforward, although such a figure can be reasonably calculated for quite large businesses, such as retailers and hotel chains; the key issues are the ease and speed with which a replication can be put together. There is also a need for such calculations to check on whether a higher value can be achieved by the business in a form other than its present one; this involves looking at selling-off individual PLBs as separate entities (*break-up value*), or selling-off the assets piecemeal (*liquidation value*). Finally, there is a need to check on the value of the underlying assets of the business, because this has implications for the security underpinning the business itself and also the potential financing needs of the company; for example, if the debtors' portfolio turns out to be a very risky one, not only is there a possibility of losses through bad debts, but there is also an implication for short-term financing requirements.

As with the preparation of profit and cash flow forecasts, we shall obviously have a far better prospect of performing a succesful valuation of the assets if we have access to internal information; not the least of these advantages will be the ability to inspect physically the assets themselves. To start with, we shall look at the issues involved in determining the realisable value of the assets. A crucial point to be addressed in discussing such a concept is the circumstance of the realisation; is the asset sale to be a forced one (emergency liquidation), a gradual liquidation or will it involve the break-up of the company? Clearly, value will normally be at its lowest when a rapid liquidation is required, and highest when profitable businesses are disposed of as part of a break-up. Forced liquidation price will rarely be of interest unless the valuation object is thought to be in financial distress.

Break-up valuation

If we are to look at the idea of break-up values, we are simply recognising the principles behind valuation that we apply elsewhere in this book. Essentially, the value of any business is dictated by its future cash-generating potential. A company will be worth more as a series of separate businesses than as a whole if either cash flow can be gained by cutting out all central overheads by each PLB providing its own services, or if those individual businesses can be made to generate additional cash flows by being run in a different manner. Such an eventuality may come about because of greater incentives, freedom from centralised decision-making, increased co-operation between management and workforce, greater use of initiative, freedom of access to external capital rather than reliance on rationed internal funds, or simply by synergystic gain from combination with some different company. Obviously, business units can themselves be parcelled together in a way that maximises value; if, for example, we are investigating the possible break-up of a conglomerate group that amongst its businesses has a consumer electrical appliances division and a gas fire manufacturing division, we may well find that the optimal value is created by combining these two operations into a consumer products company, which is sold off. The general rules are simple (even if their application is not); first, find the value of each PLB as a 'stand-alone' unit. This can be compared with the realisable value of the unit's assets to see whether there is a *prima facie* case for discontinuing the activity. Second, search out any alternative combinations of business units – it may be that a business which appeared to be worth abandoning is actually worth keeping in conjunction with some other activity. At this stage, we should therefore have some idea of whether each PLB is worth more as a 'going concern' than as a liquidated activity. One important (but sometimes not fully investigated) point is that before deciding on the closure of any PLB, *all* the alternatives should be investigated, and these include internal efficiency improvements, external marketing improvements, investment opportunities, sale to management/workforce and sale to some other company.

Having analysed the liquidation alternative (and presumably deciding to take appropriate action), let us assume we are now left with those businesses that have a going concern value greater than their liquidation value. The third step is now to compare the value of the entire company in its 'as is' state with the value of the company less the cash flows from any disposed PLB plus the potential disposal proceeds of the PLB in question. If the former is less than the latter, then the PLB should be retained; otherwise its disposal should be considered. All this is summarised in Figure 5.3.

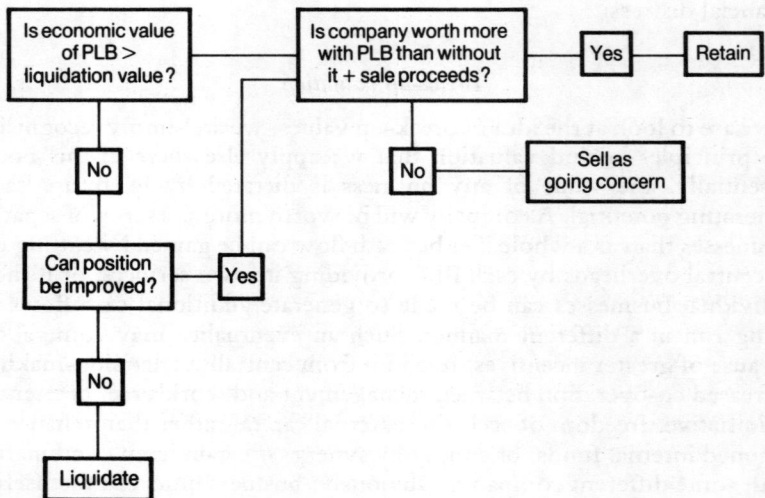

Is economic value of PLB > liquidation value? → Is company worth more with PLB than without it + sale proceeds? → Yes → Retain

Is economic value of PLB > liquidation value? → No

Is company worth more with PLB than without it + sale proceeds? → No → Sell as going concern

Can position be improved? → Yes

Can position be improved? → No → Liquidate

Figure 5.3 Analysis of liquidation, disposal and retention alternatives.

There are several points to watch when appraising this break-up valuation. The first of these are the overhead costs that would be borne by the independent PLB and the remaining business (this is discussed in Chapter 4); note that we might rationally expect some synergy in overheads. The second issue is that of inter-PLB transfers of goods and services. However these are priced for management accounting purposes,[9] when considering the value of a PLB as an independent entity any such goods and services must be priced at an 'arms length' market price (recognising such factors as selling costs and quantity discounts), because if the entity is sold off, any trading that continues with the rest of the group will be conducted on such a basis. The third point concerns the tax implications; the disposal itself may potentially give rise to a tax liability if proceeds are different from costs. The other tax consideration is the tax shield value of the PLB to the business as a whole. To the extent that the profits of the individual activities comprising a business combination are not perfectly positively correlated, a tax advantage can arise by virtue of the fact that losses in some activities can be offset against profits in others; the break-up of the combination obviously reduces this potential. Furthermore, there may be differences in the tax shields on borrowing if either the borrowing capacity of the combination is different from the sum of the borrowing capacities of the individual parts, or if the financing cost of the debt changes;[10] the issue of debt tax shields is discussed in Chapter 6. If financing costs alter, there will, of course, be a cash flow change reflecting the difference in interest charges on the debt; this really reflects risk transfer between debt and equity holders.[11]

The determination of liquidation and replacement values

Having discussed issues relating to break-up realisable values, we shall now look at the determination of liquidation or piecemeal sale values of assets, and their replacement values. In general, such values can only be arrived at with any accuracy by direct inspection. It is obviously possible for outside valuers to arrive at crude 'guestimates' in cases where the company has a reasonably simple structure (for example, this may be practicable in the case of high street retailers), but the dangers of the approach can be anecdotally illustrated by several recent examples, including Polly Peck (where just prior to the suspension of the company analysts were estimating that a substantial asset value per share would be realised on any break-up of the company). For the purposes of this section, we shall look first at how the balance-sheet value relates to realisable and replacement asset values, and then look at the additional information that a valuer who had access to internal information might need.

Fixed assets
Running through the assets in balance-sheet order, property values are normally stated as a recent valuation rather than historical cost. As the date of such valuation is disclosed, it is possible to arrive at an approximate current value by the application of property price indices; transaction costs on buying or selling would need to be allowed for in arriving at replacement or realisable values. However, it is important to realise that professional property valuations are prepared on the assumption that an open market exists with willing buyers and sellers. It is perfectly possible that it might take some considerable time to find such a buyer. Furthermore, the valuations will have been prepared on a property-by-

property basis. If, say, the break-up and piecemeal sale of the property portfolio of a major high street retailer was being contemplated, attempting to sell such a large amount of property at once might have a significantly depressing effect on values, particularly if there was some geographical concentration of the assets. There is also the question of special purpose properties, such as industrial plants and ports. Attempting to define a realisable value for such cases is fraught with difficulty, because of the need to consider the possibilities of alternative use and any attendant land clearance and alteration costs involved; special surveys would be the only way of accurately arriving at such values.

Other fixed assets, such as plant and equipment, vehicles and fittings are normally carried in the balance sheet at historical cost less depreciation. However, certain assets (for example, the British Airways aircraft fleet) are sometimes shown at valuation, although companies are often reluctant to use such an approach because of the accompanying need for higher depreciation charges. Unless a recent valuation of assets is available, balance sheet values of these assets are a very poor guide to either liquidation or replacement value. The answers to the questions that need to be asked about these assets can rarely be found from the annual report. We really need to know the production technology employed, and how this relates to that employed by competitors (if the technology is outdated, balance sheet value might considerably over-state realisable value), the state of repair of the assets, the degree to which these assets are moveable and the degree to which the assets have a specialist use. Perhaps the best illustration of the last two points is the sale of, say, a complex chemical plant; unless there is a buyer for the operation as a going concern, the liquidation value of the assets is likely to be just the scrap value of the equipment, and if there was any toxicity problem the entire fixed asset value could be negative.

Investments
Any investments shown on the balance sheet are simply valued at market prices, if the investments are easily saleable. Note that the market value of such investments at the accounting year end is a mandatory disclosure, but any revision to current market values requires a detailed breakdown of the investments held; this information will be available only from the accounts or any other source if investment held is a substantial one (more than 2 per cent if the investment is in a listed UK company). However, if such a substantial stake in a listed company is owned, we would need to consider the likely impact of any sale (or purchase, in the case of replacement cost) on market prices; furthermore, it must be remembered that some stakes in quoted smaller companies can be virtually unsaleable in any quantity, unless there is a matching purchaser for the shares. In the case of investments in unlisted companies, valuations would need to be prepared on a 'willing buyer' basis and on a forced sale one if liquidation values were being considered.

Intangible assets
Intangible assets present some conceptual difficulty; if we are seeking a break-up valuation, then the values of such assets are obviously implicit in the values ascribed to each PLB. If liquidation values are being investigated with a view to a piecemeal sale of the assets, some intangibles, such as 'goodwill' are, by definition, valueless, because there is no 'going concern' to possess such a thing. However, other intangibles, such as brand names and patents, may well have a liquidation value. Replacement costs of such items are often impossible to estimate; clearly a patent cannot be replicated (at least not in EC, and many other, countries), whereas a brand could be, at least in theory, by spending a great deal on marketing and allowing for the time value cost of the whole process.

Current assets
With the exception of stocks, the book, liquidation and replacement values of most of the current assets are likely to be fairly close to one another, unless inflation rates are high. Besides the obvious issue of bad debts, another one that needs to be considered is the definition of cash and liquid assets. In general, the netting-off of cash balances is not permitted by accounting regulations, but positive balances are combined in the consolidated balance sheet of the company. The problem here is identifying just where the cash is located. It is perfectly possible that a large chunk of a healthy-looking cash balance is locked into a country with tight exchange control regulations; this is the sort of issue that can be addressed in a valuation with access to internal records, but not otherwise.

Stock values can either be very objective and close to both realisable and replacement values (as in the case of the large supermarket chains), or extremely subjective (contract work in progress valuation being the best example). In between these extremes, we have the cost of manufactured stock. The general accounting rule is that stocks should be valued at the lower of cost or realisable value; unfortunately, in the case of manufactured goods, 'cost' is highly subjective, because SSAP 9 requires cost to include manufacturing overheads. As overhead allocation is a very arbitrary process,[12] it follows that the resultant stock values are also arbitrary. A point that needs to be considered here is that the realisable values of the stocks of regularly produced branded products are fairly easy to estimate; on the other hand, the realisable values of specialist products may not be. Related to this, fashion goods of any sort can have very low realisable values; in theory, these should be written down in the accounts, but in practice complex issues arise here because the true value of such stock may not be apparent at the time when the accounts were prepared. Again, a valuer with an internal perspective can investigate these issues, whereas anyone valuing from an external one cannot.

These stock valuation problems can look trivial compared to the problem of estimating values of long-term contracts. According to SSAP 9, the balance sheet value should be cost (which will include overheads, and can even include capitalised interest charges), less amounts taken to the profit and loss acount,[13] less any provisions for foreseeable losses. Any payments due on these contracts should be disclosed separately under debtors. Key issues that need to be thought about include degree of completion and the likelihood of any problems, including both construction difficulties and possible claims against the company. Those who enjoy horror stories can find a great deal of interesting reading in this area. When we move to try and work out the realisable or replacement values of these contracts, we can find ourselves venturing into the realms of the meaningless. Normally, these contracts will only be worth anything if they are completed; contractors who attempt to 'realise' such 'stocks' by walking away from the job are unlikely to receive much in the way of cash, but may well receive some interesting correspondence from solicitors. In a sense, then, these contracts have only a going concern value, which is best measured by the remaining revenues receivable, less the additional costs, all suitably adjusted for the time value of money.

Liabilities

We can now turn our attention to valuing the liabilities. In the case of short-term liabilities, such as trade creditors, taxation and bank overdrafts, realisable and replacement values (which still make sense as concepts applied to liabilities) are likely to be similar to book values, provided appropriate adjustments are made for time value of money. However, long-term liabilities can have a substantially different 'replacement value' or 'realisable value' if the interest payments on them are fixed. Imagine a company was fortunate enough to issue fixed interest debentures when interest rates were only 5 per cent pa, and that since then they have doubled. This debt will be recorded in the accounts at its par value, yet the fair value of this debt in the capital markets will be considerably less than this;[14] in fact, this value is both the realisable value (i.e. the amount for which this debt could be liquidated) and the replacement value (the amount that could be raised for this annual interest charge) of the debt.

Note also the implications of this for the profit calculation; ideally, profit numbers should reflect current interest charges (because this reflects the current opportunity cost of capital), which is not generally the case where fixed interest debt has been used. This turns out not to be a problem for the DCF valuation method, because the discount rate chosen reflects both current cost of capital and target gearing levels. The final point that we need to be aware of concerning liabilities is taxation; *actually* realising assets could give rise to a substantial tax charge.

Replacement costs

It should be evident from the above that although, in most cases, we can start from accounting values and derive sensible estimates of realisable (liquidation) values, the same cannot be said for replacement costs. We come back to the point made above – replacement costs are really of conceptual value only, in so far as they prompt the question 'how much would it cost to establish this business from scratch?' Provided this is less than the economic value of such a business, replication of the activity will be preferable to takeover as a way into the market and, as such, replacement value should form an upper bound to the values of such businesses. However, as we have seen, 'replacement value' in this sense includes the full costs of replication of the service capacity of the business in question, and includes such tenuous items as the value of key personnel, brands, goodwill and so on. In the case of the corner shop, the local garage or even some larger businesses, such things are easily estimated, whereas in the case of businesses with high barriers to entry (e.g. pharmaceuticals) or businesses where a great deal of importance is attached to key individuals, the opposite is true.

One measure of replacement cost used by financial analysts is the q ratio; this is simply the ratio of the market value of the company to the estimated replacement cost of the *physical* assets. One problem with this is the definition and calculation of replacement costs; none the less, this is a measure used by US analysts, and Copeland and Weston (1988) report that 'in recent years the q ratio has been running at 0.5 to 0.6', and note that for companies in the natural resource industries it has been as low as 0.2 because of the values of reserves in the ground (before readers rush out to launch a takeover bid for British Gas, they should be aware of the impact of extraction costs and the time value of money on such values). In fact, this is one argument advanced for both the number of takeovers that take place, and the observed takeover premia; we discuss this in more detail in Chapter 9.

The q ratio phenomenon appears to be inconsistent with either the theory of opportunity value of assets or with managers behaving in a rational manner. We might rationally expect the q ratio to be *greater* than one, because the firm will have valuable non-physical assets and (hopefully) be investing in positive net present value projects; the theoretical upper bound on value would be the lower of the economic value and the replacement cost of both physical and intangible assets. An intriguing puzzle is why managers bother replacing assets if the market value of the firm is less than replacement value? This is an interesting question worthy of further research; possible explanations include the insufficiently profitable use of assets by incumbent managers (but note that the ratios above are *average* ones), industry differences (for example, there may be industries where it would not be worthwhile replacing the assets, but where economic value exceeds realisable value; Concorde is an example of this), or simply the over-estimation of the replacement costs *of service potential* of the assets by analysts and others. Whilst US data is available, there is no readily accessible source of q ratios for the United Kingdom, although services such as *Datastream* can be used to derive price to accounting-book value ratios. Furthermore, *Acquisitions Monthly* publishes data on the net asset values and asset price multiples in bid situations, where that information is available.

Where asset valuations are regularly used

Before leaving our discussion on asset valuations, we should note that some types of business are normally valued by reference to their asset bases and not by their earnings; the most obvious examples include property companies, oil companies and investment trusts. Note that discounted cash flow approaches can be used in such cases, but they are not always helpful. They are likely to be very useful in the case of oil and property companies, but will generally not be so in the case of investment trusts, where in the case of quoted investments the asset values will already reflect consensus market valuations. On average, investment trusts and property companies trade at a discount to net asset values; with oil companies, both extraction costs and the period of extraction need to be estimated using DCF principles.

Conclusion on asset values

As we have seen, the historical book value of the assets, stated in the accounts, is of no direct use in the determination of business asset values; we are concerned with replacement costs, realisable values and economic values.

Realisable values are of concern because if the break-up or liquidation value is higher than the economic value achievable by following the optimal set of strategies, the business should either be disposed of or liquidated.

Replacement cost means the replication cost of the business. As we have noted, in practice this can be difficult to estimate but, in the case of acquisitions, there is a need for some attempt at the calculation to check whether the business in question can be replicated for a lower cost than the acquisition price. It can also serve as a useful indicator to incumbent management teams; if the replacement cost of the assets is greater than the current market value of the business (in other words, if the q ratio is less than 1.0), this provides a signal to those managers that business value may not be being optimised by current strategies.[15] Furthermore, such firms may prove to be tempting takeover targets.

SUPER PROFIT VALUATION

Our final accounting-based valuation technique is the super profits method. This approach has a variety of interpretations but all of them essentially capitalise above-average returns and add them to the asset value. As an example, assume that we wish to value Edwards Williams

Ltd*, a manufacturer of rugby balls. The firm has been having some success recently, and is forecast to earn a profit of £380,000 in the current year. The net asset value of the company is £2 million and the current 'acceptable' return on capital employed is thought to be 15 per cent pa. The so-called super profits are defined as £380,000 less the required return on the asset base (15 per cent × £2 million = £300,000), which nets out at £80,000 pa. These are then capitalised at some super profit multiple, typically somewhere between three and five times; for this example, let us assume five times is used. This gives us a capitalised super profit figure of £400,000, which is added to the net asset value of £2 million to produce a valuation of £2.4 million.

The problems of applying this method should be apparent – it attempts to apply the worst features of the PE and asset valuation approaches and, furthermore, exists in something of a data vacuum. The approach is a rather old-fashioned one, which seems to try to fuse economic and accounting theories of value; sadly, it fails dismally. Not only is the theory seriously flawed, it no longer appears to be used in practice. Let us examine the problems in more detail. To take the theoretical objections first, the model assumes that a business earning 'normal' profits (in the economic sense) is worth only its asset value. Now, in a world where accounting values represented the current opportunity value of the assets, this would be valid. Unfortunately, as we have seen above, the accounting net asset value will only represent such a figure by coincidence and not by design. Second, to be valid, earnings would also have to be defined in an economic sense, which would require a cash-flow-based definition, rather than an accruals accounting-based one. Third, even if these issues could be resolved, we would be left with the problem of determining a satisfactory super profits multiple (note that satisfactory rates of return can be determined, provided asset values and earnings are properly defined).

Turning to the practical problems of the method, it is unclear why this approach has any advantage over the earnings multiple method. Both require the derivation of a capitalisation multiple but, as we have seen, the PE methodology at least has *some* theoretical validity because we can always derive a PE multiple consistent with the alternative DCF approach to valuation (and, as we have also seen, this can be simply done in the case of constant growth factors); the same is not true of the super profits approach. Second, there are ready sources of proxy or analogue PE multiples, both for non-acquisition situations and for those involving acquisitions. There are no such sources for super profit multiples. Finally, in the context of unquoted company valuation, the method has been dismissed as unsatisfactory in the case of *Buckingham* v. *Francis*. In conclusion, there is nothing to be said in favour of the method, and a great deal to be said against it.

CHAPTER 6

DISCOUNTED CASH FLOW MODELS – ESTIMATING THE DISCOUNT RATE

So far, we have taken the opportunity cost of capital as given, and we have largely ignored the question of risk. In fact, the two are inter-related; it might seem self-evident that the more risky a company is, the greater the return required, but whilst this is partly correct it is by no means a universal truth. To understand why something that appears to be a statement of the obvious truth is not always so, we need to appreciate the concepts behind what has become known as *modern portfolio theory* (MPT).[1] In essence, MPT is an elegant mathematical formulation of the old proverb 'do not put all your eggs in one basket'; in short, it states that the relevant measure of risk is *portfolio* risk and that an additional investment needs to be evaluated in terms of the additional return it generates relative to the additional risk it imposes on the portfolio. It is therefore possible to imagine (at least in principle) that on occasions, an opportunity may arise that is in itself extremely risky, but that none the less reduces the risk of a portfolio of investments. As a very simple example, consider a medium-sized partnership of accountants, who offer a range of accounting and tax planning services; the business is not particularly risky but can suffer in a recession. Meanwhile, in the same town, there is a company receivership practice. Demand for receivership services is volatile (and therefore the practice is risky), but it is counter-cyclical. If we look at an acquisition of the receivership practice by the accountants, we find that the addition of an individually risky business can reduce their overall risk exposure.

RISK AND PORTFOLIOS OF INVESTMENTS

Whilst the mathematics of portfolio theory is outside the scope of this book,[2] it is useful to pick up some of the major implications of the theory. First, rational investors will hold well diversified portfolios (it helps to think of institutional investors as the role model here). Second, given that this is so, on individual investments they will be concerned not with the *total* risk of such investments, but with the *additional* risk that they impose upon the portfolio; the greater the number of different investments held, the more this will be true. We can depict this relationship in Figure 6.1.

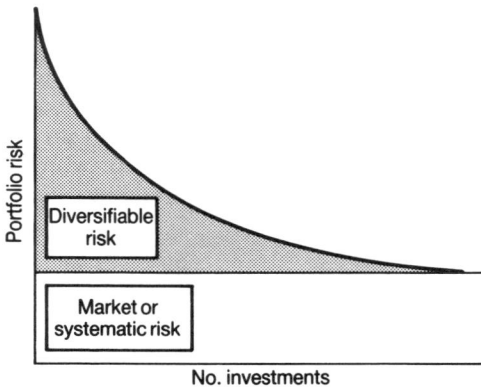

Figure 6.1 Diversifiable and systematic risk.

As can be seen, increasing the number of investments in a portfolio decreases the risk to a point, but it is impossible to diversify away all risk. Certain types of risk are easily disposed of simply by holding large numbers of different investments. These can be viewed as company-specific risks, and examples include the technical failure of a newly developed product, the loss of key personnel, legal actions and, to add interest, major scandals or press revelations. By contrast, the sorts of risk that cannot be diversified away are mainly those of an economic nature. To a greater or lesser extent all firms are affected by bad news on the economic front (although in the case of receivership practices this may have a positive effect), but some are affected more than others. Remember that it is the additional contribution to portfolio risk that matters; company-specific risks tend to cancel each other out in a large portfolio, but *all* the investments in the portfolio will be moved in the same direction to some extent by these common economic factors. In a well-diversified portfolio this exposure is the important component of additional risk.

Clearly, some companies suffer from this type of economic exposure more than others; for example, those firms where product demand is discretionary, such as tour operators, hi-fi manufacturers and fashion retailers are much more vulnerable to economic downturns than those where product demand tends to be non-discretionary, such as food manufacturers, food retailers and utility companies. Thus when we say that a firm is 'risky' we should distinguish between *diversifiable risk* (sometimes known as *specific*, or *non-systematic risk*) and *non-diversifiable risk* (known variously as *systematic, non-specific* or *β risk*). As investors can diversify away the former type of risk for the expense of some transactions costs, but cannot get rid of the latter type of risk, it is *only* this latter, non-diversifiable, risk that they should expect to be compensated for. The question is how much compensation should they reasonably expect?

A RISK PRICING MODEL

At this point, we skip a lot of clever mathematics and note that given some critical assumptions, it is possible to derive a risk pricing model that prices the required return by using a single index of risk called β.[3] This model is known as the *capital asset pricing model* (CAPM), which tells us what the expected return on any investment, R_i, should be:

$$R_i = RF + (\beta_i \times MRP)$$

In the above expression, RF is the expected 'risk-free' rate of return (which in a single period context can be approximated by the return on treasury bills) and MRP is the *market risk premium*. This is the return we expect from holding a portfolio that represents the entire market of risky investments (the *market portfolio*), less the expected risk-free rate of return (put more formally, $MRP = R_{\text{market portfolio}} - RF$). Strictly, the CAPM requires that *all* assets are marketable and divisible, but in practical terms 'the market portfolio' is normally taken to be the stock market, and the return on this portfolio is approximated by the return on an arithmetic value-weighted price index with dividends reinvested. In the United Kingdom, the index that is normally used is the FT All Share Index (FTASI); in the United States, the Standard and Poor 500 Share Index[4] is used.

Whilst the assumptions underlying the CAPM may be regarded as anywhere between simplifying and preposterous, the critical factors are whether the assumptions lead to a model that is a good predictor of share returns and whether we have a practically useful model. First, we shall take a brief look at the assumptions themselves. These are:

1. No transactions costs.
2. All assets are infinitely divisible and marketable.
3. Short sales are allowed.
4. No personal taxes.
5. All individual investors are price takers and cannot influence the price of any risky asset by their actions.
6. Investors are concerned only with risk and expected returns.
7. Unlimited borrowing and lending can take place at the risk-free rate.
8. All investors have homogenous expectations concerning risk and return.
9. Investors have the same single period investment horizon (note that this can be ten days or ten years; all that matters is that it is the same horizon).

Now clearly some of these are unrealistic. However, an interesting question is *how* unrealistic? For example, imagine we are enjoying a quiet pint in the local pub, when in walks a finance academic inviting us to believe that we can borrow at the risk-free rate. In fact, we are just about to tell him that he is obviously mad, when we suddenly pause and reflect on our mortgage rates relative to the current yield on gilts. Having had second thoughts on the sanity of this character, we shall doubtless offer to buy him a drink and find out a little more about the model. In fact, we could go through each of these assumptions and argue about how well they *approximate* reality for the majority of 'the market', which is comprised mainly of institutional investors. However, we shall not do so here, as our principal concern is with how well the model actually works; interested readers are referred to Elton and Gruber (1991, pp. 284–5).

It should also be noted that many of these assumptions can be relaxed *independently* without violating the basic conclusions of the model. For example, we can do away with the short sale requirement. Perhaps most importantly, we can also develop a version of the model to take account of personal taxation; the good news is that under certain circumstances the model remains unchanged (Litzenberger and Ramaswamy, 1979[5]). We can also, given certain further assumptions, extend the model to a multi-period setting. Whilst it must be tempting for many practitioners to reject such a model out of hand for being 'unrealistic', the potential appeal of the CAPM is its simplicity. *If* it works, we have the prospect of being able to calculate the required rate of return on any risky investment by reference to just three factors. All we need to know are the risk-free rate, the market risk premium and the β of the individual investment. Risk-free rates of return are readily observable, we can estimate the market risk premium (see below) and we can also obtain β from published sources for any company quoted on most of the world's larger stock markets. This leaves us the rather trickier issue of whether the CAPM adequately describes returns on stock market investments; in other words, *does* it work?

Tests of the CAPM

Unfortunately, the strict answer to the question of whether or not the CAPM is 'true' is that it is doubtful that we can ever know. The problem is that we simply do not know the composition of the *true* market portfolio – all we have are proxies for this. The arguments here are complex (although interesting)[6] and a large number of tests can be viewed as investigating whether the CAPM gives us a useful estimator of equity returns. Most of the available evidence relates to the New York Stock Exchange. A brief summary of the findings is that there appears to be no reward for bearing non-diversifiable risk (exactly what the CAPM predicts) and that return is a linear function of systematic risk (again as predicted by the CAPM); however, the problem is that the return line is flatter and has a higher intercept than the basic form of CAPM predicts[7] (Figure 6.2).

In fact, the evidence suggests that the so-called *zero* β *CAPM* may be a better model of returns than the basic version of the CAPM. The zero β

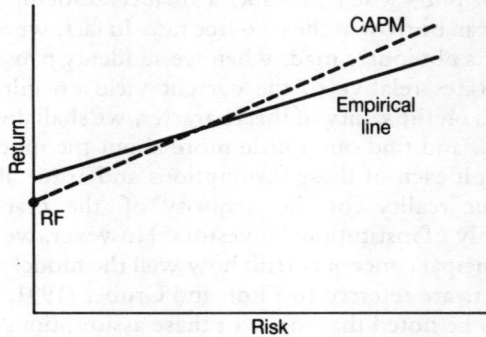

Figure 6.2   The empirical and theoretical security market lines.

version is of the same form as the basic model, but describes expected returns (in terms of the return (RZ)) that can be obtained on a portfolio of investments with a β of zero, and the return on the market portfolio (R_m):

$$R_i = RZ + \beta_i (R_m - RZ)$$

The zero β version may be, more accurate[8] but easily applicable it is not; commercially available β factors (at least for the United Kingdom) usually use the basic CAPM and, in addition, the return on the zero β portfolio involves complex calculations whereas treasury bill and gilt rates (proxies for the risk-free rate) are easily obtained. We shall therefore stay with the basic CAPM, which probably offers a reasonable approximation of the opportunity cost of capital. However, it is worth bearing in mind that for companies with either very high or very low β, the CAPM may tend to either over- or under-estimate expected returns, respectively.

Although we shall be using the basic CAPM, it must be acknowledged that we shall be applying it to derive long-term discount rates. The theoretical development of the model is based upon the assumption of a single period. Extending this into multiple periods technically requires a fairly restrictive set of assumptions (for a detailed analysis see Constantinides, 1980). In practice, these difficulties tend to be ignored because of the computational complexity they introduce; we shall follow that practice here, but it is worth pointing out that this does imply that β, the risk-free rate and the market risk premium are known and constant (see Fama, 1977).

Using the CAPM

If we are prepared to accept the approximation of reality that the CAPM represents, we find ourselves in a very useful position, as we are now able to estimate the cost of equity capital for any company quoted on any major stock exchange. We have already noted the availability of the necessary data. Let us take the case of British Telecom (BT); the β of this company can be obtained from the London Business School Risk Measurement Service, which also gives us some other information about the shares. For example, the following information can be gleaned from the September 1991 edition of the service (published quarterly):

	Market Cap (£m)	β	Variability	Specific risk	Standard error	R-squared
BT	21,419	0.78	25	18	0.10	48

First, we can work out the cost of BT's equity provided we know the return required on long-dated gilts (this is obtainable on a daily basis from the *Financial Times*; issues relating to the choice of an appropriate gilt rate are discussed below) and the market risk premium. We shall assume that the current risk free rate is 10 per cent, and that the market risk premium is 6.3 per cent. The derivation of the latter figure is explained later (see page 117). Given these data inputs, we can calculate the cost of BT's equity as:

$$R_{BT}(\%) = 10 + (0.78 \times 6.3) = 14.9\%$$

The other data given by the service are the *variability* (which tells us the standard deviation of the returns on BT shares), the *specific risk* (which is the standard deviation of returns attributable to the diversifiable part of the risk), and the R-squared (which is a statistical term that describes what percentage of the variability is explained by market risk factors). In this case, 48 per cent of BT's total risk is explained by general market risk factors.[9] The 'standard error' referred to is that of the β. Applying the normal rules of statistical inference allows us to conclude with 95 per cent confidence that the true β of BT lies between the mean and plus or minus two standard errors. Whilst this may make the observed β appear unreliable, it should be noted that we are more normally interested in the βs of portfolios of companies. A statistical property of these βs is that portfolio βs are far more accurate than the βs of individual companies.

Later on in this chapter (see page 120ff), we shall explore the area of how we can use such publicly available data in the estimation of the required rate of return (in other words, the discount rate)[10] for investment on individual business activities. Before we do so, we shall take a look at some of the more sophisticated models, which have less restrictive assumptions than the CAPM and can be used as alternatives in the estimation of the discount rate.

Alternatives to the CAPM

There is a general class of these alternatives, called *multi-index models*, which contrast with the single index CAPM. The basis of these models is the *Arbitrage Pricing Theory* (APT), which is derived in a perfect market framework where the arbitrage transactions of informed investors result in the fair pricing of fundamental risk factors. Unfortunately, APT does not give us a theoretical framework for the determination of these factors, although it does exclude some factors by definition (for example, returns in previous periods cannot be 'factors', because if they were, this would imply market inefficiency – something incompatible with the theory itself). We are therefore forced to try and find these factors by trial and error. As an example, Chen *et al.* (1986) examined the relationship between macro-economic variables and returns and suggested that industrial production, unanticipated inflation, the term structure of interest rates and bond default risk premia were important factors.

More recently, Burmeister and McElroy (1987, 1988) have conducted further tests of the APT, and found that the model explains stock returns better than the CAPM; specific factors found by them were default risk on bonds, the term stucture of interest rates, unanticipated inflation, change in economy-wide expected sales and the return on the 'market portfolio' not captured by the first four factors. Whilst this list looks similar to that of Chen *et al.*, the factors are measured in a slightly different manner. At present, considerable research still needs to be done in this area before we have a convincing set of results with which to work, but it does appear to be the case that inflation, term and default risk structure of interest rates, and industrial output all have some role as risk factors.

The issue of interest here is whether we have a model that can be used to calculate costs of capital. The CAPM gives us the relationship between return and a single risk factor. That risk factor was systematic risk, and the unit price of that risk is the market risk premium (MRP). The unit (or index) of risk exposure for individual investments is given by β. In an Arbitrage Pricing Model (APM), there are a number of factors (estimates vary, but most investment houses using the model settle on about five factors, with some using up to seven), each of which has a price (MRP_j, for each factor, j), with each security having its own set of factor βs. If we take a simple example, with two risk factors (say a general market risk premium (MRP_1) and an inflation risk premium, (MRP_2), our empirically derived model might now look like this:

$$R_i = RF + \beta_{1i}MRP_1 + \beta_{2i}MRP_2$$

To see the possible application of this model, let us assume that Sluggish* is in an industry that is not particularly exposed to general economic factors (and has a β_1 of 0.6), but does suffer from having 'sticky' prices, finding it hard to raise its prices quickly in an inflationary period. The β_2 of the company might therefore be 1.5. Lastly, assume that RF is 8 per cent, the general market risk premium is 5 per cent, and the inflation risk premium is 2 per cent. This would give us a cost of capital for Sluggish of:

$$R\% = 8 + (0.6 \times 5) + (1.5 \times 2) = 14\%$$

Now imagine this with five risk factors; we would have the unenviable task of finding five β factors for each investment, finding the appropriate five risk factors and their associated market risk premia, and then we have the additional problem of requiring all these parameters (which would almost certainly have been estimated from historical data) to remain stable over the life of the cash flow analysis. By contrast, the CAPM needs one risk premium (see this page below for a discussion of how we can estimate it) and the β factors are available from published data sources (again, see below); we also know from research that β factors are reasonably stable over time. As yet, we do not have sufficient evidence to comment on APT; whilst it is better at explaining *past* returns than the CAPM, we do not know whether it is a more efficient estimator of *future* returns. Although it must be accepted that the CAPM is a simplistic approximation of the returns generating process, an analogy can be made with a large-scale road map. This may well be a simplistic approximation of a complex landscape, but if it gets us home it presumably works well enough.

There is also another problem with APT, which is quality of data. To be able to derive sensible relationships between returns and macro–economic variables, we need sound measures of the latter. Without wishing to comment on the United Kingdom in particular, one might just wonder what happens when government statistics are released one month and then revised the next. Should we measure reaction to the original version, the revised version or what? In fact, the only UK test of the APT to date (Abeysekera and Mahajan, 1987) failed to provide any conclusive evidence on the applicability of the model to the United Kingdom.

As a conclusion to this discussion, the APT shows great promise[11] but is probably at too early a stage in its development to be of any use to practioners, except perhaps those in the United States. By contrast, there is enough data available in many European countries and in the United States to allow the CAPM to be used fairly easily. For that reason, for the purposes of this book we shall use the CAPM to estimate costs of capital; it may not be perfect, but it is probably the best practical alternative at the moment. Accordingly, we now turn our attention to two practical considerations, estimating the risk premium and estimating the βs for individual companies.

ESTIMATING THE RISK PREMIUM

That there is a considerable range of estimates of the risk premium tends not to reassure the practitioner. Part of the confusion is because of the different time horizons assumed of the investor. For example, the London Business School suggests that the long-term (fifty-year) UK average risk premium measured by the return on the stock market over and above the return on treasury bills is of the order of 9 per cent pa. By contrast, the ALCAR Group Ltd (a UK subsidiary of a US consultancy firm) suggest that the *projected* risk premium for the UK market may be as low as 4.5 per cent; however, the latter rate is calculated for use in long-term investment appraisal and is therefore the premium over the long-term risk-free rate. If we believe that there exists either a *liquidity premium* (because of the fact that long-term gilts have a greater exposure to interest rate changes than short-term ones) or an *inflation risk premium* (because our estimates of future inflation are more uncertain the further we look into the future), the yield curve on gilts will be upward sloping (i.e. long-term interest rates will be greater than short-term ones) on average. We would therefore expect a smaller difference in returns between long-term gilts or bonds and equities than we would between treasury bills and equities. Ibbotson Associates report that over the period 1922–88, the average return on US treasury bills was 3.6 per cent, whereas the average return on treasury bonds was 4.7 per cent. Unfortunately, the figures do not work out as neatly for the United Kingdom; using data from 1945–90, BZW show a return of 5.29 per cent on gilts against 6.98 per cent on treasury bills. However, the reason for this is almost certainly the failure of the market to forsee the rates of inflation that were to occur in the 1970s. If we take the last 15 years, from 1975–90, BZW report a *real* rate of return on gilts of 4.5 per cent against a real rate on treasury bills of 2.9 per cent. Given these differences between long- and short-term rates, it is therefore apparent that we must be careful to compare like with like when looking at risk premia; clearly our problem is to establish long-term discount rates and we therefore need to be concerned with the risk premium over a long-term gilt/bond rate. This raises the question of the definition of 'long-term'; complicated questions arise here concerning the 'duration'[12] of equities versus the 'duration' of gilts and of the time horizons employed in the appraisal, but as a general rule of thumb, ten to twenty years is probably appropriate.[13]

Turning to the risk premium for the United Kingdom, taking BZW figures for the very long term – 1918–90 – gives a real rate of return (gross income reinvested) of 1.0 per cent on gilts against 7.1 per cent on equities, which suggests a long-term real risk premium of 6.1 per cent. If we adopt the view that the years 1918–45 were unrepresentative of our expectations of the future and therefore choose the period 1945–90, we find that the real risk premium increases to 7.2 per cent, whereas using the period 1965–90 gives us a real risk premium of 5.4 per cent (this is also very close to the 5.5 per cent found over the last 15 years). Finally, using the average of the compound returns on successive twenty-five-year holding periods since 1918 gives us a real premium of 6.3 per cent.[14]

In the recent Ofwat consultation paper on the cost of capital for the water industry (Office of Water Services, 1991), a slightly different approach is taken in that the geometric mean of the returns on equities less those on gilts is used; this produces a long-term premium (1919–89) of 5.86 per cent pa in real terms (using the period 1946–89 gives the highest premium of 7.78 per cent whilst using 1969-89 gives the lowest premium of 5.32 per cent). Both the BZW and Ofwat figures (the source for these is Treasury data) seem broadly in line with US experience; for example, Copeland *et al.* (1990) 'recommend using a 5 to 6 per cent market risk premium'.

The above appears to suggest that on balance the appropriate real premium for the United Kingdom is between 5.5 and 6.5 per cent. Real rates of interest appear to remain at a high level in historical terms and the current risk premium seems to be declining, but against this we should note that a possible problem with the BZW data is a bias towards the returns of larger firms. The empirical evidence shows us that the returns on smaller companies have historically been somewhat greater than the returns on larger firms (the issue of the cost of capital for smaller companies is discussed below). Taking all this into consideration means that it is difficult to present a convincing case for a single number being the 'correct' risk premium; however, for this book we shall boldly adopt the average of the range and recommend using a *real* risk premium of 6 per cent for UK investment. Note that if the long-term inflation rate is expected to be 5 per cent, this equates to a money or nominal premium of 6.3 per cent.

Implied costs of capital for UK companies

At this point, we shall pause and consider the implications of our discussions so far on the likely discount rate for high, medium and low risk companies. We shall turn our attention to β estimation in a moment, but for now let us consider the case of UK companies that are financed entirely by equity, and assume that a β of 1.4 represents 'high risk', a β of 0.6 represents 'low risk' and a β of 1.0 is 'average risk'. We concluded in Chapter 2 that an appropriate risk-free real long-term rate of interest based on 1991 yields was 4.2 per cent pa. We also saw later in that chapter that such yield rates are quoted on a semi-annual basis, and that the conversion formula involved squaring one plus the six-monthly rate (and subtracting one). Our risk-free rate is therefore:

$$[1 + (0.042 \times \frac{6}{12})]^2 - 1 = 0.04244 \text{ or } 4.25\%$$

From the above discussion, we have a real risk premium of 6 per cent; using the CAPM, it therefore follows that we arrive at at the following discount rates for companies in various systematic risk categories:

High   R = 4.25 + (1.4 × 6) = 12.65%
Medium   R = 4.25 + (1.0 × 6) = 10.25%
Low   R = 4.25 + (0.6 × 6) = 7.85%

These are real rates of return; our recommendation from Chapter 2 was to estimate all cash flows in money terms and discount at a rate expressed in money terms. Supposing that our estimated inflation rate is 5 per cent pa, we obtain the following money costs of capital:

High   R = (1.1265 × 1.05) − 1 = 0.183 or 18.3%
Medium   R = (1.1025 × 1.05) − 1 = 0.158 or 15.8%
Low   R = (1.0785 × 1.05) − 1 = 0.132 or 13.2%

However, this is only part of the story as we have not yet considered the effects of gearing. None the less, the above may be viewed as representing the range of equity costs of capital that will be experienced by the majority of UK companies given a long-term inflation rate of 5 per cent pa. An important qualification is that at the time of writing (the second half of 1991), UK interest rates were particularly high in real terms. Such rates are subject to continual change, in contrast to our estimate of the market risk premium, which was based upon a long-term analysis. It is therefore essential that any cost of capital used is revised on a regular basis to take account of any changes in the long-term required risk-free rate of return. A further point here is that, as we have seen in Chapter 4, real rates of return should be similar in all countries. To some extent the view could be taken that the United Kingdom is somewhat out of line with other countries; if this is the case, this rate may decline to a figure possibly closer to 3 per cent. The only practical advice is that the long-term risk-free rate of return should be monitored continually.

ESTIMATING β

Having discussed the problems of estimating the risk premium, we now turn our attention to the other vital component necessary to estimate the discount rate – β. It might seem that we simply need to find the β of the company we wish to value. This is not the case, for a variety of reasons; first, even if we can easily obtain the β from one of the many published sources, it would be subject to some measurement error. Furthermore, it would be the β of the entire business; this is fine if we wish to value a company with a single line of business, but not very useful if we wish to value a company, like ICI, with many different interests. Some of these will have a high level of systematic risk, whilst others will have a low systematic risk. It cannot be over-emphasised that *all* businesses should be valued in a manner that tests whether value is being maximised; this means that we must value each line of business separately on a 'stand-alone' basis, which in turn implies that we must use the discount rate that the market would apply to that line of business if it were an independent company. *It is therefore essential to realise that for valuation purposes each principal line of business must have its own β factor.*

An additional problem that may be encountered is the fact that the business we wish to value may be unquoted and therefore will not have a published β. For all these reasons, the normal approach we need to use is the *proxy* β method. In outline, this requires us to find a sample of companies that are representative of the business line we wish to value, calculate the β of the sample and adjust for any known differences between the sample and our line of business. These known differences will mainly be related to financing structure (financial gearing) and cost structure (operational gearing).

If we take the simple case where the company we wish to value has two principal lines of business (PLBs) and has no financial gearing, and where the proxy companies we wish to use also have no gearing, the cost of capital for each business is easily found by using an average of the β factors of the proxy companies and applying this in the CAPM (an important property of βs is that the β of a portfolio of investments is the weighted average of the βs of the investments making up that portfolio). Only two problems would need to be addressed; first, the suitability of the proxies (ideally, the proxies should be representative in terms of activity, size and market positioning, but in practice some compromises will be necessary) and second, the screening of the sample for 'outliers'. An 'outlier' is a company where the β factor seems out of line with the rest of the sample, and out of line with expectation. As an example, suppose we were attempting to derive the cost of capital for a firm that operated theme parks and had a series of leisure companies with βs ranging between 1.15 and 1.3, except for one company which had a β of 0.5. We would be justified in excluding this case from our sample because given the discretionary nature of spending on leisure activities we would expect the β to be above one.

In the majority of cases we would expect to encounter some form of debt financing; accordingly, we now turn our attention to adjusting β for financial gearing, and then to the calculation of the weighted average cost of capital for each PLB.

FINANCIAL GEARING AND COST OF CAPITAL

Unfortunately, adjusting the cost of capital to allow for the impact of differing debt levels is a difficult and contentious subject. It is also unavoidable, because whether we use a weighted average cost of capital (WACC), price–earnings or some more sophisticated approach (such as the adjusted present value model discussed on page 126), we cannot escape making *some* assumption about the effect of gearing on company value.

The basic effect of gearing on cost of capital

We shall start our analysis with the well-known Modigliani and Miller framework discussed in most finance texts.[15] For simplicity, we shall assume that we are investigating the cost of capital of a single product company, with no growth potential, which pays out all its free cash flow as dividends and interest; a firm in this situation will have an investment equal to its depreciation charge. These unrealistic assumptions can be relaxed later to allow for a more plausible setting. Let us suppose that our firm has an equity market value (E) of £5 million and a debt market value (D) of £5 million. Interest rates on this debt, which we shall initially assume to be risk-free, is 10 per cent, and the operating cash flows are expected to be £3.5 million pa, with depreciation (and hence investment) of £1 million per annum; assume that the rate of corporation tax is 50 per cent and that depreciation and interest payments are tax allowable. What can we say about the cost of equity and debt capital?

First, the cost of debt capital, r_d, is obviously 10 per cent before tax, or 5 per cent after tax. The returns to equity holders (all dividends in this case) will be (using our definition of cash flow components from Chapter 3);

Operating cash flow (OCF)	£3.50m
Depreciation (DEP) (= Investment)	(1.00)
Free cash flow pre-tax (FCFPT)	2.50
Tax 50%	(1.25)
Free cash flow (FCF)	1.25
Net interest (NI) [10% × £5 m × (1 − 0.5)]	(0.25)
Dividend (DIV)	1.00

This implies a cost of equity capital of 1.00/5, or 20 per cent pa, and as the firm has a total market value of £10 million (debt plus equity), a WACC of 12.5 per cent. The latter can be arrived at either by realising that the total cash flow is the free cash flow figure of £1.25 million, which is divided by the £10 million combined market value of debt and equity, or by splitting the two 'reward' streams, as we have done above, to derive the after tax costs of each class of capital, which can then be weighted by the market values of the two types of financing, thus giving us:

$$(20\% \times 5/10) + (5\% \times 5/10) = 12.5\%$$

Generalising from this, we can see that equity holders get:

$$[FCFPT - (r_d \times D)] \times (1 - T_c) = FCFPT(1 - T_c) - (r_d \times D) + (T_c \times r_d \times D)$$

where T_c is the corporation tax rate expressed as a decimal. In case this seems like a gratuitous equation, it in fact offers a very important insight, because it allows us to see how the equity cost of capital varies with different levels of gearing. It is intuitive that the riskiness of equities increases as gearing increases; the problem is to calculate by how much. In the above example, we assumed that gearing was 50 per cent (we shall measure gearing as the ratio of the market value of debt to the market value of debt plus equity); what would the result have been if gearing had been zero? Turning to the above expression for the reward to equity holders, we can derive the market value of equity by dividing the dividends paid to the shareholders (the left-hand side of our above equation gives us this figure) by the required rate of return on equity in a geared company; because we already knew that the answer to this calculation is £5 million, we concluded that the implied return (call it r_{eg}, for return on equity in a geared company) was 20 per cent. Looking at the right-hand side of our expression, we can see that the first term gives us the cash flow that the equity holders would have received in the absence of gearing, the second term gives us the interest payment made and the last term gives us the value of the annual tax relief on debt. We assumed that debt was risk-free, and that implies that all cash flow streams associated with the debt should be discounted at the risk-free return on debt capital, r_d. Meanwhile, back at the stock market, the debt holders receive the income that is the cost to equity holders represented by the second term in our expression.

What does all this tell us? First, the interest payment itself is merely a transfer of wealth from one class of security holder (equity) to another (debt); slicing up cash flow in this way contributes nothing to corporate value. However, the last term, $T_c r_d D$, is a real gain in value because it effectively represents a subsidy on debt from the government. We argued that this should be discounted at r_d, and when we do so we get the result that the present value of the tax offset is $T_c D$ (remember that we assumed no growth, and thus all our present value calculations involve perpetuities). In the absence of gearing, the value of our ungeared company, V_u, would be simply $FCFPT(1 - T_c)$ discounted at the cost of equity for an ungeared firm, r_{eu}. As the value of a geared company, V_g (debt plus equity), must be greater than the present value of an ungeared company by $T_c D$, we have:

$$V_g = V_u + T_c D$$

We can now apply this to our case of 0 per cent gearing and find the implied cost of equity. $T_c D$ is 50 per cent × £5 million, or £2.5 million. As V_g was £10 million, V_u must be £7.5 million. We also know that V_u = $FCFPT (1 - T_c)/r_{eu}$, so solving for r_{eu} gives us:

$$r_{eu} = 1.25/7.5 = 0.1667, \text{ or } 16.67\%$$

Of course, this result depends upon a number of assumptions, the most critical of which are the absence of liquidation costs (this in turn means that the cost of debt financing does not increase as gearing levels rise, although, as we shall see later, the introduction of 'risky' debt does not change our central conclusion) and that individuals, as well as firms, can borrow and lend at the risk-free rate (this is necessary to allow arbitrage between debt and equity, which can be carried out through the use of what is often quaintly referred to as 'home-made' gearing[16]); this rather onerous assumption is relaxed later. An additional assumption, which we shall discuss in more detail later, is that debt income and equity income are taxed at the same rate. It is on this issue of personal taxation that many of the difficulties in estimating the effect of gearing on cost of capital are encountered.

Implications of the Modigliani and Miller analysis

Forgetting for the moment issues concerning arbitrage and personal taxation, what implications do we have from the above, and what problems does this present? The main implication is that in the absence of liquidation costs and personal taxes, high gearing should be the dominant pattern because the maximisation of corporate value is found when gearing is 100 per cent. This appears not to accord with reality, although some highly geared management buyouts are interesting examples. The other implication is that WACC declines in a linear fashion as gearing rises. The most obvious problem is that in reality lenders will require higher levels of return to compensate for increased risk as debt levels increase; indeed, this is exactly what we should expect to happen according to the CAPM. Rubeinstein (1973) and Buckley (1981) have shown what will happen to the cost of capital when we allow for the presence of risky debt, with the perhaps surprising result being that although the cost of borrowing will rise at high levels of gearing, the optimal structure is still 100 per cent debt and WACC still declines linearly with increases in gearing. This relationship is expressed by:

$$\text{WACC} = r_{eu}[1 - T_c \times (\frac{D}{D+E})]$$

Whilst this may be valid for reasonable levels of gearing, it is worth pointing out some real world problems, which may help to explain why the result might be invalid at high gearing levels. First, when companies increase their gearing levels, they increase the probability of making losses in any one year, and this means a delay in obtaining the tax relief on debt interest (a situation sometimes called *tax exhaustion*). Indeed, *in extremis*, should the company go bankrupt it will never obtain these benefits; the effect is that the expected present value of the tax relief on debt does not increase linearly with gearing. Second, if liquidation is a costly process we should expect the value of the geared company to decrease by the present value of the expected liquidation costs. Third, lenders to highly geared companies often impose restrictive covenants, which limit managerial actions particularly in terms of dividend payments; this might be viewed as a cost of higher gearing, which again serves to reduce the value of companies with high levels of debt.[17] As our purpose here is the calculation of costs of capital, rather than the derivation of optimal capital structure, we shall not attempt to integrate these factors into our analysis. Instead, we shall proceed under the assumption that such costs are unlikely to be of major significance for companies with reasonable levels of gearing. However, should it be suspected that such an assumption is invalid, it becomes important to build in some reduction in value to take account of these costs; a possible methodology is that of adjusted present value, discussed on page 126.

The impact of capital structure on the discount rate

Having given a brief outline of the ideas behind gearing and cost of capital, we now turn our attention to a more detailed analysis of the impact of capital structure on the discount rate used in valuing PLBs.

We know that the β of a portfolio of investments is a weighted average of its constituents βs. We also know the relationship between the value of geared and ungeared companies; furthermore, we can view a geared company as consisting of a portfolio of debt and equity. Putting all this together and expressing the relationships in terms of β gives us the following (see Schnabel (1983) and Buckley (1981) for a detailed derivation):

$$\beta_{eu} = \beta_{eg} \times \frac{E}{V_g - TD} + \beta_d \times \frac{D(1 - T)}{V_g - TD}$$

The β subscripts, eu, eg and d refer to the equity of an ungeared and geared company, and the β of debt, respectively. In the absence of personal tax (which we shall discuss in a moment), T is the rate of corporation tax and is equal to T_c in the previous formulae. Note also that the bottom row in the weighting given to the geared equity and debt βs is equivalent to the value of an ungeared firm. The importance of this formula is that in allowing us to model the relationship between geared and ungeared βs, it enables us to use proxy companies with levels of gearing different from that of the PLB we wish to value, and also lets us examine the effect of different financing alternatives upon value. Suitably armed with this formula, we can demonstrate three different routes to valuing a PLB, the first two of which involve discounting the FCF at a WACC; the third uses a different approach, known as *adjusted present value*.

To illustrate all this, we shall use the example that we used to demonstrate the Modigliani and Miller propositions, with a few minor modifications. We now assume that the risk-free rate is 8 per cent, the market risk premium is 10 per cent , the β of debt is 0.2 and the β of equity is 1.2. Note that this leaves r_{eg} and r_d unchanged from our original example at 10 per cent and 20 per cent, respectively. Applying our formula for ungeared equity β, we obtain:

$$\beta_{eu} = 1.2 \times \frac{5}{10 - (0.5 \times 5)} + 0.2 \times \frac{5(1 - 0.5)}{10 - (0.5 \times 5)} = 0.8667$$

According to the CAPM this gives us a cost of equity capital for an ungeared firm of:

$$r_{eu} = 8 + (0.8667 \times 10) = 16.67\%$$

This is the same rate that we concluded above. We also have two routes for deducing the WACC; the first was the 'traditional' method that we have already used, which simply involved weighting the equity and debt in proprtion to their market values, which we concluded resulted in a WACC of 12.5 per cent. The second method of arriving at WACC is to use the formula that related WACC to the return on an ungeared company. Using this results in:

$$WACC = 16.67 \times [1 - 0.5(\frac{5}{5 + 5})] = 12.5\%$$

However, once we allow the introduction of more complex forms of financing (these are the subject of Chapter 7), the 'traditional' approach to estimating WACC is normally easier to use.

The value of the entire firm can now be calculated by discounting the free cash flow at the WACC. Because in this case, we have a perpetuity, the value is simply £1.25m ÷ 0.125 = £10m. The equity value is found by deducting the market value of debt (£0.5m ÷ 0.1 = £5m) from the value of the firm.

An alternative to WACC

A totally different approach is that the *adjusted present value rule* (APV) suggested by Myers (1974), which makes use of the basic relationship between the value of geared and ungeared firms. As we know that the value of a geared firm is the value of an ungeared one plus the present value of the tax relief on debt interest, we can conclude that the value of any company, PLB or project consists of its value if it is financed entirely by equity (known as the *base case PV*), plus the present value of the tax relief on debt interest (known as the *tax shield PV*). Valuing our company according to this rule we get:

$$V_g = \frac{1.25}{0.1667} + \frac{5 \times 0.5 \times 10\%}{0.10} = £10m$$

At first, this appears to be a simple repetition of the above analysis. However, the real value of the APV approach compared to the WACC method is that it allows us to cope with changing capital structures and (perhaps more importantly) the possibility of tax exhaustion, because we can simply model the expected tax savings in the year when we think they will be realised.

The problem of personal tax and cost of capital

Having presented three alternative models for valuing PLBs based upon free cash flow, we now turn to the confusion caused by the introduction of personal taxes. Schnabel (1983) shows that with personal taxes, T in the expression for the ungeared equity β becomes:

$$T = 1 - \frac{(1 - T_c)(1 - T_e)}{(1 - T_d)}$$

Where the subscripts e and d denote personal taxes on equity and debt respectively. In the case where these are zero, T is simply T_c, as it is where T_e and T_d are the same. Unfortunately, if we take a tax regime with the characteristics of the United Kingdom's imputation system, we find that T_e depends upon whether the returns to shareholders take the form of capital gains or dividends. If we take the extreme position, and assume that all share returns take the form of capital gains with equity and debt being held either by tax exempt institutions (such as pension funds) or by individuals who are above the capital gains tax exemption limit (and indexation is ignored), we find that T_e is equal to T_d; in such a case, the tax advantage to debt is described by the corporation tax rate. At the other end of the spectrum, if we take the view that all return on equities takes the form of dividends then the tax credit received by individuals means that equity income is tax free for basic rate tax payers (provided that the advance corporation tax (ACT) payable by the company is fully recoverable against mainstream corporation tax), whereas debt interest income is not. Given a corporation tax rate of 33 per cent and a basic rate of 25 per cent, this suggests that the tax advantage to debt could be as low as 10.7 per cent; exactly the same result is obtained by pension funds, which can reclaim the tax credit and receive debt interest income on a tax free basis. It would therefore appear that we have to make some assumptions about the long-term dividend distribution policy of the firm, the likelihood of tax exhaustion and the tax position of our shareholders and debtholders in order to achieve an estimate of the value to the firm of debt tax shields.[18] As an example of how this might be made to work, imagine that we have a payout ratio of 40 per cent and that our gearing ratio is expected to remain constant at a level where we believe there is no serious possibility of tax exhaustion. Also assume that all profits are earned in the United Kingdom, that the ACT is fully recoverable and that shareholders are all pension funds. T_e will now be a weighted average of dividend income (a negative tax of one-third) and capital gains tax (nil), so that T_e is (40 per cent $\times$ -0.3333 plus 60 per cent $\times$ 0), which gives us a negative tax of 13.33 per cent. Plugging this into our formula for T yields:

$$T = 1 - \frac{(1 - 0.33)(1 + 0.1333)}{(1 - 0)} = 0.241 \text{ or } 24.1\%$$

This does not allow for the lag in receiving tax relief on debt interest (which reduces the value of the tax advantage) or the lag in receiving ACT offset (which, in so far as it represents a timing disavantage, leads to a small cost of T_e for taxpayers).[19]

As if all this is not complicated enough, we not only face a real world where there is a multiplicity of domestic tax paying positions, but there are also likely to be overseas investors subject to different taxation and quite possibly the firm will have overseas subsidiaries, which arrange borrowing outside the United Kingdom; this will be subject to *local* tax relief. All that we can conclude is that for most UK companies that can claim full ACT offset, and where there is no significant likelihood of tax exhaustion or bankruptcy, the present value of the domestic debt tax shields is likely to be between 10.7 and 33 per cent of the value of any perpetual debt, depending on investors and payout policies; for the higher figure to be achieved, we would need to assume zero dividend payout and no lag in obtaining tax relief. Furthermore, these percentages will decline as gearing increases, because the present value of expected bankruptcy costs will reduce the value of the firm, as will the fall in present value of the expected tax shields attributable to any increase in the probability of tax exhaustion. One solution is to attempt the incorporation of realistic assumptions on average tax rates and likely payout policies into the analysis, as in our example above; any calculations for overseas borrowing would need to take account of the tax relief available in the relevant country. The other possible solution is to assume, somewhat heroically, that the market conditions necessary for dividend irrelevancy hold, which requires that dividends and capital gains are taxed equally, on average. This is the position taken by Ashton (1989a); in such a case, the value of the debt tax shields is the same as we calculated for the 100 per cent payout case, i.e. 10.7 per cent.

Our problem here is to present a solution that is helpful to practitioners. Taking a UK imputation tax perspective, the honest answer is that the answers to two important questions are as yet unknown. These questions are: (i) what is the value of UK tax shields? and (ii) does the dividend payout policy of the firm affect the cost of capital? Whilst the answer to both questions is an empirical matter, some helpful guidance can be offered. It appears reasonable to conclude that the tax advantage of debt is a company (or PLB) specific variable. To establish the extent of this advantage, the key questions which need to be addressed are:

1. What is the company/PLB effective corporation tax rate?
2. What is the *expected* tax shield advantage on interest payments obtainable in any year?
3. What is the average tax paying position of shareholders/debtholders?
4. Is all the ACT recoverable?[20]

An example of how these issues may be considered is given in the case study in Chapter 7. We should also note that these problems afflict *any* attempt to arrive at a company valuation and are therefore inescapable, because whether we use WACC, APV or PE methodologies we are making some assumptions about debt tax shields and costs of capital. This is an important point because it is frequently forgotten that any PE ratio is in part a function of an implicit cost of capital.

Before leaving this section, one way around the problem of tax exhaustion caused by the presence of unused capital allowances is for companies to lease assets instead of purchasing them. The cost of such leasing finance is discussed in Chapter 7.

THE COST OF CAPITAL FOR FOREIGN ACTIVITIES

In theory, the principles we have outlined so far in this book can be applied to the valuation of foreign businesses. Looked at from the shareholders' perspective, the alternative to their company investing in an overseas subsidiary is for them to purchase equities in the country concerned. The relevant costs of capital are therefore the local risk–free rate and the local risk premium (these rates would reflect local inflationary expectations); in fact, if all capital markets were free of exchange control regulations, we should expect to observe similar real risk–free rates in all countries. In addition, we might expect similar risk premia in all countries, although this assumes the availability of similar portfolios in each market. A more thorough approach to this problem is the calculation of country-specific βs based upon a 'world' market. World market indices are available (e.g. *Financial Times*, Morgan Stanley Index), but care must be taken concerning the weightings attached to each country; for example, the Morgan Stanley Index is heavily biased towards the US market. We should also be aware of the fact that using a 'world' market index or assuming constant real risk premia across countries presupposes that international equity markets are integrated. Fortunately, there is some support for such an assumption to be found in Wheatley's (1988) paper, which examines twenty-six years of data from eighteen different equity markets, including the United States and United Kingdom.

An added problem once we move away from the major developed stock markets is the relatively short time series available for the estimation of βs and risk premia; many markets included in a world index have emerged fairly recently (e.g. Taiwan, Turkey) and/or there have been dramatic changes in the relative performances of some of these markets (the most obvious example being Japan). Because of the difficulties that can be encountered in some of these markets (and, of course, the fact that some PLBs may be in countries where no market exists) an alternative to using a local CAPM approach is the use of proxy costs of capital derived from other markets (typically the United States and United Kingdom, being the largest markets apart from Japan) and adjusted for anticipated local inflation. Countries where data are available on local βs, risk-free rates and risk premia include most Western European countries (generally, it should be expected that the reliability of the data is correlated with the size of the market), Australia, Japan, Hong Kong, Canada and the United States; useful data sources include BARRA International; Erasmus University, Rotterdam; Datastream and Standard & Poor.

Note that with this approach no attempt is made to adjust the discount rate for specific risk factors associated with the foreign location of the project (such as political risks). These types of risk are best accommodated through cash flow adjustments (see Chapter 9). When estimating the discount rate we are merely looking for a return that compensates for the *systematic* risk of the investment. In developed markets, the theoretical arguments for doing this are clear because as we have noted above, investors always have the alternative opportunity of direct investment. In countries with no developed markets it is difficult to defend any particular approach to the problem; none the less, we shall make an attempt by using an analogue country argument. Insofar as countries have similar characteristics, it might be reasonable to assume that the opportunities for investing in country A (which does have a developed market) should give similar returns to those obtained in the economically similar country B (which does not); naturally, this argument looks reasonable when applied to some countries and pretty thin when applied to others (a particular case being that it is difficult to find suitable 'analogues' for many Eastern European countries at the moment). Finally, we should note that similar arguments apply if a PE methodology is being used to value the company; again it is not advisable to load the PE multiple for risk. However, note that the use of PE multiples to value foreign businesses is particularly problematic because of inter-country differences in generally accepted accounting principles (see Chapter 5).

THE COST OF CAPITAL
FOR SMALLER COMPANIES

As we noted above, the BZW share returns data are biased towards larger companies. The BZW Index shows an average return (with gross dividends reinvested) over the thirty-six years to December 1990 of 13.8 per cent pa. In fact, since 1962 the BZW Index has been based upon the FT Actuaries All Share (FTA) Index; prior to this it was based upon thirty shares. Dimson and Marsh (1991) in their discussion of the Hoare–Govett Smaller Companies (HGSC) Index give exactly the same 13.8 per cent return on the FTA Index, although they had to produce a 'reconstructed' version of the FTA Index prior to its introduction in 1962. Now the London market happens to be heavily biased towards larger stocks;[21] the FTA (like all the indices used in this chapter) is a value-weighted index that is therefore heavily influenced by the largest UK companies. The fact that, historically, smaller companies have outperformed larger ones is well known; whether this merely reflects the lower liquidity of the shares of such companies or a genuine outperformance is debatable. However, the difference in performance appears not to be explained by risk (see, for example, Dimson and Marsh, 1989, 1991). Just how large the outperformance is depends upon the time frame chosen. A comparison of the Dimson and Marsh 'reconstructed' FTA and HGSC Indices for the thirty-six years to December 1990 produces a premium of 4.2 per cent pa, whilst an analysis based upon the period for the twenty-eight years from December 1962 (when the FTA Index began life) produces the considerably smaller premium of 2.7 per cent.

For the United States, Ibbotson and Sinquefield (1986) show a return on the smallest quintile of New York Stock Exchange stocks of 2.8 per cent above that observed on all NYSE stocks on a value-weighted basis; this result is based upon geometric average rates of return over the period 1926–85. This figure might lead us to expect a premium towards the lower end of those reported for the United Kingdom in the previous paragraph.

The real point, of course, is that it is future returns that matter. As this small companies effect is now very well known, let us suppose that the lower figure of a 2.7 per cent real premium is representative of the long-term expected small company premium. The HGSC Index applies to the lowest 10 per cent of stocks by market capitalisation, so we have an idea of the size of company that might be affected. We should not expect that the cost of capital will suddenly shift by the amount of any premium as soon as the firm crosses the 10 per cent capitalisation line, although Keim's (1983) US research suggests that the effect is not linearly associated with size.[22] If the firm we wish to value is a small one, and we believe we should take account of the small firms effect, this can be done by adding in the required premium *after* allowing for risk. Note that such a position results in a technical violation of the CAPM, which assumed that only *systematic* risk was included in risk pricing.

βS AND OPERATIONAL GEARING

In the same manner that financial gearing is associated with the level of β, we also find that operational gearing influences β. Operational gearing is the ratio of fixed costs to revenues, so that firms with a comparatively high level of fixed costs would be said to have high operational gearing. In principle, it is possible to calculate the relationship. Brealey and Myers (1991) show that as the PV of an asset (A) is the PV of revenue (rev) less the PV of variable expenses (VC) and fixed expenses (FC), which on rearrangement gives:

$$PV(rev) = PV(FC) + PV(VC) + PV(A)$$

and as the β of the revenue stream will also be a weighted average of the component βs, we have:

$$\beta_{rev} = \beta_{FC} \times \frac{PV(FC)}{PV(rev)} + \beta_{VC} \times \frac{PV(VC)}{PV(rev)} + \beta_A \times \frac{PV(A)}{PV(rev)}$$

If we assume that revenue and variable cost βs are identical, and that by the invariate nature of fixed costs we might reasonably approximate the β of the stream as zero, we have, upon rearrangement:

$$\beta_A = \beta_{rev} \times (1 + \frac{PV(FC)}{PV(A)})$$

Unfortunately, Brealey and Myers (1991) fail to point out that this little formula suffers by being practically unusable because we do not know the present value of the asset until we know its β, which is necessary to derive the value of PV(A). This, of course, was precisely what the formula was trying to establish in the first place. None the less, the formula is of conceptual value when using the proxy β approach because we can see that a different level of operational gearing from the proxies leads to a change in β. As regards the proxy companies, the asset present value would correspond to the value of the firm in an ungeared state, and in so far as the fixed costs are observable, given a β of zero the relevant discount rate would be RF. Given the difficulty of estimating all the variables, the only practical advice that can really be given is to choose proxies with operating structures similar to that of the valuation object.

USING PROXY βS – AN EXAMPLE

Imagine that we wish to arrive at a cost of capital to value the large unlisted family concern of Tulip Design Ltd,* a company that operates in the flower arranging industry. The company is all-equity financed and the valuation has been asked for by the board prior to a decision on whether to sell or float the company. Inspection of the flower arranging industry shows that there are only two listed companies, FA plc and AoF plc; details of these companies are as follows;

Company	β	Variable interest debt (£m)	Equity (market value) (£m)
FA plc	1.0	100	500
AoF plc	0.9	50	500
Total		150	1000

To simplify matters, let us assume that the value of debt tax shields to both of these companies is 26 per cent (see the arguments above), the real risk-free rate is 4 per cent and the market risk premium is 6 per cent in real terms. Expected inflation is 4 per cent pa and, given the relatively small size of Tulip Design Ltd, we believe that any purchaser would expect a small company premium rate of return of 2.5 per cent (general issues relating to valuation for flotation and valuation of unlisted companies are dealt with in Chapter 9). In the case of variable interest debt it is normally reasonable to assume that book (or par) value is a proxy for market value.

The first step is to calculate the β of our proxy portfolio. This is simply a market-weighted average of the individual equity βs:

$$\beta_{portfolio} = \frac{(1.0 \times 500) + (0.9 \times 500)}{1000} = 0.95$$

We then ungear this β, using the formula:

$$\beta_{eu} = \beta_{eg} \times \frac{E}{V_g - TD} + \beta_d \times \frac{D(1 - T)}{V_g - TD}$$

Assume that the debt β implied by the borrowing rate of our two proxy companies is 0.2. This gives us an ungeared equity β of:

$$0.95 \times \frac{1000}{1150 - (0.26 \times 150)} + 0.2 \times \frac{150(1 - 0.26)}{1150 - (0.26 \times 150)} = 0.875$$

Our basic ungeared equity cost of capital for Tulip Design Ltd in real terms given by the CAPM is:

$$4 + (0.875 \times 6) = 9.25\%$$

Adding on the required small company premium and stating in money terms (using the relationship described above) gives us:

$$\{1.04 \times [1+ (0.025 + 0.0925)]\} = 16.2\%$$

As Tulip Design Ltd has no gearing, this is also their weighted average cost of capital, which can be directly applied to the free cash flows of the business to value the company.

A more complex example, using actual UK published data, is given at the end of Chapter 7 (see page 147).

WHAT TO DO WHEN NO PROXIES EXIST

This is the most difficult problem of all to handle in practice; hopefully, this sort of situation does not occur too often, but it does sometimes. For example, imagine we were trying to value British Telecom immediately before it was privatised. There were clearly no reasonable proxies for BT in the UK market at that time. What alternatives might we come up with?[23]

The first alternative is to look for an industry that has similar economic characteristics – say another utility. However, at the time in question there were no other listed UK utilities, so that method would not have worked. The next alternative is the use of an overseas proxy, the obvious market choice being the United States. This would probably give a satisfactory result, but it must be borne in mind that because of economic differences between countries (in particular, consumption differences), low β shares in one country will not always be so in another, although our comments on costs of capital for foreign investments might lead us to expect broad similarities.

A further possibility is direct estimation through modelling the returns on the project against returns on the market as a whole. In theory, this is quite easy to arrange through the use of a spreadsheet model and probabalistic analysis. In case any reader feels brave enough to try this approach, the formula for calculating β is:

$$\beta_i = \frac{(\text{Correlation of } i \text{ with the market}) \times (\text{standard deviation of } i)}{\text{Standard deviation of the market}}$$

The correlations and standard deviation referred to are of returns. Now whilst it is perfectly straightforward to make up a textbook example to demonstrate how this works, *actually* comparing the *returns* on the investment with those of the market for various different states of the world is not something to be undertaken lightly. It can therefore only be recommended as an absolute last resort.

A better alternative to direct estimation is the use of *accounting βs*. The accounting β can be estimated by regressing the change in accounting profits of the firm in question (in this case, BT before privatisation) against the change in accounting profits of a sample of firms typical of the market as a whole. To do this in practice would require the use of an accounting database service such as *Datastream*. Naturally, this is a 'quick and easy' approach to the problem (although probably not that quick, on reflection), but US research has suggested that accounting βs and share return βs are related (Beaver and Manegold, 1975).

In reality, confronted by such a problem we would probably try several of these approaches to cross-check on the accuracy of our answer.

SUMMARY

As we have seen, although the CAPM is not a perfect approach to calculating the cost of capital, it is probably the best alternative currently available, at least outside the United States. In terms of practical application, the easiest route is usually to look for proxy or analogue companies for each PLB and adjust the β factors of those proxies for their gearing levels to give the β of the underlying business. This should be the β that those firms would have if they were financed entirely by equity.

This β is then used in the CAPM to give a risk-adjusted all equity discount rate for the PLB; at the time of writing, the real risk-free interest rate appears to be just over 4 per cent, whilst the real risk premium can reasonably be taken as 6 per cent. The PLB's own gearing level then needs to be taken into account; this can be achieved either through the adjusted present value model, where the present value of the debt tax shields is added to the PLB's value if financed entirely by equity, or by calculating a weighted average cost of capital for the PLB. In calculating the value of the debt tax shields, or in arriving at the WACC, we need to be aware that this is a company-specific factor, which depends, *inter-alia*, upon:

1. The effective marginal rate of corporation tax.
2. The expected tax shields in each year.
3. The tax paying position of debt and equity holders.
4. The dividend payout policy.
5. Whether or not the ACT is recoverable.

APPENDIX: VALUING SUBSIDISED LOANS

The basic approach to this problem is to use the APV model to value both the net present value of the subsidised loan and the value of the debt tax shields on the loan. These are then added to the 'base case' NPV, which will have been derived from applying the 'all-equity' rate (derived using ungeared βs) to the free cash flows of the PLB.

To illustrate this, we shall use the example of Gnome plc,* which is considering an investment in Ruritania. The government has offered the company a ten year loan of 50 per cent of the initial cost of any investment made at an interest rate of 10 per cent pa. The fair market rate on such borrowing is 15 per cent. Gnome plc is considering the purchase of a truck factory, which the government is privatising; the cost of the enterprise is 10 million Ruritanian dollars (R$). Gnome's all equity discount rate is 18 per cent for such a venture, and using this rate to discount the project's free cash flows (net of Ruritanian tax at 25 per cent) has resulted in a base case NPV of −R$ 0.5 million. To this we need to add the value of the subsidised loan. This is:

Year of cash flow	Capital flow	Interest	Net	Present value at 15%
0	+5 m		+5.0 m	+5.000 m
1–9 inclusive		−0.5 m	−0.5 m	−2.386 m
10	−5 m	−0.5 m	−5.5 m	−1.360 m
Total				+1.254 m

(Note that discounting a 15 per cent loan at 15 per cent gives an NPV of zero; in other words, only loans obtained at a rate other than the fair one have a NPV different from zero.

The value of the debt tax shields (assuming these are certain to be achieved at 25 per cent pa, there is a one-year tax lag and taking the market borrowing cost of 15 per cent pa as the discount rate) is:

Year of cash flow	Interest	Tax relief (1 year lag)	Present value at 15%
1	−0.5 m		
2–10 inclusive	−0.5 m	0.125 m	0.519 m
11		0.125 m	0.027 m
Total			0.546 m

The APV of the project is therefore:

$$APV(R\$m) = -0.5 + 1.254 + 0.546 = R\$ 1.3 \text{ million}$$

As this is positive, the purchase should go ahead. The value of Gnome's equity position will be the R$5 million it invested plus this APV, giving a PLB value of R$ 6.3 million. Note that the WACC approach is not much help here because gearing is not constant; furthermore, valuing the loan subsidy via WACC fails to consider the appropriate cost of capital to apply to such an arrangement. APV is by far the simplest method of valuing items of this nature.

CHAPTER 7

ESTIMATING THE COST OF COMPLEX FINANCING ARRANGEMENTS

The last twenty to thirty years has seen a great deal of innovation in capital markets. Complex financing arrangements now abound, and include convertible loan stocks, swaps, caps, collars and other 'branded', products offered by some of the large US investment banks. Our problem is to value such financing packages (as we generally wish to discover the value of the equity) and also to work out the cost of capital of such forms of financing. Two general observations are in order; first, as we saw in the previous chapter, unless there are some external value influencing factors associated with financing (generally these will be debt tax shields, liquidation costs and any government subsidised loan arrangements), the *total* value of the business is unaffected by how it is financed. In effect, with the exception of these external factors, financing arrangements affect how the cash flows of the business are divided but not how such cash flows are created. Second, if we understand the principles of discounted cash flow analysis and option pricing, we can value any type of financing package currently on offer. Options are an important part of the modern financing scene; any form of finance that gives one or other party the right to do something (but not an obligation) involves an option. Examples include convertible loan stocks (a simple convertible allows the holder to exchange debt for equity) and caps (which allow the holder to have the interest rate set at a maximum level). For as long as we are concerned only with ordinary shares and 'plain vanilla', or ordinary, debt, we do not need to know how to deal with options.[1] Once we move away from such a simple setting, we need to understand the basic principles of options and their pricing.

An option can be defined as the right to buy (a *call option*) or the right to sell (a *put option*) an asset at a set price on some specified future date. To understand how to value such an instrument, we first need to understand the wealth position of the holder of such an option at the expiry date (the *exercise* date). As an example, we can see the position of the holder of a call option on a share in Asda plc, with an exercise price of 43 pence, expiring in January 1992, in Figure 7.1. The option price on 12 November 1991 was 7 pence. Essentially, the holder gains when the price of the shares at expiry exceeds the exercise price plus the cost of buying the option (known as the *premium*). The option will be exercised if the market price of the shares exceeds the exercise price; otherwise, the holder will allow the option to expire unexercised (in other words, the option turns out to be valueless). Figure 7.2 shows the position of the seller or *writer* of the option; he or she gains if the share price is less than the exercise price plus the premium (which the writer will have received); the bad news is that potential losses are unlimited if Asda's price climbs.

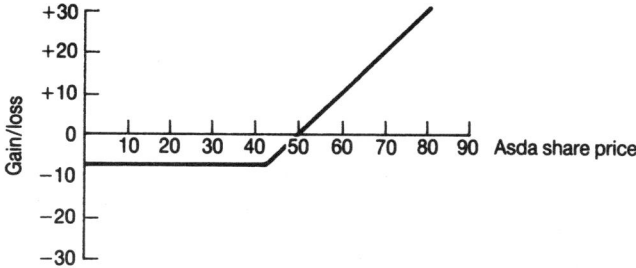

Figure 7.1   Call option purchase.

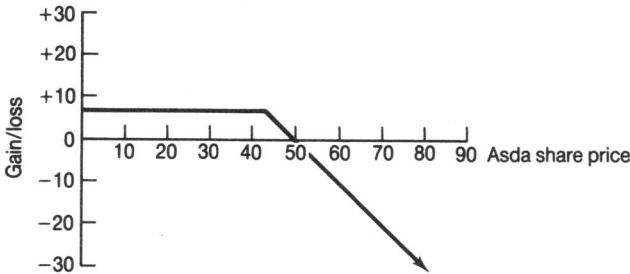

Figure 7.2   Call option sale uncovered.

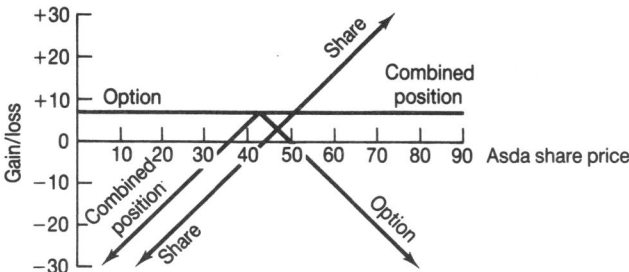

Figure 7.3   Call option sale and share owned.

However, consider the position of Ms Liffey, an institutional fund manager who holds Asda shares and has written a call option on them when the share price was 43 pence. Her position is shown in Figure 7.3, from which we can see that if the price rises above the exercise price, the loss on the call option (which will be exercised against her) is offset by the rise in value of the shares that she holds; in addition, she keeps the option premium so that her net position is a gain of this amount. If the share price falls, she is protected against any loss *provided* that the fall in Asda's share price below the exercise price is no greater than the amount of any premium she has received. In effect, she is in a risk-free position (later, we shall see that by altering the ratio of shares and call options she can maintain a risk-free position no matter what happens to Asda's share price). It is this ability to use options to hedge against losses that drives the option pricing model. We shall now take a brief look at the development of such a model.[2]

A BASIC OPTION PRICING MODEL

The easiest way to understand option pricing is through a simple single period two state example. Suppose the current share price of JPR plc★ is £3 per share. JPR is a specialist company in the pharmaceutical industry, and its future depends upon the success of a new drug, the 'Williams', which is currently undergoing final trials, the results of which will be known in one year's time. If the outcome of these trials is successful, the share price will jump to £4 per share; if the drug fails the share value will fall to £2.50. Our problem is that we hold 1,000 shares in JPR, which we would like to retain but find the short-term risk position unpalatable. Fortunately, there is a ready market in call options on JPR shares, including those with an exercise price equal to the current share price (such options would be said to be *at the money*). Now, if the share price rises to £4, a call option with an exercise price of £3 will be worth £1 at expiry, one year from now. Conversely, the same option is worthless if the share price falls to £2.50. If we now look at the proportionate change in the values of the option and share that occurs, we find the following:

$$\frac{\text{Option price range}}{\text{Share price range}} = \frac{£1 - £0}{£4 - £2.50} = 0.667$$

This number is the *hedge ratio* or *option* δ; the former name is the most descriptive because it tells us how many options we need to write to establish a risk-free position. Imagine that we sell 1/0.667 options (i.e. 1.5) for every share we hold in JPR. What would our position be if either of the two possible outcomes occurred?

	Share price £4	Share price £2.50
Value of shareholding	£4,000	£2,500
Loss on exercise of option	(1,500)	0
Net position	2,500	2,500

We would thus find ourselves in an identical situation whichever state occurred; in other words, the position is a risk-free one. What is the fair return on such a position? The answer must be the risk-free rate of return. Suppose that this rate is 10 per cent pa. The net investment we have made is 1,000 shares at £3 each, less the receipts from selling 1,500 call options at £c each. Thus the value of the call option must be the amount that equates the value of this net investment to the end of period return:

$$2500 = (3000 - 1500c) \times (1.10)$$

Multiplyirfg out and solving for c gives us the value of each call option, which is £0.4848. Of course, in the real world we have more than one period over which the share price can change, and the process can be viewed as a continuous one. If we extend our model into continuous time, we end up with the *Black–Scholes Option Pricing Model* (see Bookstaber (1981) Appendix to Chapter 4).

THE BLACK-SCHOLES OPTION PRICING MODEL

Our need is to be able to value a simple call option, under a set of reasonably realistic assumptions. The formula given below represents the only piece of serious maths in the entire book – fortunately, as this model is widely used in practice, we can normally make use of one of the computerised option pricing packages, which are easily obtainable. The model we shall use to give the value of this call option (C) is that developed by Black and Scholes, which looks like this:

$$C = SN(d_1) - Xe^{-rt}N(d_2)$$

Once we break this down into its constituent parts, it becomes rather less intimidating than it first appears. First, ignore for the moment the terms $N(d_1)$ and $N(d_2)$. S is the current share price, X is the exercise price and e^{-rt} is a continuously compounded discount factor for t years at a risk-free rate of r, where t is the number of years to expiry of the option.[3] Suppose that we knew for certain that the share price would remain at the current level (which would need to be above X in this case). We can see part of the logic for the formula because under these conditions, the value of the call becomes the share price less the present value of the exercise price, which is only payable when the option is exercised at expiry. Moving now to the realistic case of risky share prices, the point about call options is that, as we have seen in the simple example above, by holding shares and selling suitable quantities of call options (the ratio is given by the hedge ratio), it is possible to establish a risk-free portfolio, which should therefore give a risk-free rate of return. The relevant variables are the natural logarithm of the ratio of the current share price to the exercise price $[\ln(S/X)]$, the time to expiry, and the volatility of the share (expressed in terms of its standard deviatioñ, σ). The relationships between these variables are captured through $N(d_1)$ and $N(d_2)$, which are cumulative probabilities. $N(d_1)$ is the same as the hedge ratio in our simple two-state model (so we need to write $1/N(d_1)$ call options for every share we own) and $N(d_2)$ can be interpreted as the probability that the option will finish 'in the money' (Copeland and Weston, 1988, p. 276). To convert values of d_1 and d_2 to probabilities we need tables that give the areas under a normal curve (see Appendix B, page 234). The values of d_1 and d_2 are given by:

$$d_1 = \frac{\ln(S/X) + (r \times t)}{\sigma.\sqrt{t}} + [0.5 \times (\sigma.\sqrt{t})$$

and

$$d_2 = d_1 - \sigma.\sqrt{t}$$

To see how all this works, we shall return to the example of the Asda call options given at the beginning of this chapter. Let us assume that the current Asda share price is 48 pence, there are 78 days to run before the expiry of the option, that the correct standard deviation of Asda's share price is the 31 per cent given by the LBS Share Price Database (September 1991), and that the risk free rate (continuously compounded) is 10 per cent pa. In addition, we need to know that there are no dividends payable on these shares before the expiry of the option (see below for an explanation of what to do when there are dividends). First, d_1 and d_2 are:

$$d_1 = \frac{\ln(48/43) + (0.1 \times 78/365)}{0.31 \times \sqrt{78/365}} + (0.5 \times 0.31 \times \sqrt{78/365}) = 0.9884$$

$$d_2 = 0.9884 - (0.31 \times \sqrt{78/365}) = 0.845$$

Turning to the area tables given in Appendix B (page 000), when $d_1 = 0.9884$ we can see that the corresponding area ($N(d_1)$) is 0.8389, whilst for d_2 the area is 0.7995. Plugging these numbers into the Black–Scholes model gives us an option value (C) of:

$$C = (48 \times 0.8389) - (43 \times e^{-0.1 \times 78/365} \times 0.7995) = 6.62 \text{ pence}$$

The actual market price was 7 pence, which is the rounded price; considering the slightly cavalier assumption we made, this might be viewed as a good approximation.[4]

Having unwrapped and played with our new toy, we should perhaps take a look at what use we can make of it.

FINANCING INSTRUMENTS INVOLVING OPTIONS

It turns out that even apparently simple debt financing can have options built into it. Many debenture and loan stock issues, particularly in the United States, have what are known as 'call provisions', which allow the company to buy back the loan stock at a set price (designed to protect the firm against interest rate falls in the case of fixed interest securities), which essentially amount to the debt holder having 'sold' the company a series of call options. Similarly, many loan agreements stipulate a 'cap' to interest rates which is also an option-like arrangement. In so far as both of these are priced through an interest rate premium on the bond or loan, their incorporation into a WACC is simple, and we do not really need option pricing formulae to do so. However, there are two important sources of finance without such a simple solution – warrants and convertible unsecured loan stocks (CULS).

A warrant is a pure option, in that it allows the holder to buy shares in the issuing company at a specified price on a certain date(s). Warrants are normally associated with bond issues (from which they can be detachable and separately tradeable), new equity issues (e.g. Lloyd's Bank German Investment Trust), or dividend distribution (e.g. BTR). CULS are similar to a combination of a warrant and a loan stock, where the warrant is not detachable and separately tradeable. The coupon rate on the loan stock will be less than the current rate on comparable corporate loan stocks, reflecting the value of the attached warrant. To perform company valuations, we need to know the cost of capital of these forms of financing and their fair market value, because the value of the equity is the value of the firm less the value of any claims on that firm.

Using the Black–Scholes model to value warrants

So far, we have an option pricing formula; we now wish to use this for pricing warrants. There is an important difference between options and warrants in that the former are written by outsiders on existing shares, whereas the latter are written (issued) by the company and involve the issue of new shares; thus warrants have a dilution effect which options do not. This is easily allowed for, and subject to certain assumptions (the most onerous for our purposes being that the firm pays no dividends before exercise) the relationship can be shown to be:[5]

$$W = \frac{N_S}{N_S + N_W} \times C$$

where N_S and N_W are the number of shares and warrants in existence at present. As an example, suppose that BRT plc* has a current share price of £3.50, has 100 million shares in issue and issues 10 million warrants (one warrant carries an entitlement to one share) with an exercise price of £5 and an exercise date five years from now. Let us assume that the risk-free rate on five-year gilts is 10.25 per cent and the standard deviation of the share price is 25 per cent pa[6] (as we have noted, historical standard deviations are available along with β factors from services such as the London Business School Risk Measurement Service). The β of the shares is 1.0, and the market risk premium is 6 per cent.

Before we can value the warrants, we need to note that the gilt yield quoted is *not* a continuously compounded rate. In fact, as we have seen in Chapter 2, a gilt yield of 10.25 per cent (given the semi-annual coupons on gilts) equates to an APR of:

$$APR = [1 + (0.1025/2)]^2 - 1 = 0.1051 \text{ or } 10.51\% \text{ pa}$$

To convert an APR to a continuously compounded rate (CCR), we need the natural logarithm of one plus the APR:

$$CCR = LN(1.1051) = 0.1 \text{ or } 10.0\%$$

Using this CCR of 10 per cent, we now (i) value the warrants and (ii) calculate the implied cost of capital on the warrants.
First, calculate values for d_1 and d_2:

$$d_1 = \frac{\ln(3.5/5) + (0.1 \times 5)}{0.25 \times \sqrt{5}} + (0.5 \times 0.25 \times \sqrt{5}) = 0.5359$$

$$d_2 = 0.5359 - (0.25 \times \sqrt{5}) = -0.0231$$

Turning to our normal area tables in Appendix B (see page 234), $N(d_1) = 0.7054$ and $N(d_2) = 0.492$. Plugging these values into our option pricing formula yields:

$$C = (3.5 \times 0.7054) - (5 \times 0.492 \times 0.6065) = £0.98$$

The fair value of the warrant is therefore:

$$W = 0.98 \times \frac{100}{100 + 10} = £0.89$$

We now need to find the implied cost of capital on these warrants; the β of warrants (βw) can be shown to be related to the β of equity by the following (see Copeland and Weston (1988) for a full explanation):

$$\beta_w = \beta_e \times N(d_1) \times S/C$$

Applying this to our example gives the result:

$$\beta w = 1.0 \times 0.7054 \times 3.5/0.98 = 2.52$$

This indicates that the warrant is much riskier than the underlying equity, because of the fact it is considerably 'out of the money'. In general, the closer the exercise price is to the current price, and the longer the time to expiry, the nearer the β of the warrant will be to that of the equity.

Clearly, in the majority of cases, given the length of time between issue and exercise of many warrants, we would expect dividend payments to be made. One way of approximating a solution to this problem is to value the call option component by reducing the initial term S in the Black and Scholes model by the present value of the expected dividend.[7] We shall look at an example using this approach in our valuation of a CULS below.

Using the Black–Scholes model to value convertibles

Having established a procedure for valuing warrants, we are now in a position to approximate the cost of capital of a CULS, which we know is roughly equivalent to a warrant plus an ordinary unsecured loan stock. Unfortunately, the accurate valuation of a CULS is a very complex task because of several factors. In the first place, the exercise price on a straight option is clear cut; on a CULS, what is being surrendered on exercise is the value of the underlying loan stock. If the redemption and exercise dates are the same, and redemption is at par, no particular problem exists, but when this is not the case, the underlying value of the CULS at each possible exercise date needs to be estimated. In reality, we will also encounter problems connected with dividend payments and optimal timing of option exercise. Given that our requirement is to approximate the value of convertibles to: (i) estimate cost of capital; and (ii) estimate the residual value of the equity, we can probably get away with the short cut of valuing a convertible as a warrant (with due allowance for dividend payout) plus an equivalent unsecured loan stock.[8] We shall now look at an example that follows this approach.

The first step is to value the loan stock element, for which we need to know the yield to maturity on an equivalent straight loan stock. Let us take the case of Sussex Sportscar Manufacturing plc*, which currently has 40 million shares in issue with a market price of £2 each. To finance an expansion, it has recently issued £10 million worth of 9.25 per cent CULS. Per £100 nominal, the loan stock is convertible into forty ordinary shares at the option of the loan stock holder in five years time (this means that the effective exercise price is £2.50). Alternatively, if the loan stock is not converted, it is redeemable by the company at par in five years. The current yield on equivalent ULS issues is 12 per cent, the continuously compounded risk-free rate is 10 per cent (which, as we have seen in the previous section, equates to an APR of 10.51 per cent and a gilt yield of 10.25 per cent) and the market risk premium is 6 per cent.

Following the CULS issue, the company's shares have a β of 1.2, are expected to carry a net dividend of 12 pence in year 1 (a figure that is expected to grow by 11.2 per cent pa), and have a standard deviation of 30 per cent pa. Our objective is to work out the WACC; for this purpose we shall assume shares and debt are held mainly by pension funds and, given our discussion on tax shields in Chapter 6, we shall assume a tax relief value of approximately 24 per cent. Finally, to avoid complications concerning the value of the firm, we shall assume that the gearing level remains constant[9] and that there is no other debt in issue at present. First, the fair value of an equivalent ULS is found by discounting the five-year 9.25 per cent coupons at 12 per cent, and adding to this the present value of the £100 redemption value in five years at 12 per cent:

$$(9.25 \times 3.605) + (100 \times 0.5674) = £90.09$$

The warrant element is now valued in a manner similar to that used above, except for the inclusion of a dividend effect. Allowing for this requires us to calculate the present value of the expected dividends; estimating these dividends and discounting them at the risk-free rate of 10 per cent pa[10] gives us (assuming that the warrant is exercised *before* the share goes ex-dividend in year 5):

Year	Dividend	Discount factor (e^{-rt})	Present value
1	12	0.9048	10.86
2	13.3	0.8187	10.89
3	14.8	0.7408	10.96
4	16.5	0.6703	11.06
Total			43.77

We now proceed as before in valuing the warrant element, except that S, the current share value, is taken as today's share price less the present value of these dividends, i.e. $2 - 0.4377$, or 1.5623.

We now calculate d_1 and d_2 in the usual manner:

$$d_1 = \frac{\ln(1.5623/2.5) + (0.1 \times 5)}{0.30 \times \sqrt{5}} + (0.5 \times 0.30 \times \sqrt{5}) = 0.3799$$

and:

$$d_2 = 0.3799 - (0.30 \times \sqrt{5}) = -0.2909$$

Therefore $N(d_1) = 0.6480$ and $N(d_2) = 0.3859$.

Applying these values in the call value formula gives:

$$C = (1.5623 \times 0.6480) - (2.5 \times e^{-0.1 \times 5} \times 0.3859) = 0.4272$$

Now for each £100 of loan stock, there will be forty shares if the warrants are exercised, which would create $100,000 \times 40$ or 4 million shares. Thus the value of each warrant is:

$$W = \frac{40}{40+4} \times 0.4272 = £0.3884$$

As forty of these attach to each £100-worth of CULS, we have a warrant value of £15.54, thus giving us a total CULS value of £15.54 + £90.09 = £105.63 per £100 nominal.

Having calculated fair values, we now need to calculate the costs of capital. On the ULS element, this is simply the equivalent yield, less the assumed tax shield, which gives us 12 per cent $\times (1 - 0.24) = 9.1$ per cent. On the warrant, using the formula for β given above, we obtain:

$$\beta_w = 1.5623/0.4272 \times 0.648 \times 1.2 = 2.84$$

This implies an expected return of (noting that the CAPM requires the risk free rate expressed as an APR):

$r_w = 10.51 + (2.84 \times 6) = 27.6\%$ pa

The expected equity return is:

$r_e = 10.51 + (1.2 \times 6) = 17.7\%$ pa

Finally, we are in a position to work out the company's WACC:

Finance	Market value	Annual cost (%)	Cost × market value
Equity	£80 million	17.7	14.168
CULS:			
warrant element	1.554m	27.6	0.429
ULS element	9.009m	9.1	0.820
Total	90.563	17.0*	15.417

*15.417/90.563%

Note that the weighted cost of the convertible is 11.8 per cent.

Before leaving the topic of convertibles, a common feature of such instruments is the 'forced conversion' clause, which allows the company to redeem the bonds for equity if the shares have stood above the effective exercise price for a number of days (usually between 30 and 60). In effect, this gives the company a call option on the CULS, which in principle can be valued using option pricing models. However, this is an extremely complex process because the exercise date is unknown. For our purposes, we can probably ignore this effect, but in practical terms it means that the warrant element is less valuable than it would be without such a feature.

SWAPS

Another prevalent feature of modern financing is the swap. Reduced to basics, the swap is merely the exchange of one set of cash flows for another. The swap can be a currency swap or an interest rate swap. In the former, a company typically borrows in one currency and 'swaps' the liability for one denominated in a different currency; both principal and interest rate differences are exchanged. As an example, the 1990 accounts for J. Sainsbury plc showed that they borrowed Y5000 million at 5.875 per cent, which was swapped into a $32 million dollar loan at 7.7 per cent. Although it is possible to value this swap arrangement, in efficient and frictionless markets its NPV should be zero; however, imperfections and regulatory and tax arbitrage opportunities sometimes allow borrowing to be arranged more cheaply in some countries than in others. For our purposes the effect of such an arrangement is that Sainsbury's obligations are now denominated in dollars. From a valuation and cost of capital perspective, we can reasonably conclude that a sensible treatment is to value Sainsbury's loan using US dollar rates of interest (this gives us a 'quasi-market value'); the cost of this capital is the US dollar rate less the tax shields received on such borrowing, weighted by the quasi-market value of this US dollar debt.

The interest rate swap involves no exchange of principal, but just the exchange of interest rate obligations. For example, BlueChip plc* can borrow £100 million fixed at 12 per cent pa for five years, or alternatively can borrow at LIBOR plus 0.25 per cent. Because of its size, Lesser plc* cannot borrow on fixed rate terms so advantageously, paying 14 per cent for a loan of this size and duration but can borrow at LIBOR + 0.75 per cent. Because of their differing cash flow patterns and economic exposure, BlueChip would really like to borrow at variable rates whilst Lesser wants to borrow at fixed rates. A swap might be arranged so that BlueChip borrows fixed rate money, Lesser borrows at floating rates and the terms of the swap are that Lesser pays BlueChip 13 per cent fixed, whilst BlueChip pays Lesser LIBOR plus 0.5 per cent. Compared to their alternative borrowing strategies, both gain; BlueChip pays:

$$12\% - 13\% - \text{LIBOR} + 0.5\% = \text{LIBOR} - 0.5\%$$

(compared to the LIBOR + 0.25 per cent it would have had to pay), whilst Lesser pays:

$$13\% - (\text{LIBOR} + 0.75\%) + (\text{LIBOR} + 0.5\%) = 13.25\%$$

(compared to the 14 per cent it would have had to pay).

Impressive a gain as this might be, unless markets are not terribly smart, surely there must be *something* missing? There is; basically, BlueChip has taken on some of the default risk of Lesser, which was why the market wanted a much higher long-term premium than the short-term one. Whilst such effects can be valued, as can differential interest rate expectations, the simplest approach for our purposes is to treat such swaps as zero NPV investments and value the debt of BlueChip as though it were floating rate (which is effectively what has been created), and that of Lesser as though it were fixed rate. Tax shield values should be based upon the expected tax savings, which for floating rate debt requires an estimate of future interest rates. In general, the best way of estimating these is to look at the yield curve on government debt (corporate debt can be used if the market is large enough, as in the case of the US) and work out the implied future interest rates, in a manner similar to that used in Chapter 2 to estimate the future inflation rate. For example, if we wish to work out the implied interest rate (the spot rate) for year 2, and we know the one-year rate together with the yield on two-year debt, we can solve the following:

$$(1+\text{yield on 2 year debt})^2 = (1+1 \text{ year spot rate}) \times (1+2 \text{ year spot rate})$$

If government debt is used to estimate such rates, an appropriate risk premium would need to be added.

LEASING

It is fairly easy to show that in a world of rational lenders, leasing simply displaces borrowing capacity. In fact, it is now generally recognised that the correct way to evaluate financial lease contracts is to calculate the difference in cash flow resulting from leasing versus direct acquisition, and to discount these differences at the marginal after tax cost of borrowing (see Brealey and Myers, 1991, Chapter 12). This is because the opportunity cost of capital on the lease agreement is the same as the company's cost of other (straight) debt capital. In general, leases only have a positive net present value to the lessee when there is some tax advantage involved, and this can only occur when the lessor is in a less favourable tax paying position than the lessee; the most usual reason for this is temporary tax exhaustion (normally because of unused capital allowances) on the part of the lessee.

In terms of the treatment of leases in the WACC calculation, the theoretically correct approach is to weight this after tax opportunity cost of borrowing by the value of the lease contract. However, from a practical perspective it will normally be difficult to establish the necessary numbers and an acceptable short cut under most circumstances will be to weight the after-tax cost of the company's debt capital by the book value of the lease. Of more serious concern is the presence of off-balance-sheet lease arrangements not captured by the provisions of SSAP 21; to the extent that these arrangements are known about, some estimate of such lease values should be included in WACC and gearing calculations.

ESTIMATING THE DISCOUNT RATE – A CASE EXAMPLE

Let us assume that in January 1991 we were attempting to value Western Supermarkets Ltd* (WSL), which is the food retailing arm of Glyndwr Foods plc*. WSL is positioned towards the 'quality' end of the market, and Glyndwr wishes to appraise the value of this subsidiary in order to assess alternative strategies for its future. Glyndwr has a β of 0.85 and a gearing, based upon market weights, of 18 per cent debt and 82 per cent equity. Research (London Business School Risk Measurement Service), has shown the following:

Item	Market Capitalisation (£m)	Equity β	Standard deviation (%)
Food retailing (average)	917 (average)	0.82	22
Argyll	2253	0.67	23
Morrison (W)	335	0.78	27
Tesco	3569	0.80	24

Note that for simplification, a rather small selection of proxies has been used, but some companies have been excluded for reasons of market positioning (Kwiksave and Budgens), or because their βs appear out of line with the sector as a whole (e.g. William Low, with a β of 0.43). Sainsbury's has been excluded because of its diversification into DIY and the USA, but this is probably rather 'purist' since its β is not that much higher than Tesco's, at 0.82.

From the *Financial Times*, the average yields to redemption on UK gilts were 11.02 per cent (five years) and 10.5 per cent (fifteen years) and on corporate debentures and loans the yields were 12.37 per cent (fifteen years) and 12.63 per cent (five years). Summary data from the 1990 published accounts, together with supplementary information from the International Stock Exchange Yearbook, for the three companies are as follows:

Item	Argyll (£m)	Morrison (£m)	Tesco (£m)
Short term loans and overdrafts	59.4	74.7	2.1
Current portion of LT debt	67.5[a]	7.6	–
Commercial paper and unsecured loans	–	64.5	–
Total short-term interest bearing debt	126.9	146.8	2.1
Fixed interest loans	–	0.2[b]	165.2[c]
Variable interest loans	21.0	–	–
Finance leases	33.3	–	55.6
Convertible loan stock	60.04[d]	–	106.9[e]
Total long-term interest bearing debt	114.3	0.2	327.7

[a] From Argyll's accounts, this would appear to include £63.5m of commercial paper.

[b] Repayable in 1995 with a £30,000 premium; interest 10.75 per cent.

[c] Comprises: 4 per cent unsecured loan stock, 2006 par value £125m, book value £65.6m

10.5 per cent bonds, 2015 redeemable at £100m book value £99.6m

[d] 4.5 per cent 1987/2002 convertible at 295 pence, or redeemable by the company at a declining premium, or at 123.5 per cent in 1992 at the bondholder's option.

[e] 4 per cent 2002. Convertible at 174 pence, or redeemable by the company at a reducing premium between 1987 and 1993, provided the share price is at least 226 pence, or at 127.625 per cent in 1992 at the bondholder's option.

NB: with regard to the convertibles, it should be noted that the company redemption option is present to allow the company to force conversion, because the detailed conditions require the company to give a period of notice before redeeming the bonds.

Finally, Glyndwr's management feel that given the nature of the business, on a 'stand-alone' basis WSL would support a gearing of 20 per cent debt to 80 per cent equity; given the size of the subsidiary, fixed interest debt costs would be around 12 per cent pa. A quick look at the average dividend payout ratios for large supermarkets suggests a figure of just over 30 per cent; assuming that debt and equity holders are UK tax exempt institutions, applying our tax effect formula from Chapter 6, and recognising that the tax on equity is:

$$(30\% \times -33.3\%) + (70\% \times 0\%), \text{ or } 10 \text{ per cent } negative$$

gives us:

$$T = 1 - \frac{(1 - 0.33) \times (1 + 0.10)}{(1 - 0)} = 0.26 \text{ or } 26\%$$

Thus the tax shield on debt would be approximately 26 per cent of any interest charges.

Case study solution: Step 1 – Ungearing proxy βs

We are now in a position to calculate the cost of capital for WSL. The first step is to ungear the proxy company βs to arrive at an 'all-equity' cost of capital. When performing the calculations, it is useful to ungear each company in turn to detect any 'outliers' in the sample. An additional factor to bear in mind is that in the ungearing process convertibles are only considered in terms of their value as straight debt, although where the value of the 'equity' portion is significant, this can be added to the market capitalisation of the company's shares. We should have used a five-year average for the ungearing, but we have used only the 1990 position for simplicity. Finally, note that, ideally, the long-term core overdraft should be used in the calculations; arriving at such a figure would mean investigating both interim and final accounts for a number of years, with the aim of taking out any short-term financing requirements (in theory, all the overdraft should be for short-term financing, but UK practice means that the overdraft is often used as a source of long-term finance). In the example below, we assume that *all* of the overdraft is used for short-term financing, and hence it is excluded from the calculation.

The ungeared β for each company is calculated below:

Argyll

Variable interest bank loans	£21.0m
Commercial paper and short term debt	£67.5m
Leases	£33.3m
4.5% convertible: loan portion (see below)	£63.0m
Total	£184.8m

The convertible debt portion has been valued by assuming redemption in

December 1992 at £123.5 per £100 nominal, and discounting the coupon and redemption values at 12.6 per cent (the corporate average yield), thus:

$$PV = \frac{4.5}{1.126} + \frac{4.5 + 123.5}{1.126^2} = 104.95 \text{ per £100 nominal}$$

Multiplying the £60 million par value by 104.95/100 gives approximately £63 million.

The final figure we need to calculate is Argyll's debt β. Unlike equity βs, debt βs are not published, but if we knew Argyll's borrowing cost we could compare this to a risk-free equivalent rate and deduce a β by substituting the various figures into the CAPM. A more reliable method is to use credit ratings where these are available; the method we use here is to assume that the two major supermarkets we are using as proxies can all borrow at the same rate as Sainsbury's, which is the only supermarket with quoted fixed interest debt at the time of writing. Sainsbury's debt trades at a yield of about 0.95 above the equivalent life gilt yield.[11] Assuming Argyll could borrow on these terms, plugging the relevant rates into the CAPM and assuming that the long-term inflation rate is 5 per cent, and therefore given our previous discussion the market risk premium in money or nominal terms is 6.3 per cent, gives us the following (note that the left-hand side is the return required on supermarket debt):

$$11.02 + 0.95 = 11.02 + \beta(6.3)$$

Solving for β gives us a debt β of 0.15.

Using the Buckley formula described on page 125 to ungear Argyll's β by assuming a tax shield effect is similar to that of WSL gives us:

$$\beta_{Argyll} = 0.67 \times \frac{2253}{(2253 + 184.8) - (0.26 \times 184.8)} + \\ 0.15 \times \frac{184.8(1 - 0.26)}{(2253 + 184.8) - (0.26 \times 184.8)} = 0.64$$

Repeating this process for Morrison's gives us the following debt value:

Morrison's	
Short-term loans	£64.5m
Variable interest bank loans	£0.2m
Total debt	£64.7m

As Morrison's is a smaller company, we shall assume it can borrow at the corporate average rate for debentures, which represents a short-term premium of about 1.6 per cent to gilts. Using the CAPM logic applied to Argyll gives us an implied debt β of:

$$11.02 + 1.6 = 11.02 + \beta(6.3) = 0.25$$

Ungearing Morrison's β we therefore have:

$$\beta_{\text{Morrison}} = 0.78 \times \frac{335}{(335 + 64.7) - (64.7 \times 0.26)} +$$

$$0.25 \times \frac{64.7(1 - 0.26)}{(335 + 64.7) - (64.7 \times 0.26)} = 0.71$$

Finally, we can calculate Tesco's ungeared β:

Tesco

4% deep discount loan stock (present value at 12.4% corporate rate)	£55.1m
Finance leases	£55.6m
4% convertible (PV of coupons and redemption at 127.625 in 1992)	£114.7m
10.5% bonds (2015) PV at Sainsbury's premium (above) of 0.95% over the gilt rate of 10.49%	£93.4m
Total	£318.8m

We have already assumed a debt β of 0.15 for Tesco, therefore we can ungear the β as for the other cases:

$$\beta_{\text{Tesco}} = 0.8 \times \frac{3569}{(3569 + 318.8) - (318.8 \times 0.26)} +$$

$$0.15 \times \frac{318.8(1 - 0.26)}{(3569 + 318.8) - (318.8 \times 0.26)} = 0.75$$

We are now in a position to bring all this together and calculate an ungeared equity β for the whole sample. Note that the ungeared βs are fairly tightly grouped, and we appear to have no worries concerning outliers. We can summarise our data as follows:

Company	Ungeared β	Market Capital (£m)	'Raw' β	Debt value
Argyll	0.64	2253	0.67	184.8
Morrison	0.71	335	0.78	64.7
Tesco	0.75	3569	0.80	318.8
Total		6157		568.3

Given our somewhat heroic assumptions on debt βs, we can calculate the average debt β of our sample as:

$$\frac{(184.8 \times 0.15) + (64.7 \times 0.25) + (318.8 \times 0.15)}{568.3} = 0.16$$

In a similar fashion, the raw equity β of our sample is:

$$\frac{(0.67 \times 2253) + (0.78 \times 335) + (0.80 \times 3569)}{6157} = 0.75$$

Taking all this into our de-gearing formula gives us the underlying business risk β for our sample, which is:

$$0.75 \times \frac{6157}{(6157 + 568.3) - (568.3 \times 0.26)} +$$

$$0.16 \times \frac{568.3(1 - 0.26)}{(6157 + 568.3) - (568.3 \times 0.26)} = 0.71$$

Step 2 – Regear the equity β for WSL's capital structure

The above β (0.71) is the β that WSL should have if it was financed entirely by equity. If we were about to value the company using an APV approach, we would use this to calculate a discount rate and add in the value of the debt tax shields, together with any other financing 'side-effects', such as issue costs. However, in this case we want to know the WACC for WSL.

We know that the cost of equity capital for a geared firm is higher than that for an ungeared one. Previously, we wanted to find the equity cost of capital of an ungeared firm from that of geared proxies; this time, as we know the cost for our PLB in an ungeared state, we wish to reverse the procedure. This is simply achieved by rearranging the Buckley formula from Chapter 6 to give:

$$\beta_{eg} = \frac{\beta_{eu}(V_g - TD) - \beta_d[D(1 - T)]}{E}$$

Substituting in our numbers for WSL (denoting the value of the geared firm is 100 per cent) gives:

$$\beta_{eg} = \frac{0.71[100 - (0.26 \times 20)] - 0.16[20(1 - 0.26)]}{80} = 0.87$$

Note that the assumed borrowing cost of 12 per cent is in line with the average sample β of 0.16 used in the regearing calculation. We can now calculate a geared equity rate for WSL by substituting in the CAPM:

$$r_{eu} = 10.49 + (0.87 \times 6.3) = 15.98, \text{ or approximately } 16\%$$

Step 3 – calculate the WACC

Given the assumed borrowing costs, gearing levels and debt tax shields for WSL, we obtain a weighted average cost of capital of:

$$\text{WACC} = (16 \times 80\%) + [12 \times (1 - 0.26) \times 20\%] = 14.6\%$$

At this stage, we should highlight the fact that a number of corners have been cut. In particular, we should have used five-year average accounting numbers, we should really have used credit ratings to estimate debt βs and we have taken no account of the difference in risk between unsecured loan stocks and secured loans. We should really have made sure that the assumed discount rates and βs were compatible; essentially, what we have here represents a short cut approach to the problem. None the less, it provides a useful illustration of some of the real world problems we might expect to encounter.

CHAPTER 8

DISCOUNTED CASH FLOW VALUATION

If we could forecast the cash flow for every year to infinity, this chapter would be very short. We would only need to note that the forecasting principles to be applied were those described in Chapter 4, the target variable to be forecast was the free cash flow (FCF) and the discount rate to be used could be calculated according to the principles set out in Chapters 6 and 7. Of course, the real problem is that we cannot make a reasonable forecast of the specific FCF more than a certain number of years out. We are therefore forced to make a simplifying assumption about the nature of the change in these cash flows, one alternative being that the FCF grows at a constant rate in perpetuity. This allows us to estimate the *terminal* or *horizon value* of the business at the forecast horizon (that is, the end of the explicit forecast period). There are alternative methods of estimating this value; we could assume continuous replication, erosion of economic rents (this simply means that after a certain time the economic advantage of the business is diminished to the extent that only zero NPV projects are available to it), or the familiar prospective PE multiple. We shall look at the merits of each of these in turn. Before doing so, we shall reconsider the explicit forecast and its preparation.

THE EXPLICIT FORECAST PERIOD

The key considerations concerning the forecasting of profits and cash flows were discussed at length in Chapter 4. There we noted the importance of economic and company background factors and detailed the information required to prepare the forecasts themselves. In particular, we concluded that a forecast needed to be prepared for each principal line of business (PLB), because environmental and corporate considerations are likely to differ between each of these. Furthermore, each PLB has its own level of systematic risk, which needs to be reflected in the discount rate.

A key point is that the skills necessary to forecast free cash flows successfully are exactly the same as those required to forecast earnings; we noted that in most businesses, the accuracy of the forecast was likely to be most sensitive to the sales revenue estimate. It is perhaps worth recapitulating on why the free cash flow is the key variable we need when making a DCF valuation. If the company did not have to invest in any fixed assets or increase its working capital investment, all of the operating cash flows after tax could be paid out as dividends; in such an event, there would be nothing else to be done with them. However, real businesses need to invest to maintain the existing asset base (note that because of inflation and the 'lumpy' nature of investment flows, this investment is not the same as accounting depreciation) and to expand. Sales, profit and cash flow growth can only come about through investment. This is true even in inflationary conditions, where working capital investment is needed to maintain short-term operating capacity.

In this growth situation, if we simply took the expanding after-tax cash flows from operations and discounted them, we would over-estimate the value of the firm because we would fail to take account of the sacrifice necessary to achieve the expansion. That sacrifice is measured by the cash flow retained in the firm and not paid out as dividends. As we noted in Chapter 3, in the case of a business financed entirely by equity, where investment was made directly (that is no cash is placed on deposit) and no new shares were issued, free cash flow and dividend would be identical. However, given that businesses can use cash deposits, borrow, receive and make interest payments, and issue new equity, dividends and free cash flows normally differ. In Chapter 3, we defined free cash flow and here we give an example taken from the British Vita accounts of 31 December 1990[1] (see Figure 8.1 for the relevant extracts):

Cash flow British Vita (£000)

		1990	1989
Sales turnover	TR	635,948	589,605
Cash operating expenses			
variable	VC ⎫		
fixed	FC ⎭	562,863	530,342*
Operating cash flow	OCF	73,085	59,673*
Cash taxes	CT	16,695	15,826†
Operating cash flow after tax	CFAT	56,390	43,847
Working capital investment	WCAP	5,138	1,488
Investment in fixed assets	INV	35,545	58,605‡
Free cash flow	FCF	15,707	−16,246

We can also reconcile FCF and dividends thus:

Free cash flow	FCF	15,707	16,246
Less: Interest paid net of tax	NI	− 6,639	3,526†

Cash placed on deposit (increase in net cash balance)	CDI+	−11,458	
Loans repaid	D−		
Plus: Interest income net of tax	INT	+ 4,564	+ 2,765
Cash withdrawn from deposit (decrease in net cash balance)	CDI−		+13,024
New borrowings	D+	+ 8,055	+ 7,840§
New share issued	E+	+ 869	+ 5,218
Dividends	**DIV**	11,098	9,075

Notes: The dividend is that shown as *paid* in the Source and Application of Funds Statement. With the exception of turnover, given in the P&L Account, all figures are taken from the Source and Application of Funds Statement, which, along with Note 5 to the accounts, is reproduced as Figure 8.1.

The calculation of those items marked are as follows (1989 figures in parentheses):

★The OCF is the £69,893 (£58,502) 'Total funds from operations' with the £3,192 (£1,171) net interest payable (Note 5) added back. The cash operating expenses are then calculated as the balancing figure between this and the turnover.

†To calculate the interest paid and received net of tax, a 35 per cent tax rate has been assumed. The net tax relief thus obtained, £1,117 (£410), has been added back to derive the tax paid on operating cash flow.

‡The INV figure is the total of 'Acquisition of subsidiaries' £68,256 (£12,085), investment in associated companies £0 (£15,898) plus purchase of tangible fixed assets £39,037 (£34,093), less the sale of tangible fixed assets £4,048 (£2,045), the decrease of investment in associated companies £7,462 (£620) and government grants received £238 (£806).

§New borrowing is the total of the increase in long-term creditors, the increase in short-term loans and the decrease in long-term debtors.

It is this free cash flow that needs to be forecast for the chosen horizon. As we have observed elsewhere, this should be a minimum of five years and should always be for the maximum number of years possible. In general, the aim is to forecast as far into the future as is necessary to ensure that the 'steady-state' scenario, necessary to forecast the terminal or horizon value of the PLB, is a reasonable approximation of reality. By 'steady-state' we mean that return on new investment (RONI) and the proportion of earnings retained for reinvestment (RE) and hence the FCF growth rate (g) are all constant to *perpetuity*. Note that such a set of assumptions is implicit whenever a PE multiple is applied to a forecast earnings figure.[2] Whilst it is misleading to speak of *maintainable earnings or maintainable free cash flows* unless the business is a zero growth one (in which case all of the operating cash flows except those required to replace existing assets will be paid out as dividends), it is rather more reasonable to describe such a state as a 'maintainable growth rate'. Below, we investigate what constitutes a sensible set of assumptions about such growth rates.

A further difficulty is the precise interpretation of RONI; we discuss this below, but for now it is sufficient to note that it is normally *not* the same as the accounting rate of return, except under restrictive assumptions.

Group Source and Application of Funds

for the year ended 31 December 1990

	£000	
	1990	1989
Source of funds		
Profit on ordinary activities before tax less minority interests	53,907	48,036
Extraordinary items	2,040	(274)
	55,947	47,762
Items not involving the movements of funds		
Minority interest in the retained profit for the year	321	273
Depreciation	19,114	16,765
Profit retained by associated undertakings	(1,199)	(1,949)
Exchange differences and other items	(4,290)	(4,349)
Total funds generated from operations	69,893	58,502
Funds from other sources		
Sale of tangible fixed assets	4,048	2,045
Issue of Ordinary share capital	869	5,218
Increase in creditors: amounts falling due after more than one year	230	1,892
Disposal of investments in associated undertakings	7,462	620
Decrease in debtors: amounts falling due after more than one year	—	152
Increase in loans	8,227	5,796
Government grants	238	806
	90,967	75,031
Application of funds		
Dividends paid	11,098	9,075
Taxation paid	15,578	15,416
Acquisition of subsidiary undertakings (note 14)	8,256	12,085
Increase in debtors: amounts falling due after more than one year	402	—
Increase in investment in associated undertakings	—	15,898
Purchase of tangible fixed assets	39,037	34,093
Working capital movement		
Increase in stocks	2,744	4,606
Increase in debtors: amounts falling due within one year	7,354	14,354
Increase in creditors: amounts falling due within one year	(4,960)	(17,472)
	79,509	88,055
Increase (decrease) in net cash balances	11,458	(13,024)

Figure 8.1 Extracts from the Annual Report of British Vita plc, 1990.

Consolidated Profit and Loss Account

for the year ended 31 December 1990

	Notes	£000	
		1990	1989
Turnover	2	**635,948**	589,605
Cost of sales		**(476,990)**	(477,165)
Gross profit		**158,958**	142,440
Distribution costs		**(37,126)**	(33,040)
Administrative expenses		**(70,286)**	(65,273)
Operating profit	3	**51,546**	44,127
Share of profit of associated undertakings	4	**5,874**	5,353
Interest payable and similar charges	5	**(3,192)**	(1,171)
Profit on ordinary activities before taxation	2	**54,228**	48,309
Tax on profit on ordinary activities	6	**(21,081)**	(18,240)
Profit on ordinary activities after taxation		**33,147**	30,069
Minority interests		**(321)**	(273)
Profit before extraordinary items		**32,826**	29,796
Extraordinary items less taxation	7	**2,040**	(274)
Profit for the financial year		**34,866**	29,522
Dividends paid and proposed	8	**(11,724)**	(10,203)
Retained profit for the financial year	25	**23,142**	19,319
Retained by			
The Company		**2,235**	340
Subsidiary undertakings		**19,708**	17,030
Associated undertakings		**1,199**	1,949
		23,142	19,319
Earnings per share	9	**18.8p**	17.3p

INFORMATION EXTRACTED FROM NOTES TO THE ACCOUNTS	£000	
	1990	1989
5 Interest payable and similar charges		
Bank overdrafts, acceptance credits and bank loans	**8,740**	4,548
Finance leases	**242**	229
Loans not fully repayable within five years	**757**	316
Loan notes	**475**	332
	10,214	5,425
Less interest recieved	**(7,022)**	(4,254)
	3,192	1,171

Figure 8.1   (*continued*)

Transition period forecasts

Whilst ideally we would hope to be able to forecast explicit cash flows until a steady-state period can reasonably be assumed, we might often encounter the phenomenon of a period of growth of above (or below) normal long-term rates for a certain period. One useful approach in such cases is to model a transitional period between the explicit forecast period and the horizon period, using some form of change process; the easiest of these is the assumption of a linear rate of change. To illustrate the way in which such a process might be used, we shall return to the example of Pastoral Ltd given in chapter 5. The specific five-year forecast for Pastoral was as follows (all figures in £000s):

	Year 1	Year 2	Year 3	Year 4	Year 5
Operating cash flow (OCF)	3300	3267	3993	4832	4832
Projected long-term trend +10% pa (forecast average 10%)					
Depreciation (DEP)	800	820	1000	1430	1450
Taxes (paid as cash) (CT)	1085	490	0	1480	547
Investment in:					
working capital (WCAP)	0	220	710	0	290
fixed assets (INV)	200	1800	4300	200	3270
Cash flow (= OCF−CT− WCAP−INV) (FCF)	2015	757	−1017	3152	725
Projected long-term trend +10% pa					
Profit (PATS)	1415	1957	2993	1872	2835
Projected long-term trend +10% pa (forecast average 19%)					

Now, as we can see from this, the profit growth and FCF growth throughout the forecast period are somewhat out of line with one another, because of the heavy investments that have been forecast in years 3 and 5. Suppose that as a consequence of this, we refine our forecast of FCF growth and assume that the initial rate of growth is 17 per cent pa, declining over a five-year period to the long-term assumed *nominal* GDP growth of 7 per cent pa (which might be the result if we assume a real long-term growth in GDP of 2 per cent pa and an inflation rate of 4.9 per cent pa); the profit growth beyond year 10 will also reduce to 7 per cent pa. The resulting FCF figures for years 6 to 10 inclusive become (all figures in £000s):

	FCF forecast	*Growth from previous year (%)*
Year 6	848	17
Year 7	975	15
Year 8	1,102	13
Year 9	1,224	11
Year 10	1,334	9

From year 11 onwards, growth is assumed to continue at the long run rate of 7 per cent pa in perpetuity. Using our basic FCF growth model from Chapter 3, this gives us a year 10 terminal value, assuming a cost of capital (as we did in Chapter 5) of 14 per cent pa, of:

$$V_{10} = \frac{1.334 \times 1.07}{0.14 - 0.07} = 20,391$$

It is now necessary to discount the specific forecast FCF, the transition period FCF and the implied year 10 terminal value at the cost of capital of 14 per cent; this produces a year 0 value of £11,305 million. Whilst the calculations involved are tedious when carried out on a manual basis, it is a simple matter to develop a spreadsheet model to calculate present values based on a linearly changing growth rate in FCF. In general, if there is some disparity between the growth rate of FCF is the final years of the explicit forecast period and the sustainable long-term rate of growth (see below), serious thought should be given to the inclusion of some transitional period to model the rate of change.

THE CALCULATION OF THE HORIZON OR (TERMINAL) VALUE

The horizon, or terminal, value of a business is its value at the end of the explicit forecast period; in practice, the estimation of such a figure is a necessary component of any valuation. In theory, we could value our firm or PLB by taking the explicit forecast out far enough for the terminal value not to matter very much. Unfortunately, depending on growth and discount rates, this might involve us forecasting cash flows anything from fifty to one hundred years ahead, which is hardly practicable (as a quick proof for readers, what is your best forecast of your business's cash flows in the year 2075?). We are therefore forced into adopting some form of terminal value calculation.

All such models are approximations, because we do not *literally* expect a steady state to occur. In particular, it is important to realise that our real expectation is that trade cycles will take place. As such, our steady state model must reflect *average* expectations of costs and demand, in other words those that exist at the mid-point of the trade cycle. For this reason, the final year of our specific forecast period must be carefully chosen so that it reflects neither economic boom nor slump conditions.

Before we examine the various alternatives, we should perhaps look at a popular criticism of DCF valuations, which is that the majority of the value comes from the assumed terminal value of the company. Whether or not this is true depends upon the length of the specific forecast period, the growth rate of the PLB's free cash flows, and the cost of capital. In Table 8.1, we attempt to show the effect of choosing different time horizons, assuming a PLB with an average systematic risk factor (i.e. $\beta = 1.0$) financed entirely by equity. Whilst we could, somewhat conveniently,

Table 8.1 Proportion of value contributed by horizon value, free cash flow growth model

Forecast horizon (years)	Growth 3%			Growth 5%			Growth 7%			Growth 9%		
	PV PLB	PV horizon value	% Total	PV PLB	PV horizon value	% Total	PV PLB	PV horizon value	% Total	PV PLB	PV horizon value	% Total
5	7.92	4.25	54	9.55	5.52	58	11.89	7.42	62	15.57	10.47	67
10	7.92	2.34	30	9.55	3.36	35	11.89	4.95	42	15.57	7.67	49
15	7.92	1.29	16	9.55	2.04	21	11.89	3.31	28	15.57	5.62	36
20	7.92	0.71	9	9.55	1.24	13	11.89	2.21	19	15.57	4.11	26
25	7.92	0.39	5	9.55	0.75	8	11.89	1.48	12	15.57	3.01	19

recommend that the forecast horizon be extended until the terminal value is a relatively small percentage of total value, this would result in a fairly long specific forecast period for the 'average' business (average being defined as one which grows at the same rate as the economy). In fact, as we have observed above, all that is necessary is to forecast far enough ahead for a 'steady state' assumption to be a reasonable approximation of forecast reality. The real point is that *any* forecasting method makes a similar assumption, the difference being that a DCF approach does so explicitly rather than implicitly. For example, applying a PE ratio to a forecast year 1 earnings number actually assumes that 100 per cent of the value is terminal value.

Turning to our various terminal valuation alternatives, we have the choice between a simple constant growth model, a positive present value of growth opportunities model, a continuous replication model, a zero growth opportunities model and a PE valuation approach. We shall examine the merits of each of these in turn.

The constant growth model

This is simply our familiar free cash flow growth model from Chapter 3, which, adapted for our cost of capital calculation from Chapters 6 and 7, gives us:

$$V_H = \frac{\text{FCF}_{H+1}}{\text{WACC} - g}$$

V_H gives us the value of the firm at the end of the explicit forecast period (year H), so that we need to use the free cash flow for the next period (which by our steady state assumption is $\text{FCF}_H \times (1 + g)$); to find today's value of the company, we simply add the present value of this horizon value [$V_H \div (1 + \text{WACC})^H$] to the present value of all the free cash flows for the specific forecast period.

An important issue when using this formula is to understand what constitutes a reasonable assumption for g, the long-term growth to perpetuity. A serious question is whether it is reasonable to assume that growth will be much different from the rate of growth in GDP in the long-term. Taking the average industrial or retail firm operating in domestic markets[3] as our example, it is quite possible that for a time maintainable growth may exceed GDP growth (the UK supermarket chains are a case in point). However, market saturation will occur eventually; depending on the type of product, demand might then simply remain constant (in which case a working assumption is that FCF just grows in line with inflation), or increase in line with GDP growth. Which will in fact happen depends on the nature of the product or service.

The first point to note is that there is almost always an argument in such a case for using some form of transition model. An example based on a UK supermarket would suggest that after the specific forecast period, a decaying growth model might be used to handle the transition to 'market saturation', at which point a growth model where g was equal to the anticipated long-term inflation rate could be used.

The second point concerns the factors that determine the growth rate. We know from our analysis in Chapter 3 that $g = \text{RONI} \times \text{RE}$, where RE represents that proportion of earnings retained by the firm. This means that, as g declines, so must RONI, RE or both. The special problems of defining and estimating RONI are discussed below, but if we extend our supermarket example, we can see that both are likely to change because eventually the NPV of opening a new store will decrease to zero (so RONI = WACC), at which point the only need for retentions would appear to be the replacement of existing assets. In the case where RONI declines to WACC but growth occurs at the same rate as any increase in GDP (which might be the case for companies in the leisure industry, for example), then RE needs to reflect the increase in capital necessary to maintain this rate of growth.

The conclusion on growth rate estimation is that it is far too easy to adopt an unrealistically 'bullish' view of *long-term* growth prospects; in the medium term, it is quite feasible that abnormal growth can be achieved (if this is the case, we might again make use of a transition period model) but there must be considerable doubt that many firms can grow at a much faster rate than GDP growth in perpetuity. There will be some genuine outperformers, and some under-performers (where growth may be negative); however, the message should always be to question assumed growth rates that are a lot different from this average.

The present value of growth opportunities model

In Chapter 3, we noted that a PLB can be valued by calculating the perpetuity value of the sustainable current earnings after tax and adding to this the present value of the growth opportunities. We can now show that if the return on the new investment made in any period remains constant, the value of the growth opportunities can be described by the sum of the present values of each year's investment (net of any tax allowances) multiplied by the return on that new investment (RONI) less the cost of capital, divided by that cost of capital. Formally, with the cost of capital given as the weighted average cost of capital (WACC) for the PLB in question, we can calculate the horizon value by:

$$V_H = \frac{\text{ENGS}}{\text{WACC}} + \Sigma \frac{\text{INV}_t(\text{RONI}_t - \text{WACC})}{\text{WACC}(1 + \text{WACC})^t}$$

The derivation of this formula is a little complicated, and as such has been relegated to the appendix at the end of this chapter (see page 176). Note that in addition to the assumptions mentioned above, we are also assuming here that gearing remains constant (in other words, as retained earnings increase, borrowings increase in proportion, so that all new investment is financed by a constant mix of debt and equity).

At first glance, it is easy to reject this formula as not terribly useful, but some reflection shows that in fact it offers an insight into the transition period problem. We know that positive NPV investments come about because of some special advantage the firm has; this may be attributable to brand names, patents, efficiency, location or some other factor. The essential feature of all these (except, perhaps, location) is that eventually such advantages can be competed away; the question is one of timescale. That is what our formula attempts to capture; for how many years does the investment advantage continue? At the point when RONI falls to the WACC, the NPV of new investments has become zero, so the value of future growth is nil (this is one way of defining a 'mature industry'). This model therefore attempts to encapsulate the elements of our above discussion on this issue. However, there is a difference in assumption; where we used the perpetual growth model with a transition period model, the assumption is that *all* project cash flows change at the same rate. With the model we have described in this section, the assumption is that return changes progressively on all *new* investments, whilst the return on investments once in place remains constant.

Which of these assumptions is likely to prove the most reasonable in practice? The answer is that in the case of growth prospects diminishing through market saturation and/or new competition arriving, all cash flows are likely to decline at some rate. However, in the case where the expansion is into more marginal investment areas, and there are barriers to entry in existing markets, the assumptions of the growth opportunities model might be more defensible.

The continuous replication model

The assumption underlying this approach to terminal values is that the firm simply continues to invest in the same bundle of projects that it has at the end of the forecast horizon. This assumption amounts to saying that there will be no additional growth opportunities, and that the only investment necessary is that required to replace the existing asset base. Unlike the zero NPV model described below, the continous replication model assumes that the NPV on the replacement investment is the same as that on the existing investment.

If these assumptions are appropriate (and cases where this might be so include utility companies or ventures such as Eurotunnel), the terminal value in year H is simply the annual equivalent cash flow divided by the cost of capital. This calculation was described in detail in Chapter 3, with an example extended to show the effects of inflation (see the section on 'the FCF model and lumpy investment flows'); further examples are given in the discussion of accounting rates of return and RONI below. All we need note here is that following Chapter 6, the WACC should be used as the cost of capital.

The zero NPV model

This method of arriving at the terminal value assumes that all of the business's economic advantage has been competed away by the end of the specific forecast period (sometimes referred to as the erosion of economic rents). If this is the case, then the value of the firm is simply that value arrived at by estimating the value of the existing operations at the specific forecast horizon. In effect, this is a special case of the growth opportunities model, where the growth opportunities sum to zero. This suggests that the horizon value should be:

$$V_H = \frac{\text{ENGS}_H}{\text{WACC}}$$

As, in such a case, the shareholders would be strictly indifferent between further investment by the company or dividend payout, the value is also given by FCF_H/WACC. In fact, this type of final year earnings model will also give us the value of the firm in the case where the firm can still obtain a positive NPV on its existing projects, but does not have any growth opportunities. An example of this type of situation is given below.

The price–earnings multiple model

As we saw in Chapter 3, in a steady-state situation it is always possible to derive a prospective PE multiple to apply to the forecast earnings figure. The general formula, adapting that derived in Chapter 3 by recognising that the required return is the WACC, is:

$$\text{PE} = \frac{(1 - g/\text{RONI})}{\text{WACC} - g}$$

In the case where g, RONI and WACC are all industry averages such a PE ratio will itself be the industry average PE. However, for the reasons discussed in Chapter 5, it does not follow that the current industry average PE ratio will be representative of the forecast PE at the end of the specific forecast horizon, because cost of capital, growth rates and RONI figures may all change, at least in part because of inflation changes and cyclical factors. In this respect, we need to note that the steady-state scenario reflects *average* trading conditions and not those experienced during booms or recessions. Provided such factors are properly taken account of (in particular, see the comments below on accounting), it may be possible to use some average historical industry PE multiple, suitably adjusted, as a proxy for the horizon prospective PE multiple.

AN EXPLANATION OF THE RELATIONSHIP BETWEEN ACCOUNTING PROFIT AND PRESENT VALUES

Given that several of the above models require inputs either of earnings or of RONI, it is vital that we appreciate the relationships between accounting profits and 'earnings', as used in the above models, and between the accounting rate of return and RONI.

Unfortunately, accounting profits and accounting rates of return may be of surprisingly little help in estimating economic worth. As Edwards *et al.* (1987) note, 'Much of the economics literature is . . . very pessimistic about the applicability of accounting information to economic analysis'. We shall take a look at this issue using some simple examples to illustrate the main points;[4] for simplicity we shall ignore the effect of taxation throughout but discuss the implications of taxation at the end of our analysis.

The single investment case

Let us assume we wish to value Autunno,* one of Vivaldi plc's* four divisions. Initially, we shall assume no inflation, no gearing and an equity cost of capital of 10 per cent and that the product is made using a piece of machinery costing £400,000, which needs to be replaced every four years (assume that the machinery is worthless at the end of this period). We shall further assume that net cash inflows are £130,000 pa and look set to continue at that level for the forseeable future. Autunno has just replaced the machinery in question.

The value of each of Autunno's investment decisions is simply:

$$\text{NPV (£000)} = -400 + \frac{130}{1.1} + \frac{130}{1.1^2} + \frac{130}{1.1^3} + \frac{130}{1.1^4} = +12.082$$

As with our example of lumpy investment flows in Chapter 3, we can value the firm by calculating the annual equivalent cash flow that this represents, given that the firm will reinvest in such equipment every four years. The annual equivalent (AE) can be found from:

$$\text{AE (£000)} = \frac{\text{NPV}}{\text{4year, 10\% annuity factor}} = 3.812$$

As this is the annual equivalent each year to perpetuity, it follows that the NPV of the firm is 3.812/0.10 = £38.120. To find the value of the firm, we simply add this to the capital just provided to replace the machine, giving us a figure (the gross present value) of £438.12(000).

The first question is what is the return on this new investment? Clearly, if a conventional accounting definition of profit is used with straight line depreciation, the accounting rate of return will rise each year as the asset base falls. The average accounting rate of return (AARR) will be:

$$\text{AARR} = \frac{\text{Average profit (cash flow} - \text{depreciation)}}{\text{Mid-life book value of machinery}} = 15\%$$

This figure turns out to be of no real help in valuation because AARR and any other accounting-based return measures ignore time value of money. A more fruitful way of approaching the problem is to ask what return the shareholders expect, and how this relates to the new investment. Given that the company has constant cash flows, no growth opportunities and needs only to retain sufficient cash to reinvest in asset replacement, surplus cash can be paid out as dividends, in which case we shall expect the value of the firm to remain constant.

We already know that the shareholders require a 10 per cent return and, as the firm is valued at £438,120, this implies a required dividend of £43,812 pa if the market value of the firm is to remain constant. This equates to a return on new investment of £43,812/£400,000, which is equivalent to 10.95 per cent. This is not the AARR or anything like it; neither is it the internal rate of return.[5] An alternative and generally more useful way of calculating RONI in this type of continuously replicated investment situation is:

$$\text{RONI} = \frac{\text{Annual equivalent NPV} + (\text{WACC} \times \text{initial investment})}{\text{initial investment}}$$

Applying this to our example yields:

$$\text{RONI} = \frac{3812 + (0.10 \times 400,000)}{400,000} \quad 0.1095 \text{ or } 10.95\%$$

Whilst it is always possible to calculate such RONI figures, it is difficult to see the advantage of so doing; to arrive at the return figure, we need to know the NPV of the project in the first place. Once we know this, there is little point in deriving a rate of return to use in one of our valuation formulae, because it is easier to use the 'continuous replication' model. Note also that, because the investment pattern is not constant, it is not possible to use the accounting earnings figure of £30,000 pa (calculated using straight line depreciation) in any meaningful sense in the valuation process.[6]

Multiple investment projects

In general, the multiple project case involving 'lumpy' investment flows can be solved by extending the above analysis. However, we wish to show when the accounting rate of return *might* be useful for the purposes of valuing a business. Essentially, the accounting rate of return is only of use where investment flows are not lumpy in nature, the cash flows from such projects are constant (at least in real terms) and where the returns on all projects are similar. In order to illustrate this, suppose that Autunno expands each year by adopting a similar project until the end of year 3, when the expansion programme is complete. The cash flows, in £000s, will now be:

	Year 0	Year 1	Year 2	Year 3	Year 4	Year 5	Year 6	Year 7...
Investment	400	400	400	400	400	400	400	400
Inflows	130	130	130	130	130	130	130	130
FCF*	−400	−270	−140	− 10	120	120	120	120
Depreciation	100	200	300	400	400	400	400	400
Profit†		30	60	90	120	120	120	120

*Inflows − investment.
†Inflows − depreciation.

The value of the firm can now be calculated in one of two ways. First, using the 'continuous replication' model described above we know that the perpetual value of each project, continually replicated, is £38,120 in year 0 terms. One of these is added each year until year 3, giving us a NPV of:

$$\text{NPV of firm} = 38,120 + \frac{38,120}{1.1} + \frac{38,120}{1.1^2} + \frac{38,120}{1.1^3} = 132,910$$

Adding this to the £400,000 year 0 cost gives us the gross PV of £532,908, which is the year 0 value of the firm. Alternatively, we can obtain the same result by discounting the FCF figures for each year to perpetuity (this process is greatly eased by realising that the value of the firm in year 3 (and beyond) will be £1.2 million, the present value of a perpetual £120,000 cash flow from year 4 onwards).

The *accounting rate* of return from year 4 onwards will be given by the profit figure of £120,000 divided by the opening net book value of the assets, £1 million (the assets purchased over the previous four years will have net book values of £400,000, £300,000, £200,000, and £100,000 in ascending order of age); this figure now remains constant at 12 per cent. However, unless there is any future growth, there is no role for such a rate of return anyway, because all earnings are paid out as dividends. However, there is a role for the accounting profits figure since we can use the 'zero NPV model' (or, more correctly in this case, a zero growth model). As we have seen, this type of analysis could be used to give a horizon value. As a steady-state exists from year 4 onwards, the year 3 horizon value is:

$$V_3 = \text{ENGS/WACC} = 120/0.1 = £1200 \ (£000)$$

This is the same as the present value of cash flows to perpetuity.

However, so far we have ignored the important questions of growth and inflation. We shall look first at the significance of the accounting rate of return and accounting profits when the firm is growing at a constant rate.

The multiple investment project firm with growth

Extend the above example further by assuming that from year 5 onwards Autunno invests £60,000 in new projects at the start of year 5, expanding this investment by 3.75 per cent pa thereafter. The cash flows on these new investments are proportionate to those received on existing projects. All this produces the following *incremental* cash flows and profits:

Initial investment year	New invest- ment	Cash inflows in year (£000)							
		6	7	8	9	10	11	12	...
5	60.00	19.50	19.50	19.50	19.50	19.50	19.50	19.50	
6	62.25		20.23	20.23	20.23	20.23	20.23	20.23	
7	64.58			20.99	20.99	20.99	20.99	20.99	
8	67.01				21.78	21.78	21.78	21.78	
9	9.52					3.09	3.09	3.09	
10	9.88						3.21	3.21	
11	10.25							3.33	
Total cash inflow		19.50	39.73	60.72	82.50	85.59	88.80	92.13	
Total new investment	60.00	62.25	64.58	67.01	69.52	72.13	74.83	77.64	
Incremental FCF	−60.00	−42.75	−24.85	−6.28	12.98	13.46	13.97	14.49	
Depreciation		15.00	30.56	46.71	63.46	65.84	68.31	70.87	
Incremental earnings		4.50	9.17	14.01	19.04	19.75	20.49	21.26	

Notes: 1. New investment falls in year 9 because of the need to replace the year 5 original assets.
2. Depreciation is calculated on a straight line basis on the assets owned at the beginning of the year.

From this we can deduce several things. First, the firm is actually in a 'steady-state' of growth from year 9 onwards (after the first batch of assets have started to be replaced). Second, using the FCF growth formula, we can value the company at, say, the end of year 10 as:

$$V_{10} = \frac{FCF_{11}}{R - g} = \frac{13.97}{0.10 - 0.0375} = 223.52$$

Now the accounting book value of the new assets at the end of year 10 is found by calculating the net book value of each of the four assets, giving a figure of £173,914. We know that the year 11 profit is £20,490 so that the accounting rate of return on the new investment is $20,490/173,914 = 0.1178$ or 11.78 per cent (note that because of the year-end cash flow assumption underlying NPV, consistent accounting rates of return can only be found by using opening book values). We also know that in terms of the *new* earnings and investments, the payout rate $(1 - RE)$ is given by the incremental FCF divided by the incremental earnings, i.e. $13.97/20.49 = 0.6818$. The retention rate is thus $1 - 0.6818 = 0.3182$.

It should now be possible to arrive at a year 10 value for the new investment projects by using the price–earnings multiple formula that we used in Chapter 3:

$$PE = \frac{1 - g/\text{RONI}}{(R - g)}$$

Plugging in the relevant numbers gives us:

$$PE = \frac{1 - 0.0375/0.1178}{0.10 - 0.0375} = 10.91$$

As this is a prospective PE ratio, it must be applied to the forecast year 11 earnings to give the year 10 valuation. Doing so gives us:

$$V_{10} = 10.91 \times 20.49 = 223.54 \ (\pounds000)$$

Note, however, that this only works with constant rates of growth, cash flow and asset replacement. Finally, we need to discount this horizon value back to year 0 and add in to this value the present value of the year 5 to 10 cash flows and the value of the company's original set of projects. It is important to realise that the growth opportunities must be valued separately from the original (constant earnings) set because otherwise the growth rate changes over time as the new projects become a larger proportion of the firm's activities.

The growth case with inflation

Suppose that from year 7, a persistent rate of inflation of 10 per cent pa occurs; inflation continues at this level to perpetuity. A recalculation of the above numbers gives us the following accounting earnings, investments and cash flows (this time the depreciation calculation is shown to illustrate the problem of historic cost accounting depreciation):

Item	Year 7	Year 8	Year 9	Year 10	Year 11	Year 12
Cash flow	39.73	66.79	99.83	113.92	130.02	148.38
Depreciation						
purchase in t−1	15.56	16.15	18.42	21.03	24.0	27.39
t−2	15.00	15.56	16.15	18.42	21.03	24.00
t−3		15.00	15.56	16.15	18.42	21.03
t−4			15.00	15.56	16.15	18.42
Total depreciation	30.56	46.71	63.46	65.84	79.60	90.84

Incremental accounting earnings	9.17	20.08	34.69	42.76	50.42	57.54
New investment	64.58	73.71	84.12	96.00	109.56	125.03
FCF	−24.85	−6.92	15.70	17.92	20.46	23.35

First, we need to note that none of this poses any problems for the FCF growth model, provided a true steady-state has been reached. This still occurs in year 9, because the replacement cost of the assets is automatically reflected in the FCF figure. Growth is now at the nominal rate of 14.13 per cent pa (3.75 per cent in real terms) and the nominal cost of capital is now 21 per cent pa. This gives us a horizon value of the company in year 10 of:

$$V_{10} = \frac{20.46}{0.21 - 0.1413} = 297.82 \ (\pounds000)$$

In year 7 price levels, this is equivalent to the value we calculated above. If we now take our earnings figure and attempt to derive a PE ratio on the basis of year 9 or year 10 data, the result will *not* be compatible with that obtained by the FCF model. This is because the accounting book values and depreciation charges reflect two different rates of inflation, 0 and 10 per cent. However, once we reach the point where a *constant* inflation rate has uniformly affected all asset and depreciation figures,[7] then a PE multiple can be successfully applied. Taking year 11 as the point where this is achieved, we first need to sum the net book values of the assets, which results in a value of £212.09 (000). This implies an accounting rate of return of 50.42/212.09, which is equivalent to 23.77 per cent. Applying this to our PE formula produces the following ratio:

$$PE = \frac{1 - 0.1413/0.2377}{0.21 - 0.1413} = 5.9$$

We can now value the company in year 10 by applying this PE multiple to the prospective (year 11) earnings:

$$V_{10} = 5.9 \times 50.42 = 297.7 \ (\pounds000)$$

Apart from a minor rounding error, this is the same value as was achieved by the FCF method. It is also worth noting that inflation has the effect of increasing the retention rate (in this case to 40.6 per cent) because replacement cost is greater than that provided for with historic cost depreciation.

Finally, we must emphasise the fact that the PE approach only works if a consistent inflation rate is experienced throughout the life of all the assets held *and* during the horizon value period. The alternative, if we wish to use a PE methodology, is to restate all asset values and depreciation charges in horizon period price levels to give a real earnings figure, and then carry out the exercise using a real RONI, RE and *g* to give an appropriate multiple of real terms. This is generally the safer approach to apply, although we still need to know the age structure of the assets to estimate the inflation-adjusted horizon depreciation and asset value figures.

Conclusions on the use of accounting numbers in the valuation process

In general, numbers derived from accounting data can only be used where the investment flows are constant. We also require constant rates of growth, inflation and returns on new investment. The latter group of requirements constitute the standard assumptions of most of the horizon valuation methods (including, implicitly, the 'traditional' PE approach) and as such may not be unreasonable. However, the requirement that investment flows are constant may cause difficulties. Whilst both the growth opportunities and continuous replication models can cope with the situation where growth is not constant, those that rely upon accounting data inputs cannot. In this respect, we must also emphasise that some care is needed in defining RONI in such a case with the growth opportunities model.

The good news is that it appears that the circumstances under which accounting numbers are of most use are those that are often assumed to apply beyond the explicit forecast horizon. The bad news is that such a situation will almost certainly *not* have applied to any historic periods that may have been under review when preparing the forecast. Empirical results on whether such historic numbers are of any use in predicting economic value are somewhat thin on the ground, but a recent study by Kelly and Tippett (1991) suggests that the accounting rate of return 'is a potentially poor proxy for the future economic return'. The further bad news is that to make any sense of the accounting numbers we really need to know the age structure of the assets themselves. This is not a problem for a valuation being conducted with access to internal information, but it is so for an 'external' valuation. The best advice that can be given here is to look back through past annual reports in order to try and establish past patterns of asset replacement and the likely age of the assets.

Finally, we should note that our example is a simple illustrative one that has offered virtually no scope for 'creative accounting'. Reality may be somewhat different, providing many potential pitfalls for the naive external valuer reliant upon published accounting data. In so far as it is possible, accounts should always be restated on an 'objective' basis (from the valuer's perspective) before starting the analysis.[8]

TAXATION AND HORIZON VALUES

We need to consider the impact of taxation in those horizon models which assume growth. The continuous replication model automatically does this provided that the cash flows considered are those that arise after tax. In the case of the FCF growth and the PE multiple models, the steady-state period must be set in such a way as to ensure that it is the after-tax cash flows that are expanding at a constant rate. Where writing down allowances are less than 100 per cent pa and assets are retained for a long period of time, this can necessitate the specific forecasting of cash flows for some time into the future.

MODELLING THE PLB

By this stage, we have a set of cash flows for the specific forecast period, a horizon valuation and depending on the methodology chosen, possibly a transition period forecast as well. Taking our example of Autunno (the growth case but without inflation – which is the same result we would obtain with a *constant* inflation rate throughout, with all figures stated in real (year 0) terms), we have the position shown in Table 8.2.

Note that the original cash flows and growth cash flow terminal values have been modelled separately and then added together to give the horizon value.

The next step in the process, not shown here because of the simplicity of our example, would be to extend the model to produce the forecast profit and loss accounts and balance sheets at each year end. This was discussed in Chapter 4 but as we noted there, an important reason for producing such forecast accounting statements is to serve as consistency and logic checks on the process.

Finally, we should always perform a sensitivity analysis or 'scenario modelling' exercise as described in Chapter 4. All the key variables should be analysed in this way; such variables include not only the items discussed in Chapter 4 (sales, margins and so on) but also key value determinants like RONI, growth in FCF, amount of working capital, amount of fixed asset investment and the cost of capital. Where there is a mixture of growth opportunities and existing business (as in the case of Autunno Ltd), each has to be analysed separately in order to examine the effect of changes on value.

In the case of multi-line of business entities interactions between business areas, in particular the question of covariance, must be considered when performing any senisitivity or scenario analysis at company level.

VALUING THE BUSINESS

Having valued the PLB and analysed the sensitivity of the value to changes in the key variables, it is a relatively simple step to value the firm as a whole. We have already discussed the issue of optimal asset utilisation in Chapter 5, and noted that we should value each PLB in terms of its 'as is' value, and its value to the business (in other words, its value adopting optimal strategies and taking account of any economies of scale or scope achievable by the business as a whole). We further concluded that as long as this value to the business was greater than the disposable value of the

Table 8.2 Autunno Ltd

LR growth pa 3.75%   Discount rate 10%

	Year 0	Year 1	Year 2	Year 3	Year 4	Year 5	Year 6	Year 7	Year 8	Year 9	Sum of Specific forecast	Horizon value	Total value Year 0
FCF original	-400.00	-270.00	-140.00	-10.00	120.00	120.00	120.00	120.00	120.00	120.00		1200.00	
FCF increase		-270.00	-140.00	-10.00		-60.00	-42.75	-24.85	-6.28	12.98		215.47	
FCF Total	-400.00			-10.00	120.00	60.00	77.25	95.15	113.72	132.98		1415.47	
Discount factor	1.00	0.91	0.83	0.75	0.68	0.62	0.56	0.51	0.47	0.42		0.42	
Present value	552.72	-245.45	-115.70	-7.51	81.96	37.26	43.61	48.83	53.05	56.40	-47.57	600.30	552.72
Value of PLB at year end		878.00	1105.80	1226.38	1229.01	1291.91	1343.86	1383.09	1407.68	1415.47			
Accounting data													
Earnings		30.00	60.00	90.00	120.00	120.00	124.50	129.17	134.01	139.04			
Prospective PE	18.42	14.63	12.29	10.22	10.24	10.38	10.40	10.32	10.12	9.81*			

*Note that while the prospective PE on both existing and new earnings is the same from year 9, the combined ratio changes as the proportion of earnings from new investment increases.

activity, it should be retained. Assuming that we have gone through this process and are now attempting to value the company as a whole, what observations can we make?

First, the value of the firm is the sum of the present values of the individual component PLBs, or their disposable values (appropriately discounted and with full allowance for selling costs) if these are greater than such going concern values. Note that whilst the correlation of cash flows between different PLBs affects the probability distribution of values, the *expected* present value of the firm will simply be the sum of the present values of each PLB.

Second, we need to add in the value of any *financial* assets owned by the business. Discounted FCFs at the WACC properly value the operational aspects of the company but any items like trade investments, cash invested in government bonds and so on will not have been included. Given our conclusions that markets are largely price efficient (unless we have 'inside' knowledge), the appropriate value for such financial assets must be their current market value.

Finally, we often need the value of *equity* rather than the value of the firm as a whole. The financing structure of the firm simply divides up the value of the firm between various claimants, so that the value of the equity is the total value of the firm less the value of the other claims, such as debt, convertibles and preference shares. As the valuation of debt and convertibles has already been dealt with in Chapters 6 and 7, we can summarise the whole process as shown in Figure 8.2.[9]

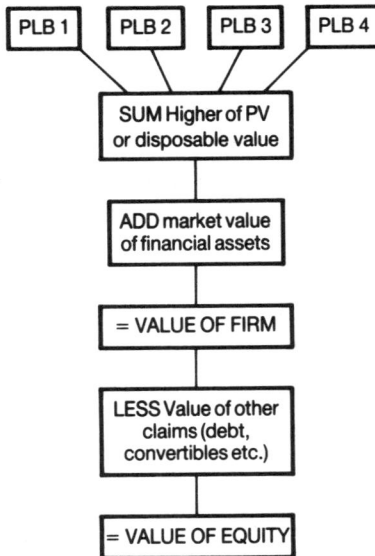

Figure 8.2 Valuing the multi-business company.

APPENDIX: DERIVATION OF
GROWTH OPPORTUNITIES MODEL

In the case of the zero growth firm, we know that ENGS = DIV and that with gearing the value of the firm is given by:

$$V_0 = \frac{ENGBT(1 - T)}{r_{eu}} + TD = \frac{ENGS}{WACC}$$

Where ENGBT = earnings before tax and ENGS = earnings after tax = ENGBT(1 − T). All other notation is as defined in Chapter 6. Now suppose growth opportunities arise requiring an investment in year t of INV_t, after allowing for the value of any capital allowances. Taking a horizon of N years, provided that gearing (and hence WACC) remains constant, we can write the value of the firm as:

$$V_0 = \frac{ENGS_1 - INV_1}{(1 + WACC)^1} + \frac{ENGS_2 - INV_2}{(1 + WACC)^2} +$$

$$\ldots \frac{ENGS_N - INV_N}{(1 + WACC)^N} + \frac{V_N}{(1 + WACC)^N}$$

If we assume that the return made on any one year's investment is constant at $RONI_N$, we get:

$$V_0 = \frac{ENGS_1 - INV_1}{(1 + WACC)^1} + \frac{ENGS_1 + (RONI_1 \times INV_1) - INV_2}{(1 + WACC)^2} +$$

$$\ldots \frac{ENGS_1 + (RONI_{N-1}) \times INV_{N-1}) - INV_N}{(1 + WACC)^N} + \frac{V_N}{(1 + WACC)^N}$$

This can be written as:

$$V_0 = \sum_{t=1}^{N} \frac{ENGS_1}{(1 + WACC)} + INV_1 \left(\frac{RONI_1}{(1 + WACC)^2} + \ldots \frac{RONI_1}{(1 + WACC)^N} \right.$$

$$\left. - \frac{1}{(1 + WACC)} \right) + INV_2 \left(\frac{RONI_2}{(1 + WACC)^2} + \ldots \frac{RONI_2}{(1 + WACC)^N} \right.$$

$$\left. - \frac{1}{(1 + WACC)^2} \right) \ldots + \frac{V_N}{(1 + WACC)^N}$$

Which on summation gives:

$$V_0 = \sum_{t=1}^{N} \frac{ENGS_1}{(1 + WACC)^t} + \sum_{t=1}^{N} INV_t \left[\left(\sum_{T=t+1}^{N} \frac{RONI_t}{(1 + WACC)^T} \right) \right.$$

$$\left. - \frac{1}{(1 + WACC)^t} \right] + \frac{V_N}{(1 + WACC)^N}$$

Our purpose here is to calculate the horizon value of the firm, so our summation should be to infinity. Doing so means that the first term becomes simply ENGS/WACC, the last term, which discounts V_N to the present, becomes insignificantly small and similarly:

$$\frac{RONI_t}{(1 + WACC)^T} = \frac{1}{(1 + WACC)^t} \times \frac{RONI_t}{WACC}$$

Substituting these into our above expression yields:

$$V_0 = \frac{ENGS_1}{WACC} + \sum_{t=1}^{\infty} INV_t \left(\frac{RONI_t}{(1 + WACC)^t} - \frac{1}{(1 + WACC)^t} \right)$$

Multiplying through gives us the expression we seek for the growth opportunities model:

$$V_0 = \frac{ENGS_1}{WACC} + \sum_{t=1}^{\infty} \frac{INV_t(RONI_t - WACC)}{WACC(1 + WACC)^t}$$

However, in the case where growth from new investment is only expected to continue for N years into the future, the summation is simply continued to year N instead of infinity. When we are calculating horizon values using this type of model, we typically assume N to be a number of years beyond the horizon, with the horizon value, V_H, being given by:

$$V_H = \frac{ENGS_H}{WACC} + \sum_{t=H+1}^{N} \frac{INV_t(RONI_t - WACC)}{WACC(1 + WACC)^t}$$

CHAPTER 9

OTHER ASPECTS OF
VALUATION

In this chapter, we look at some special situations where value is determined by issues other than the existing state value of the business as a going concern. In Chapter 5, where we discussed asset valuation, we have already looked at the value of the business in alternative form, i.e. we proposed analysing break-up and liquidation value of each PLB to check on whether or not each activity was achieving the best possible value as a going concern. In this chapter, we look at the special cases of the additional value created by takeovers and mergers (which for simplicity we shall refer to throughout this chapter as simply 'mergers'), and the problem of valuing minority stakes.

In the case of mergers involving listed companies, successful acquirers normally pay a figure in excess of the current market price, which can be viewed as a control premium paid to purchase certain special benefits; we discuss the value of these benefits below. As we have seen in earlier chapters, the market value of listed companies should reflect the going concern value of firms following existing and currently planned strategies. The value of one share represents a proportionate value of this amount. The same cannot be said of unlisted companies, where shareholdings tend to be concentrated in the hands of relatively few individuals; we therefore look at the special case of valuing minority shareholdings in such firms from a non-legal and non-taxation perspective.

Finally in this chapter, we also take a brief look at the so-called 'trade norms' sometimes applied in valuing businesses.

THE VALUE OF MERGER BENEFITS

There is considerable evidence to suggest that many acquiring firms pay premiums that may be too high; estimates of these premia vary considerably, but in a recent UK study Limmack (1991) reports premia as high as 37.1 per cent which is similar to Firth's (1980) finding of 38 per cent, whilst in the United States Jensen and Ruback (1983) find an average premium of 30 per cent; Eckbo and Langohr (1986) report 53 per cent on French cash offers, versus 20 per cent for those in exchange for securities (evidence on bid premia is discussed in more detail in Chapter 10).

Recent anecdotal examples of firms paying too much for their targets include Marks and Spencer's acquisition of Brooks Brothers,[1] and Boots' acquisition of Ward White (*FT*, 14 November 1991). *Acquisitions Monthly* (November 1989, August 1991) reports the following average bid premia for the United Kingdom over the past five years:

Year	Bid premium over price 1 month before offer (%)
1986	46
1987	39
1988	38
1989	36
1990	32

Whilst this appears to suggest a continued downward movement in such premia, the first two quarters of 1991 show a marked increase; *Acquisitions Monthly* reports that the average premium in the second quarter of 1991, 'reached an unprecedented 60 per cent' and suggests that 'Share offer premiums continue to be affected by the bidders' decreasing share price'. This phenomenon is roughly what we might expect if bidding firms were paying too much for their victims.

Given the sort of premia discussed above, we might view such amounts as extremely demanding in terms of the merger benefits required, and this begs the question of whether firms are over-optimistic in their estimation of these benefits. Accordingly, we shall attempt to investigate the sources of such benefits. The first of these is synergy, which basically assumes that the profitability of a business combination is greater than the profitability of the two component companies added together because some efficiency gain will result from the merger.

Synergy

Synergy might reasonably be expected to occur because of economies of scale. Such benefits can relate to production, through the more intensive use of plant and equipment (the implication here may well be the rationalisation of some of the post-combination assets of the firm), by increased throughput from moving the labour force further down the so-called 'experience' or learning curve (for example, the Boston Consulting Group claims that this is an important factor in the claimed association of market share and profitability[2]), or by increased purchasing power in raw materials markets. Other cost benefits relate to administration costs and marketing and distribution costs. Gains may also be experienced in the area of research and development. The common feature of all these benefits is that they are likely to be associated with horizontal integration, i.e. a merger between firms in the same industry. The cash flow saving resulting from these benefits can normally be estimated without too much difficulty, although over-optimism needs to be guarded against. In particular, the acquiring company management should not just be asked to quantify such savings, but should also be asked to specify when and how such savings will be achieved. As such business combinations will be in common lines of business, the existing cost of capital can normally be used as the discount rate, but due allowance must be made for changes in gearing (see Chapter 6). However, certain types of cost reduction have a lower systematic risk than normal synergystic savings. Near certain fixed cost savings can be discounted at a lower rate because, as we saw in Chapter 6, the β stream of fixed costs should be similar to the β of debt (in fact, if the benefit was *absolutely* certain (an extremely unlikely event) the appropriate discount rate would be the risk-free rate of return). We must be careful to emphasise the words 'near certain'; it should be borne in mind that in the long term few costs are really fixed, and it is the long term that is of interest to us here.

Second, some synergystic benefits might be expected to occur in vertical integrations. A vertical integration is one where companies at different stages of the manufacturing process combine; examples include clothing retailers taking over their suppliers and computer manufacturers buying software houses. Benefits here might include the elimination of selling costs and obtaining security of sourcing or outlets; besides the gain in terms of risk elimination, a direct result might be the need for lower stock levels. Note, however, that in all these cases it is possible in principle to obtain similar benefits by co-operative trade agreements; mergers might actually be an expensive and inefficient way of realising such benefits. When valuing these benefits, the general comments on value made above are relevant; however, the discount rate chosen now needs to reflect the systematic or market risk of the PLB where the savings arise.

Third, there may be benefits in terms of financial synergy. Financial synergy comes about when either direct borrowing costs or transactions costs are reduced. It is worth examining why such savings may come about in a little more detail. The evidence clearly suggests that size is an important factor in the determination of corporate cost of capital, for several reasons. In the case of any capital issue offered through the markets, the transactions cost of the issue tends to vary in inverse proportion to the amount being raised. Along with this, access to certain markets can only be obtained by companies of a certain size; examples include the ability to list shares on foreign stock exchanges (thereby widening the investor base) and issuing bonds on the Euromarkets. Additionally, the shares of larger companies will be more marketable (in a liquidity sense), resulting in a lower bid–ask spread which, rationally, should lead to a reduction in any liquidity premium required by shareholders. It is also possible that both equity and borrowing costs are reduced for larger firms because of the wider availability of information on such companies. Large firms are very much in the public eye; they are studied by a significant number of analysts, by the financial press and may also be rated by credit rating agencies, such as Moody's. All this means that for either an equity investor in, or a potential lender to, a large firm, the costs of acquiring information are considerably reduced compared to the cost for smaller firms. Even if these smaller firms are listed, they may be studied by comparatively few analysts and it may be unlikely that there will be much publicly available information on such companies, except for the published accounts. Furthermore, in this situation there is a greater risk of 'informed' investors being able to deal at the expense of the 'naive' or 'uninformed'; this should lead to an increase in the bid–ask spread for such firms (Glosten and Milgrom, 1985), again implying an increased cost of capital. Note that financial synergies of the type discussed here will be size driven, and as such it does not matter whether the merger takes the form of a vertical, horizontal or conglomerate integration.

Another reason why borrowing costs tend to be lower for large companies may be because of risk reduction. This might, in part, be due to the enhanced visibility of the company, but it is more likely to be associated with benefits from diversification. To the extent that a diversified company is less prone to a costly liquidation, it may be able to borrow more and, as we know from Chapter 6 that this *may* give rise to increased valuable tax shields, a gain in the value of the combined equity may result. Furthermore, a similar benefit may result without any increased gearing if the combined firm is more likely to benefit from debt tax shields because of lower profit volatility. However, the argument that lower borrowing costs are achieved for reasons other than the avoidance of liquidation costs or the gain of realised tax shields is suspect. This is because the reduction of risk achieved by debt holders is simply offset by a loss in the value of limited liability achieved by shareholders. It should be noted that this argument applies to the positions of *existing* debt holders; if two firms merge, the value of the outstanding debt will tend to increase because each firm now effectively guarantees the other's debt position. As, in the absence of other synergies, the value of the two firms remains the same in total, if the value of the debt rises, the value of the equity should fall (it is possible to prove this using the option pricing model discussed in Chapter 8; see Galai and Masulis (1976) for an explanation). In the case of *new* debt issued by the combined firm, both debt and equity holders will merely receive a fair return for the systematic risk they are taking on. It must always be borne in mind that rational investors will hold diversified portfolios; a pure conglomerate merger does them no favours because they can replicate the investment portfolio that the combined firm represents themselves for a minor payment in transactions costs. However, as we have noted above, the tax shield issue and the ability to avoid costly liquidations changes this result, although it does not seem credible to believe that the effect could be large enough to justify anything other than a marginal bid premium.

Tax shield and transactions costs savings are best dealt with through the APV model described in Chapter 6.

Strategic value from mergers

In addition to the desire to benefit from synergy, there are several strategic motives for mergers, some of which are rational and some of which are irrational. In this sense, 'rational' means value adding; in other words, the acquirer must gain a positive net present value from the business combination. It is helpful to dichotomise strategic reasons into defensive and aggressive ones. Defensive reasons can include protection from cyclical exposure or exposure to one industry, protection of markets or supplies, buying needed expertise, capacity reduction or the need to achieve a certain minimum size and the requirement to move away from a concentration in a declining industry.

Some of these have been discussed under 'synergy' above, and some can be immediately dismissed as irrational motives from the investors' perspective, although they may well be rational from a managerial one. If we take the general case of diversification, we have already observed that management are merely performing a task that shareholders can do for themselves. There are clear and powerful incentives for management to diversify, as they receive added protection from cyclical and industrial exposure,[3] although unless subsequent performance is satisfactory there is always the danger of the market 'disciplining' an under-achieving post combination firm. Our task here is to investigate under what circumstances it might make sense for managers to do this rather than the shareholders.

Liquidation costs
First, as liquidations are costly affairs, business combinations that diversify away some risk do offer something to the shareholders. However, they gain only the present value of the reduction in *expected* liquidation costs. In a US study, Warner (1977), estimates that the average bankruptcy costs for a sample of eleven US railroads was in the order of 1.4 per cent of their market value five years before bankruptcy. By contrast, Altman (1984) gives a much higher figure of 11–17 per cent of the market value three years prior to bankruptcy for his sample. If we wanted to predict the expected bankruptcy cost for other US companies from this data, we would need to multiply this percentage by the probability of the company becoming bankrupt, and discount this figure back to the present, which is likely to produce a small figure. Whilst it is unwise to extrapolate too much from small sample US studies, we might adopt a slightly cynical attitude to claims that the avoidance of expected liquidation costs is a justification for the observed level of bid premia.

Taxation
Second, diversification may allow the realisation of some tax shield

benefits on increased borrowing; this point was discussed above. However, other taxation benefits may be related to this argument. To some extent, corporation tax has option-like properties in that taxation authorities receive a positive payment when the firm makes a profit, but do not make a payout themselves when the firm makes a loss (Ball and Bowers, 1986); it is true, of course, that carry-forward provisions and the like exist, but these still represent a timing disadvantage. If two firms with less than perfectly correlated profit flows merge, the value of the taxation authority's 'option' is reduced, because to some extent the losses of one part of the firm can be used to offset the profits of the other; as the value of the taxing authority's position is reduced, it follows that that of the shareholders must be improved. However, it must be concluded that whilst there are undoubtedly some benefits to diversification that can be achieved only through merger, they are unlikely to be particularly large. In fact, a recent empirical study by Morck *et al.* (1990) finds that acquisitions driven by a diversification are associated with poor post-merger performance, which is precisely what we would expect if acquirers paid a high premium to acquire marginal benefits. It may also be the case that these benefits are lost in the additional problems generated by managing a business outside the realms of existing experience.

Threat elimination
Clearly, the combination of firms to eliminate threats (be these to outlets, supplies or market share) might yield some benefits to the shareholders of combining companies. For example, it has long been recognised in the economics literature that collusion in price setting leads to the increased profitability of the co-operating parties.[4] One way of achieving such an effect is through merger; the resulting shareholder gain is, of course, achieved at the expense of society in general, which is why many countries have legislation in place to prevent the abuse of oligopolistic and monopolistic positions. However, many of the actions available to government (such as the referral of a bid to a monopolies and mergers commission) are discretionary, and to some extent this means that companies may be able to realise such benefits by judicious use of lobbying and so on.

The perverse position of declining industries
The management of firms in stagnant or declining industries often wish to diversify into other activities; this is understandable, but rarely reflects the interests of the shareholders. Unless management has a competitive advantage in the area they wish to move in to (and in general this is unlikely to be the case), they may well do better to concentrate on extracting the best results possible from the industry they are currently in (one sad consequence of some recent diversifications of this type has been a managerial neglect of core businesses) and pay out surplus cash to the shareholders as dividends. There are two possible exceptions to this; first,

there is the perversity of legislation in many countries (including the United Kingdom) which only allows dividends to be paid out of past or current profits. This can prevent loss-making companies in declining industries from rationalising assets and distributing the proceeds to shareholders, which would be the economically efficient solution; however, in some countries (again including the United Kingdom) this difficulty can be avoided, for example, by including an application to the courts to allow a capital restructuring. The second problem, which will affect companies with a large percentage of higher rate tax payers amongst the shareholders, is the tax implication of such a payout. As companies in such a situation may well be loss makers, any ACT paid may be irrecoverable, and a large tax burden would be imposed upon the shareholders. It may therefore be efficient for the firm to diversify because of tax considerations; unfortunately, such reasons can be used as effective smokescreens for management acting in its own best interest.

Aggressive reasons

Turning to the aggressive strategic reasons for acquisitions, we again find market share to be one such reason, along with an ability to employ price increases; this general class of gains is sometimes referred to as the 'product-market-power argument' (Krinsky *et al.*, 1988). In addition, we have considerations such as the extension of existing markets (including overseas expansion), joint ventures, the purchase of growth opportunities, acquiring assets at a discount, the purchase of valuable brands, the acquisition of technological advantage and the purchase of valuable options. In general, a great deal of care is needed in the evaluation and appraisal of these areas; the closer the expansion activity is to the firm's existing business, the more likely it is that management will understand the processes involved and be able to value them. Note that with several of these reasons, expansion can take place through direct investment (sometimes called *organic growth*) or through acquisition; we therefore return to the issues raised in Chapter 5 when we discussed the replacement, or replication, value of assets. As we noted there, the general experience is that market values are less than replacement costs of the physical assets; this relationship is measured through the q ratio. If this is less than 1.0, it may be cheaper to adopt the acquisition route rather than the direct purchase one. Given that the observed US ratio has sometimes been less than 0.6, some commentators have suggested that the q ratio phenomenon may partially explain the size of observed bid premia. A US study by Bartley and Boardman (1984), using a sample of thirty-three matched pairs, reports that the average q ratio for target companies, at 0.57, was significantly less than that observed for non-targets (0.75); a further US study by Chappell and Cheng (1984) supports this view that q ratios are important factors in mergers. The theoretical issues relating to q ratios have already been discussed, but it is worth re-emphasising that both the achievable returns (measured by NPV) and the true replication costs of the business (including the non-physical assets) need to be considered.

Brand values

As regards brand purchase, brand values have again been the subject of discussion in Chapter 5. Such values are implicit in the going concern price of the business, and if capital markets are operating efficiently their values should be reflected in the existing market capitalisation of the acquisition target. The key question to be addressed is why the brands are worth more to the acquirer than they are in the hands of the extant management. To some extent, the answer might lie in the efficiency of the brands' current managers (efficiency considerations are discussed below) and to a degree increased value may result from a more intense use or marketing of the brand. None the less, problems can arise for acquirers here; first, brand values can easily be over-estimated (many commentators feel that Ford paid too much for Jaguar's brand name, for example), and a more intensive development of a brand can, in some cases, devalue it through the loss of 'exclusivity'.

Cross-border synergies

An area where particular strategic issues may be important is in cross-border acquisitions. Harris and Ravenscraft (1991) suggest that cross-border acquisitions allow multi-national enterprises (MNEs) to capitalise on monopoly rents and propose that a particular area of interest is that of research and development activity. This is because 'R&D creates both a barrier to entry and monopoly power through patents.' Furthermore, markets are inefficient in allowing technology transfer because licensing arrangements and the like can be abused. In addition, the need to recover extensive R&D costs requires larger markets. Other reasons for MNE cross-border acquisitions might include differential tax advantages, different accounting treatments between domestic and foreign reporting (in theory this should not motivate takeovers but in practice it may), and differential currency strength (although this implies that capital markets are either pricing cost of capital inefficiently or that the currencies themselves are mispriced; see Chapter 4). One of several interesting findings from the Harris and Ravenscraft paper, which went on to analyse the gains received by US victim shareholders on domestic versus foreign takeovers, is that foreign buyers, 'consistently pay substantially higher premiums for US firms than do US buyers' (in fact, 39.8 per cent against 26.3 per cent, which is significant after controlling for whether the bid is for cash[5] and whether or not there are multiple bids). They also find that cross-border takeovers tend to be more concentrated in R&D-intensive industries than domestic takeovers, and that three-quarters of their sample of cross-border takeovers occur between companies in related industries. Finally, it appears that currency strength also is an explanatory factor; when the buyer's currency is strong relative to the dollar, the bid premium is higher. Of course, it is possible to argue that such a result is not compatible with a belief in the efficiency of international capital and/or currency markets.

Valuing potential benefits
One thing that we can note from the above list of aggressive strategic motivations is the difficulty of identifying *exactly* what it is that is being acquired, in cash flow terms. In many cases, we are dealing with the acquisition of things which are effectively *options*. For example, buying growth opportunities, research expertise and products under development, and all manner of other potential benefits can all be viewed as the purchase of a right (but not an obligation) to enter a possibly profitable market in the future. Unfortunately, a DCF methodology is not particularly useful at dealing with this type of problem and a PE approach is wholly inadequate. In the end, there really are only two ways of handling this situation. Where possible, we can think about such cases in terms of option pricing; an example that does this is given below. However, given the unknowns involved and the sheer complexity of the necessary calculations, in many cases the valuation of such options will be judgemental. In effect, we will have estimated the DCF value of the firm (or PLB) and be able to match this with either the observed market price or a likely acquisition price. Clearly, if the DCF value (or value prepared on some other basis) is greater than the latter, the options are simply 'in for free'; where the latter price is greater than the DCF value, it becomes a matter of opinion as to whether the value of the options to the buyer justify the premium over the calculated value. None the less, before rushing to such judgements it is worth at least attempting to value such options (even a crude attempt is better than none at all); accordingly, we shall have a look at a simple example of how such an analysis might be conducted.

Valuing options arising on merger

Let us imagine that we are advising Samantha Grabbit of Megapredator plc, which amongst its many operations has interests in hotel and tourism. Samantha has cast her eye over the Cabernet Sauvignon Hotel Group,* which is about to be privatised by the Ruritanian Government. Having read earlier chapters of this book, Samantha has valued the group on a DCF basis and reckons that the whole operation is worth about 95 million Ruritanian dollars (R$), which is a great pity since she has strong reason to believe that the Government will not sell for anything less than R$100 million. Part of the problem is that Ruritanian tourism faces a very uncertain future; none the less, if the industry goes well the Cabernet Sauvignon Hotel Group owns some potentially valuable sites which could be exploited. The necessary development would be made five years from now (in 1997) with a cost of development amounting to around R$120 million; on the basis of *expected* cash flows, the present value of the inflows (discounted back to 1997) would only be $100 million, which suggests that the investment is not going to be worthwhile (and hence none of the associated cash flows have been included in the appraisal of current value). However, as Samantha has pointed out, the standard deviation of the value of these projected cash flows is very large, in fact somewhere in the order of 60 per cent pa.[6] It is possible, therefore, that buying the Cabernet Sauvignon Hotel Group might end up giving access to a very exciting growth market. The problem, of course, is how to value the option that the purchase of the group represents.

The additional information that we need is the cost of capital of the venture itself (let us say that this is 23 per cent pa) and the Ruritanian equivalent risk-free rate – suppose that on a continuously compounded basis this is 12 per cent pa. We also need to arm ourselves with the relevant section from Chapter 7 (including the area tables given in Appendix B, (page 234)). First, we should note that the exercise price of the option is R$120 million, and *today's* (1992) value of the asset on which we have the option is R$100 million discounted for five years at 23 per cent giving us a present value of R$35.52 million. Note that when we value an option on a share, the market price has already discounted the company's estimated cash flow at the required rate of return, so that the price already is a present value.

Now we know from Chapter 7 that the value of a call option is given by the Black and Scholes model, which is:

$$C = SN(d_1) - Xe^{-rt}N(d_2)$$

In the original model, S is the current share price, X the exercise price and e^{-rt} is a continuously compounded discount factor for t years at a risk-free rate of r, where t is the number of years to expiry of the option. In this case, all the terms have the same meaning except that S becomes the present value of the asset being acquired. As we know $N(d_1)$ and $N(d_2)$, are cumulative probabilitiy density functions; to convert values of d_1 and d_2 to probabilities we need the tables which give the areas under a normal curve given in Appendix B (see page 234). The values of d_1 and d_2 are given by:

$$d_1 = \frac{\ln(S/X) + r \times t}{\sigma.\sqrt{t}} + [0.5 \times (\sigma.\sqrt{t})]$$

and:

$$d_2 = d_1 - \sigma.\sqrt{t}$$

In this case $\ln(S/X)$ is the natural logarithm of the ratio of the present value of the asset to the exercise price and σ is the standard deviation of the asset's cash flow.

The first step in arriving at the value of the option is the calculation of the values for d_1 and d_2:

$$d_1 = \frac{\ln(35.52/120) + (0.12 \times 5)}{0.6 \times \sqrt{5}} + [0.5 \times 0.6 \times \sqrt{5}] = 0.2106$$

$$d_2 = 0.2106 - (0.6 \times \sqrt{5}) = -1.131$$

Turning to our normal area tables in the Appendix, t is the value of d_i; turning to the value for $N(d_1)$ and looking up 0.2106 we find $N(t) = 0.5832$; for $N(d_2)$, following a similar procedure we obtain a value of 0.1292. Plugging these values into our option pricing formula yields:

$$C = (35.52 \times 0.5832) - (120 \times 0.5488 \times 0.1292) = R\$12.21 \text{ million}$$

Thus we find that by going ahead with the purchase, Samantha would be acquiring an option with an approximate value of R$12.21 million; adding this to the present value of cash flows from existing businesses produces a maximum price payable of R$107.21 million. On this basis, an acquisition for R$ 100 million looks like a reasonably good deal. Of course, in the real world there are additional complications; for example, the adoption of the expansion project might in turn produce options on further expansion (for example, the extension of the new hotels). In addition, the option valuation produced above uses an option pricing model derived in the context of frictionless markets with continuous trading oportunities; a particular requirement is that a risk-free hedge can be established, by holding the asset and selling an appropriate ratio of call options on that asset. Whilst, in principle, this could be done (one way would be by offering options on a joint venture in the development, something that might be achievable through the use of a form of warrants) in practice it would be difficult to achieve. Given this problem, the use of a sophisticated pricing model to value such an option can only be regarded as an approximation. In spite of this objection, it must be clear that such an option to develop a site at a future date must have some value; an approximation of this might logically be expected to be better than ignoring the value altogether.

In addition to this concept of valuing expansion potential, there are valuable options available to acquiring management on the abandonment of projects that turn out to be losers. The options considered here are known as *put* options, because they offer the alternative of selling the asset for its abandonment value. In principle, a put option can be valued using the Black–Scholes model and the so-called 'put–call parity' relationship which simply shows that the value of a put option equals the value of a call (computed in the usual way) less the present value of the asset plus the present value of the exercise price.[7] However, some degree of caution is necessary when valuing such put options because the 'exercise price' is the liquidation value of the project. Such a figure is liable to fluctuate (something which the Black–Scholes model does not allow); a good example of how mistakes might be made here is found in the case of UK property assets. How many valuers would have anticipated correctly the liquidation value of property assets in 1991 from a 1988 perspective?

There are other cases where option pricing models can make a useful contribution; these include the flexibility to delay the adoption of a project (see Stark (1990) for a discussion) and an application to research and development expenditure (Roberts and Weitzman, 1981); as Copeland and Weston (1988) note, 'The main theme is that flexibility has value'. However, before we leave this topic one point that must be emphasised is that in the case of listed companies in efficient and informed markets, the values of such options will already be reflected in the market capitalisation of the company currently owning them.

Efficiency improvement gains

The area we are concerned with here is not efficiency gain from synergy or strategic benefit, but from the acquiring company's management realising greater value from the business than the incumbent management. Such gains can come from cost reduction, revenue increases, greater asset utilisation or more effective capital investment. Takeovers may also be a way of allowing swifter adjustment to changing market conditions (Pound et al., 1986) or an effective means of bringing about a cultural change in the organisation that in some way improves productivity or efficiency.

It is important to separate differential efficiency from the issue of general managerial inefficiency (Copeland and Weston, 1988). With the former, we are looking at the position where a management team can be managing well, but a rival team may be better at managing those particular resources; this would perhaps be an explanatory factor in horizontal mergers. In the latter case, the assumption is that management is simply inept and any competent team would do better; in so far as this may lead to a rationale for conglomerate mergers, a pertinent question is whether the acquiring management really has the necessary skills to run the business they are planning on buying. In short, we should be more sceptical about whether efficiency gains will actually be realised if management do not have a particular expertise in the business they are buying.

An interesting special case is that of the management buyout. Whilst they do have the necessary skills (one hopes), it is a reasonable question to ask why the efficiency gains have not be made already; does this imply that the changes are rather harder to implement than might be first thought, or is it simply a case of management acting in its own interest?

Finally, it is worth noting that Roll (1986) in his famous 'hubris hypothesis' suggests that managers are generally over-optimistic when evaluating takeover benefits; as such, they tend to over-bid so that most (or even more than 100 per cent) of the gains end up being received by the acquired company's shareholders. These issues relating to merger gains in practice and the bargaining area are explored in Chapter 10; for now, we should simply note the danger and look for very specific budgets for efficiency improvements, with detailed plans of how they are to be achieved. It is not good enough to make general statements like 'we could increase profits by 10 per cent just through efficiency improvements'.

Taxation considerations

There are several possible tax motivations for mergers besides those discussed earlier; perhaps the most obvious is the utilisation of past tax losses. The usual assumption here is that a profitable acquirer takes over a target with past losses; in fact, a US study finds that it is more the case of acquiring firms losses being used to offset the taxable income of firms acquired (Auerbach and Reishus, 1987). In the United Kingdom, losses made by the acquired company post-acquisition may be used to offset profits made elsewhere in the group, provided that the relevant subsidiary is at least 75 per cent owned (this is known as group relief). However, past losses may only be utilised as tax shields against the future profits of the acquired company if the business of that company is continued. There is no restriction on the profits from a subsidiary being sheltered from taxation by the use of past losses from the acquirer.

Other tax considerations for acquiring companies involve the treatment of losses when subsidiaries are sold from one group to another, the treatment of unrelieved ACT and the possible crystallisation of capital gains tax liability on the sale of any subsidiaries: a detailed exploration of taxation and mergers is beyond the scope of this book, but an outline of the main UK taxation considerations on mergers can be found in Cooke (1986), whilst the taxation implications of takeovers in other countries is covered in Cooke (1988).

The main point that seems to emerge here concerning UK takeovers is that there may be tax advantages to be gained from the merger, but only if the acquired business can be continued; in other words, it is not possible to 'asset strip' the company to the extent that there is a substantial change in the nature of the trade and still obtain the benefit of past tax losses. It should also be noted that the past losses are potentially equally valuable to any acquirer and we therefore have a taxation logic for conglomerate mergers that covers the cases of loss-making target companies or loss-making acquirers. We have already mentioned one other, concerned with the covariability of taxable profit flows, above.

Finally, we should note that there are taxation considerations involved that affect the personal tax position of the shareholders of the acquiring and acquired companies. We have already discussed the problem of firms in declining industries and the dividend payout alternative to acquisitions; in Chapter 10, we discuss the implications of cash versus 'paper' offers for the target. In addition, implications can arise from inheritance taxes; for example, in the United Kingdom it may be optimal for an individual to dispose of assets before death. This can give an impetus to the early sale of part or all of stakes in closely held family companies. The point about all of these issues is firstly that the full taxation implications need to be considered (for both target and bidder, and including the personal taxation position of the respective shareholders) and that there are bargaining implications; these are discussed in Chapter 10.

Evaluating the benefits in efficient markets

One way of valuing the benefits of a merger is to value the acquired company in its current state, add on the value of the improvements, and finally add on the present value of any synergistic benefits that might arise in the acquiring company. We have discussed above the considerations involved in evaluating these components, including the valuation of strategic options. However, if we believe that stock market prices are efficient, and we are valuing a listed company, there would be no need to perform the first part of this task, because the current market value would represent the consensus view of the fair value of the company.

This perhaps suggests that we should pay most attention to the *additional* value we expect to gain from the company. Several points emerge here; if the company is viewed by the market as being 'in play', or a likely takeover prospect, the market price will already reflect the expected value of any future bid premium. The price will also be affected by the number of interested bidders and the specificity of the benefits to be realised. This latter point is important, because the benefits of past tax losses, replacing generally incompetent management and the like can be realised by a large number of acquirers. However, industry and product specific synergies might make the firm of value to only a few potential acquirers. Furthermore, provided the necessary information is in the public domain, the values of the options we discussed above will already be impounded in the share price; valuing them a second time would be double counting. Similarly, the value of brands and the like should also be present in the share price. The message is that in an efficient markets context the bidder should concentrate on the specific value that can be added to the firm by its unique actions.

SPECIAL CONSIDERATIONS RELATING TO THE VALUATION OF OVERSEAS OPERATIONS

In Chapter 6, we addressed the problem of the determination of discount rates for overseas PLBs. There we argued that the rate should reflect the systematic risk of the investment, but should not take account of other risk factors, which are really types of specific risk, the most obvious example being political risk. Now if we are not to adjust the discount rate (or indeed the PE multiple if we wish to use an earnings capitalisation approach to the valuation) for country-specific risk factors (those that are non-systematic), it follows that we must take account of this risk in the cash flows; that is the approach we shall adopt here. In addition, the sensitivity analysis and scenario modelling approaches discussed in Chapter 4 will be of particular value here. In general, the rule is to forecast the cash flows for the foreign PLB on an expected value basis; we can then either discount this using an appropriate local cost of capital, giving today's value in the foreign currency that can be translated at current spot rates, or translate all the cash flows at predicted future spot rates into the domestic currency, which must then be discounted at a rate that allows for domestic inflation (because the inflation differential is implicit in exchange rate movements – see Chapter 4). Provided there are no exchange controls, and no foreseeable risks of such controls being introduced, the former approach will be less prone to errors. However, it should be noted that it is rarely possible to avoid forecasting exchange rates because of cross-border transactions made by the foreign PLB and because of transfer prices charged for goods and services between the foreign PLB and the rest of the group. Issues relating to exchange rate forecasting were discussed in Chapter 4; given the long-term nature of the valuation problem, it will generally be useful to make use of the economic relationships we noted between interest rates, inflation rates and exchange rates.

Forecasting local currency cash flows

Whichever method that we use to value the foreign PLB, the starting point is always to forecast cash flows (or earnings flows) in the local currency; this includes translating any non-local transactions into that currency (for example, if we are valuing a Dutch subsidiary supplying goods to other European countries, all revenues must first be translated back into guilders). It is at this stage that any political and other specific risks should be reflected through the use of probabilistic analysis; in general, the forecasting of political risk requires specialist advice (although it should be noted that experts in this area do not appear to have a particularly good track record in forecasting *radical* changes; the recent events in the former Soviet Union and Eastern Europe are good examples). However, for a useful exploration of the topic, readers are referred to Eitman and Stonehill (1989) and Shapiro (1989). Considerations involve not only the type and probability of such risks (which can range from asset expropriation to tax changes or regulatory changes), but also the degree to which such risks can be managed. Shapiro notes that some risks can be insured, environments can be negotiated, operations can be structured to overcome some types of risk, and programmes can be put in place to develop local stakeholdings; all these can help to reduce expropriation-type risks. The most satisfactory way of developing cash flow expected values is through a scenario modelling approach; plausible events are analysed, and the cash flow consequences of each evaluated. This is best performed using speadsheets. Probabilities can then be assigned to each scenario and an expected cash flow forecast derived.[8] One problem with using expected values is that the average outcome does not normally occur for any one event. For example, if the probability of a revolution (which would result in the nationalisation of the firm's foreign assets without compensation) is 0.5, it does not make a great deal of sense to say that the anticipated result is half a revolution. However, looked at from the shareholders' perspective, with a large portfolio encompassing many different possible events, the use of expected values is reasonable. From the company's point of view, the advantage of this proposed scenario/ probability methodology is that we are easily able to answer 'what if' type questions, because for each scenario we have a specific cash flow; furthermore, we can also conduct a sensitivity analysis (see Chapter 4).

Estimating the cost of capital

The second stage of the process is the estimation of the cost of capital for the foriegn PLB. The special considerations involved in setting the discount rate were discussed in Chapter 6. The appropriate capital structure to use in any weighted-average cost of capital calculation is the long-term target gearing achievable by a stand alone subsidiary in its own country of operation. Note that the weights used should reflect market capitalisations of debt and equity (in the usual manner) and that therefore local 'cultural' factors on the debt–equity mix are taken into account. Any special considerations, such as the availability of subsidised loans, or government regulations specifying the required level of equity financing are best reflected through the use of an adjusted present value framework. An example of the valuation of a subsidised loan is given in the Appendix to Chapter six. It is also necessary to remember that the relevant tax rate to be used in the computation of the value of debt tax shields and WACC must reflect local corporation tax and the personal tax regimes of the investors in debt and equity (in the case of the latter, this will normally be the tax regime of the parent's shareholders; however, in the case of a valuation for a buyout, spin-off or comparison with other (local) operations, the local personal tax regime would be relevant).

Translating value into parent's currency

We can now carry out a DCF calculation in the normal way, looking at cash flows for the specific forecast period and adding in the terminal value of the firm. As, by definition, the present value is the value today, this resultant valuation can be translated to the parent's domestic currency at the current spot rate. The final step is to consider the present value of any special benefits that accrue to the parent that would not occur if the subsidiary was truly a stand-alone enterprise. Most multi-national enterprises (MNEs) will attempt to gain some tax advantages by the judicious use of transfer pricing; the best approach when valuing any overseas operation is to ignore such gains initially, value the subsidiary on a genuine arm's length basis, and then to include the value of these gains at the final stage of the process; in effect, this is an application of the APV rule. The reason for such a recommendation is that the relative efficiency of the foreign operation is best judged by looking at the results on a stand-alone basis; tax advantages and the like are a separate financial issue.

This method of valuing the PLB in a 'local' context is perfectly reasonable provided there are no exchange regulations in force; this means that this approach is a feasible one for investments in Western Europe, the United States and several other countries. However, if we expect that there will be restrictions on capital flows the approach has to be modified to take account of the cash flows that can actually be remitted to the group, by one means or another (for example, if dividend payments are restricted, transfer prices can sometimes be used to move cash flows around). In such situations, the value to the parent can only be calculated by forecasting the cash flows remitted in the *parent's* currency, discounted at a rate that reflects the inflation rate of the parent's currency and the systematic rate of the foreign PLB. As this is a complex calculation, it is only recommended for use in this special case of effective currency control. Note the use of 'effective'; for example, it is sometimes possible to circumvent such regulations by using 'back to back' transactions.

Finally, we should again mention the issues relating to hedging, which were discussed in Chapter 4. Hedging can reduce both systematic risk and specific risk, but to the extent that shareholders can reduce the latter themselves, they will not pay the company a premium to do so (but see Eckl and Robinson (1990) for a discussion of when reduction of the latter may be of value to the shareholders). Although it is comparatively easy to hedge positions in the short term, it is difficult to provide effective long-term hedging except through devices such as financing foreign investment through borrowings in the local currency. The basic rule for coping with hedged positions is simple, because it involves no change from the position that we have discussed above, i.e. discount expected net cash flows at a rate allowing for the systematic risk of the investment. The estimation of expected cash flows should allow for the effects of any hedging, and the discount rate should allow for any changes in the *systematic* risk of the investment.

ISSUES RELATING TO NON-CONTROLLING STAKES

If the non-controlling, or minority, stake is in a listed company, no special considerations need apply. Both PE ratios and costs of capital observed from the market reflect the prices and returns on non-controlling stakes by definition. The problem in such cases is to determine the control premium to be paid; this would normally reflect the benefits to be gained from the merger (see above) and the bargaining position of both buyer and seller (see Chapter 10). However, in the case of unlisted companies, controlling stakes are a common event, whereas such things do not normally exist in the case of quoted companies because the acquisition of a controlling stake usually results in the company no longer being listed. When valuing a minority stake in an unlisted firm, two important considerations apply. First, the size of the stake is of concern since anything over 25 per cent (in the United Kingdom) allows the holder to block special resolutions; these have a specific legal significance, because although the business can continue in its day to day operations without the need for such resolutions, certain fundamental changes (such as voluntary liquidation) need the approval of 75 per cent or more of the shareholders. Second, a critical question is what exercisable influence the minority shareholders have on the company; for example, if the stake is held by the firm's financiers (say, a bank or venture capital consortium) the board is far more likely to take account of the opinions of the minority shareholder than if the stake is held by the widowed husband of one of the firm's former directors.

Valuation of non-influential minority stakes

In general principle, minority shareholders with no significant influence over the company's affairs will receive only dividends from the company; as there is no general market for their shares, it follows that an appropriate valuation method should take account only of the value of the future dividends receivable. The exception here is if there is a reasonable probability of the company being floated on a stock exchange in the foreseeable future. Assuming for the moment that this is not likely, the ideal method of valuing such a stake would appear to be some form of dividend discount model. Note that this presupposes that we are trying to establish a fair value for the shares outside the constraints imposed by legal and taxation considerations. These are specialist areas beyond the scope of this book. However, we should note that in the UK legislation exists to prevent the oppression of minority shareholders, although the definition of 'oppressive' is subject to interpretation. The Court of Appeal, in *Jermyn Street Turkish Baths Ltd* (1971) stated that, 'it is dangerous to attempt a universal definition'. However, this case did establish that a refusal to pay dividends is not in itself an act of oppression.

Before we can use the dividend growth model, it is necessary to estimate the specific dividend pattern for the forecast horizon, the long-term growth rate and the discount rate. In estimating the specific dividends for the explicit forecast period, the usual considerations expressed in Chapter 4 will apply. The choice of a realistic forecast horizon will rather depend upon the information to which the valuer has access, but if possible the recommended minimum of five years should be used. The long-term growth rate will partly be determined by the outlook for the industry in general and the specific forecast horizon used but, as we have discussed in previous chapters, the most reasonable real long-term growth assumption will typically be the real long-term increase in GDP. This figure might be in the order of 2–3 per cent above the rate of inflation (historically, Dimson and Marsh (1991) note that the Hoare–Govett Small Companies Index has shown real dividend growth of around 3.5 per cent pa between 1955 and 1990; by contrast, the BZW equity income index, which is based on the performance of larger companies, shows a real gain of just under 2 per cent pa over the same period). One approach to the problem is similar to that described in Chapter 7, which is explicitly to forecast the dividends for the specific forecast horizon, and then allow a number of years over which the growth rate linearly decays to the long-term rate – an example using this method is given below.

All this leaves us with the problem of estimating the discount rate for our model. One approach is to use the CAPM; however, there are a couple of difficulties here. First, the use of such a model assumes that the investor holds a well diversified portfolio; this is a very defensible assumption in the case of listed companies where the majority of shareholders are typically insitutions of one sort or another, but can be suspect in the case of unlisted companies. Second, the CAPM assumes that all assets are marketable and divisible. Again, the normal assumption made in its application to listed firms is that it is reasonable to apply the model to the segmented market of company shares. Clearly, it is somewhat harder to justify its application to the valuation of unlisted securities. None the less, in practice valuers have used listed company returns as proxies for unlisted companies for years, with an adjustment for lack of marketability. We shall adopt a similar approach here; the critical question is whether the discount should be applied via the discount rate or as a price adjustment as the final stage in the valuation. In practice, the approach typically used has been to value the shareholding by reference to the returns available on listed companies, and then apply a discount for non-marketability of anywhere between 25 and 50 per cent to this figure. Note that adjusting the final price has a less radical effect than adjusting the cost of capital used as a discount rate in all cases where the forecast dividend growth rate is greater than zero.

Inspection of the HGSC Index relative to the FTA and BZW indices suggests that the historical average rate of return on smaller companies over and above larger companies is somewhere in the order of 2.7 to 4.2 per cent pa; this was discussed in some detail in Chapter 6. This additional return in part allows for the lower marketability of these investments (see Dimson and Marsh, 1989); it is by no means uncommon for bid–ask spreads on such stocks to exceed 10 per cent, and on some shares the dealing of even moderately sized blocks of shares can only be carried out on a 'matched bargain' basis. As this risk appears not to be systematic risk, a reasonable approach is probably to estimate a discount rate from the CAPM in the normal way, and add on a return premium of up to, say, 4 per cent in real terms; this takes into account the alternative facing the investor of investing in smaller company shares in general.

Let us take the example of Devon Sports Tractors Ltd,* a company that specialises in the distribution of high performance tractors in the West Country. Jed owns a 10 per cent stake in the firm, which he is thinking of selling to his brother Jethro; both parties wish to agree a fair price and there are no legal or tax constraints to be considered. As tractor sales are affected by the recession at the moment, the initial dividend growth is flat; thereafter, we expect a brief boom in sales, profits and dividends, with a linear decline to the average rate of GDP growth over the following three years. This GDP growth is expected to be 2 per cent in real terms, with an inflation rate of about 5 per cent pa. The real risk free rate is estimated at 4 per cent pa, the market risk premium for FTA companies at 6.3 per cent and the β of the performance tractor market at 1.2. Our forecast dividend schedule is:

Year end	Dividend (pence)	Growth over last year (%)	Comment
1992	10	0.0	–
1993	12	20	Specific forecast
1994	14	16.7	Specific forecast
1995	16.1	15.0	Specific forecast
1996	18.2	13.0	Linear decline to 7 per cent
1997	20.2	11.0	Linear decline to 7 per cent
1998	22.0	9.0	Linear decline to 7 per cent
1999	23.55	7.0	Long-term growth 7 per cent to perpetuity

Our discount rate is calculated as:

Basic real return = 4% + (1.2 × 6.3%)   = 11.6%
Small companies adjustment = 11.6% + 4% = 15.6%
Inflation adjustment = (1.156 × 1.05) − 1   = 21.3%

The dividend valuation can now be performed as follows to give the share value at the start of 1992:

Year end	Dividend (pence)	Terminal value		Discount factor @ 21.3%	Present value
1992	10.0			0.824	8.24
1993	12.0			0.680	8.16
1994	14.0			0.560	7.84
1995	16.1			0.462	7.44
1996	18.2			0.381	6.93
1997	20.2			0.314	6.34
1998	22.0			0.259	5.70
1998	–	$\frac{23.55}{0.213 - 0.07}$	= 164.7	0.259	42.63
					93.28

Our present value per share is therefore around 93 pence. Essentially, this takes into account the 'smaller company' effect in so far as it affects the average small listed company; we now need to take into account the discount for lack of marketability. We need to bear in mind that this has partly been taken account of already, through the additional return required on smaller firms. It is easiest to see the extent of this by examining the horizon value of our example. Suppose that there was no allowance made for the size of the company; our discount rate would then have been 11.6 per cent compounded up for inflation, which would have given us 17.2 per cent. This in turn would have produced an end 1998 value of:

$$V = \frac{23.55}{0.172 - 0.07} = 230.9 \text{ pence}$$

This means that a discount of $(230.9 - 164.7) \div 230.9$, or around 29 per cent, has already been allowed for. Close attention must be paid to this because this discount will increase as the dividend growth rate becomes larger. This is one of the problems of allowing for the additional return required on smaller companies in the discount rate. Now, clearly, some compensation for lack of marketability is reasonable, but to take off, say, an *additional* discount of 35 per cent would appear to be double counting some of the small company and non-marketability effects. Unfortunately, no hard and fast rules on non-marketability discounts can be given, as there are as yet no theoretical models that would enable us to do this. What we can say is that in practice, the discount might reasonably increase for stakes of less than 25 per cent in the United Kingdom, given the significance of this in the case of special resolutions, and increase with the relative proportion of the shareholder's wealth that is tied up in this particular stake, to compensate that investor for the lack of diversification in his or her portfolio. Related to this point, because shareholders in unlisted firms are often poorly diversified, we might expect the non-marketability discount also to reflect the specific risk of the investment, as well as the systematic risk. In this context note that not all of the specific risk would be of concern, but the undiversified element of that risk. In conclusion, then, a suitable price discount becomes both firm *and* investor specific.

Valuation of influential stakes

Unless the company is to be floated on a stock exchange within the foreseeable future, valuation here follows similar principles to the position described above. However, in this case the shareholder may be able to influence the payout, investment and flotation policies of the company, and may also have other sources of income from the enterprise, such as director's remuneration. All these factors need to be considered when placing a fair value on the shares. It is also likely that anyone in this position will have access to the internal plans and budgets of the company. Because of the position of influence enjoyed by the shareholder, he or she should consider the value of the assets in alternative use. This idea of break-up and liquidation values was discussed in Chapter 5. However, for a significant group of investors, the venture capitalists, the value of stakes in unlisted companies is typically driven by a flotation objective at the end of a set period. There will also be strings attached to any financing deal, so that quite often the venture capitalist's stake is linked to the achievement of this objective. Financing arrangements of this kind are frequently found in management buyouts, so that if all goes according to plan, management end up owning the company, or a considerable part of it. However, if profits fall short of target, debt is not paid off on schedule, or flotation does not take place as planned, various rights are exercisable by the providers of finance so that they end up owning an increased share of the company; arrangements of this sort are sometimes known as 'equity kickers'.

Such venture capital investment needs to be valued in a way that takes into account the market value of the company on flotation, and this type of valuation is described next.

VALUING COMPANIES FOR FLOTATION

There is nothing particularly special about valuing a company for flotation on a stock exchange. All the principles we have discussed so far in this book are relevant to valuation in such cases, although we must bear in mind that the value is reduced by the amount of flotation costs, which usually involve a significant percentage of the issue proceeds. It is difficult to give precise percentages because these vary according to the type of issue, whether the market is the official list or Unlisted Securities Market (USM), but the costs for a placing on the USM are unlikely to be less than £250,000. For a company transferring from the USM to the main market the costs can start from around an additional £50,000 and run to around £200,000, whilst for an initial public offer on the main stock exchange the costs would start at well over £1 million and would be unlikely to amount to less than 4 or 5 per cent of the amount raised; this can increase considerably depending on the circumstances, reaching up to 10 per cent in some cases. Details of the flotation costs of recent new issues can be found in *New Issue Statistics* (KPMG Peat Marwick).

Just as in the case of the purchase or sale of any company in a situation where market players tend to emphasise earnings valuation heavily, the flotation price of a company typically tends to be arrived at by making some use of the industry-average price–earnings ratio. Whether this is reasonable from a theoretical point of view is debatable, but the facts appear to be that investment advisers pay a good deal of attention to the prospective earnings multiple attached to the projected profit numbers. This should not be taken as implying that all new issues are priced at the industry-average PE, because some qualitative factors appear to be considered by the market allowing some issues to be priced at a premium to the sector average, whilst others are priced at a discount. However, this should not be taken as implying that DCF methodologies are not used in some cases; Eurotunnel is the classic example where a PE approach was virtually meaningless. All this suggests that, although we can (and indeed should), value a flotation prospect using the DCF method, realism demands that this is checked by reference to the implied PE on prospective earnings.

A special need for such considerations is in valuing the stake held by venture capitalists. Typically, the approach used is the 'exit multiple' one, where the required equity stake is set by reference to a required rate of return (usually a rather high rate, hence the alternative name of 'vulture capital' set on the basis of the *internal rate of return* on the investment). This type of valuation of a minority stake is interesting because all the value of the equity stake is normally realised on exit, as dividends are not usually paid. However, part of the financing package normally contains various types of debt, ranging from secured debt through various classes of 'mezzanine financing' (preference shares, convertibles and unsecured debt), so that interest is received and loan principals are paid off over the life of the financing arrangement. It is also common, in the case of buyouts for example, for the individual providers of finance to take a similar percentage of equity, mezzanine and secured debt. Further discussion of points relating to management buyouts can be found in Chapter 11.

One of the difficulties of this approach to valuing venture capital stakes (which tends to be generally descriptive of that used in practice) is that the assumed exit multiple is frequently based upon the current industry average. We discussed the problems of using PE ratios in this way in Chapter 5, and should note that a better approach would be to perform the exit value calculation on a DCF basis. However, two observations are in order; first, the exit value is often being estimated some three to five years out, and calculating a DCF value on a worthwhile basis would need cash flow projections for five years beyond those dates at an absolute minimum. If we fall back on simplifying methods for estimating the terminal value (see Chapter 8), then we are using an approach that can be shown to be similar to a PE methodology anyway (see Chapters 3 and 5 for an explanation of this). Second, 'exit' implies a sale to someone, which will either be the market, via a flotation or more commonly via a trade sale;[9] in so far as practitioners may be thought likely to use PE methodologies at a future date, the use of exit PE multiples can be defended to some extent.

The general rule for valuing a stake held in a company that is likely to be floated at some point in the future is to estimate the flotation price using the methodologies developed elsewhere in this book, but bearing in mind the point about prospective earnings multiples made above. This figure is then discounted back to give today's value, and added to the present value of the dividends receivable until flotation. Note that insofar as the free cash flow and dividend valuation models are similar (see Chapter 3), we might expect that flotation has a relatively minor impact upon value. However, this ignores the crucial issue of the discount for non-marketability; furthermore, it is possible that flotation might relieve any capital rationing constraints on the company, enabling it to grow at a faster rate by adopting a larger number of positive NPV projects.

To illustrate this, we shall return to our example of Devon Sports Tractors Ltd. Suppose the company currently has 1 million shares in issue, and that the plan is to float the company on the stock market at the end of 1995, immediately after the shares go ex-dividend. Let us also assume that free cash flows and dividends are identical; we know that at the end of 1995, the value of the company in its current state is:

$$V£m = \frac{0.182}{1.213} + \frac{0.202}{1.213^2} + \frac{0.220}{1.213^3} + \frac{0.2355}{1.213^3 \times (0.213 - 0.07)} = 1.3334 \text{ m}$$

(note that the free cash flows are the prospective dividends per share multiplied by the one million shares in issue). Suppose that the flotation (on the USM) would raise a futher £3 million, through the issue of 3 million shares at £1 each, which would be invested in an expansion project with a positive NPV of £400,000 and that flotation costs would amount to £250,000. All this implies a theoretical value of the company, post-flotation in 1995, of:

Value of original business	£1.3334 million
Value of additional projects	3.4000
Less flotation costs	−0.2500
Value of business	£4.4834

This suggests a post-flotation value per share of £1.121 (£4.4834/4 million shares). We can now revise our estimate of value of Jed's shares:

Year end	Dividend (pence)	Terminal value	Discount factor @ 21.3%	Present value (pence)
1992	10	–	0.824	8.24
1993	12	–	0.680	8.16
1994	14	–	0.560	7.84
1995	16.1	–	0.462	7.44
1995	–	1.121	0.462	51.78
				83.46

The first point to note is that in terms of *basic* value, Jed has lost out, because he now has to share the value of the existing business with the new investors (who effectively bought shares at below their true worth) and has lost some value through flotation costs. However, he may have gained overall because this figure no longer needs to be adjusted downwards to take account of non-marketability discount.

TRADE VALUATION NORMS

In some industries, companies are valued as acquisition prospects on the basis of some trade convention; for example, one method used to value petrol station sites is a multiple of fuel sales. Similarly, in some service contract industries, a multiple of turnover is used, whilst in the hotel business a price per room per night sometimes forms the basis of value; in addition, professional practices are somtimes sold on the basis of fee income. Whilst such rules might offer a reasonable initial screening guide to value, it is difficult to justify their use on several grounds.

First, we have established elsewhere that value should be determined by prospects, and in particular future cash flows. Clearly, a multiple of, say, current turnover can only be the crudest of guides to long-term value. Second, such rules are easily manipulable through devices such as price discounting or heavy marketing expenditure. Third, attention must be paid to the relative cost-efficiency of the business in question, together with the possibility of improvements in this and the investment that would be necessary in order to achieve this.

In trade sales of such businesses, such factors are not *usually* ignored (although some fascinating anecdotal tales to the contrary abound) but are considered on a judgemental basis. Our recommendation on such practices must be that if trade norms are used as an initial screening device, any final purchase should only be made after a full and proper valuation has been carried out. None the less, there is no reason why trade norms should not be brought up in the negotiation proceedings if such a move is to the advantage of buyer or seller.

CHAPTER 10

THE SPECIAL CASE OF ACQUISITIONS: THE BARGAINING AREA AND FINANCING

When we are attempting to value a company for reasons other than acquisition, payment may either not arise (for example, we have advocated the valuation of any company by its own management) or, when it does, it will normally be a matter of simple cash settlement, as in the case of, say, a fund manager increasing her stake in a company that is perceived to be under-valued. However, in the case of an acquisition, the payment can include a share-for-share exchange, a quasi-equity settlement (e.g. warrants, as in the case of the Hanson offer for Beazer, or convertibles), loan notes (very common as an alternative to cash, because of capital gains tax reasons) or cash. When the consideration involves an equity exchange, the effective price paid for the company depends on the post-combination success of the new entity, because the shareholders in the acquired firm receive a fraction of the returns achieved. To understand the implications of this for the cost of buying controlling stakes, we now turn to an analysis of the bargaining area. Before doing so, we should note that the issue of bargaining *strategy* is a matter of considerable importance. Given that a proper analysis of this would necessitate delving into some complex behavioural factors and the psychological literature, bargaining strategy is beyond the scope of this book.

THE BARGAINING AREA

The price any acquirer is prepared to pay for any victim company (we shall use the term 'victim', to include the acquired company in an agreed takeover or the junior partner in a merger)[1] is in part dependent upon the form of payment to be used and the net gain arising from the combination of the two businesses (see Chapter 9). Whilst it may seem evident that the greater the degree of synergy, etc., the greater the bargaining area, it may not be so obvious why the form of payment affects this bargaining area. When a company is acquired, the amount available for division between the acquirer and victim is the perceived present value of the synergistic benefit. However, the form of payment has tax implications for some investors, because the use of cash causes a capital gains tax liability to fall upon any tax-paying shareholders in the victim company; furthermore, as we have seen in Chapter 6, if the acquirer borrows to purchase the victim, potentially valuable debt tax shields may arise (in fact, these played a considerable part in the 1980s management buyout boom). Beyond this, there is the issue of participation in the benefits of the business combination, because if any equity consideration is involved the victim's shareholders realise some of the post-combination wealth effects, be they positive or negative.

A useful starting point is to define the wealth gain arising from the business combination, which is the present value of the combination (PV_{AV}) less the present value of the two firms as individual entities (PV_A and PV_V). This gain will partly be because of business synergies and partly because of tax effects. The latter will include the value of the debt tax shields on the acquisition (if any) and the post-combination tax implications of past tax losses carried forward, unused capital allowances and so forth (the details of tax legislation are beyond the scope of this book, but for an introduction to the UK position see Cooke (1986), Chapter 11, whilst for an analysis of the international position see Cooke (1988)). In theory, the market price of the shares in the post-combination entity, P_{AV}, should be the value of the firm (PV_{AV}) divided by the post-combination shares in issue. Similarly, the share prices of the acquiring and victim firms pre-combination[2] will be:

$$P_A = PV_A \div \text{number of shares in A}$$

$$P_V = PV_V \div \text{number of shares in V}$$

Alternatively, of course, we could express all this in terms of the familiar price earnings relationship, giving us:

$$P_A = PE_A \times EPS_A \tag{10.1}$$

$$P_V = PE_V \times EPS_V \tag{10.2}$$

For the moment, we shall ignore the personal tax-paying positions of shareholders in the victim company, and note that the constraints on the bargaining area in the case of a cash offer are that the shareholders in the victim company must receive at least the pre-bid price for their shares, whereas if we assume a rational shareholder wealth maximisation objective for the acquiring company's management (more on this later) the upper bound to the price paid must leave those shareholders no worse off. When the offer involves giving the victim's shareholders part of the acquirer's equity as consideration, the definition of the bargaining area is a little more complex. The key variables are the post-combination value of the firm, and the *exchange ratio* (ER); the exchange ratio is the number of shares in the acquiring company offered in exchange for each victim company's share, thus an offer of 'five A shares for every eight V shares' would translate into an exchange ratio of 0.625. We can now move ahead and determine the bargaining area in share-for-share takeovers; the model that follows is known as the Larson and Gonedes Exchange Ratio Model (Larson and Gonedes, 1969). The expected post-merger value of a share in the combined firm, P_{AV}, is defined by:

$$P_{AV} = PE_{AV} \times (E_A + E_V) / (S_A + S_B[ER]) \qquad (10.3)$$

where: $E_{A,V}$, are earnings after tax, of acquiring and victim company shareholders (note that the earnings are those attributable to shareholders, i.e. those used to determine the EPS figures); $PE_{A,V,AV}$, are price–earnings ratios of acquiring, victim and combined companies (the use of italics denotes expected values); $S_{A,V}$, are number of shares in acquiring and victim companies, respectively; ER is the exchange ratio, expressed as the number of acquiring company shares offered in exchange for each victim company share. Note that we can also define the numerator on the right hand side of (10.3) as PV_{AV}, which would be consistent with a DCF methodology; it makes no difference to our conclusions, because the two are equivalent.

As the wealth position of each shareholder in the acquired firm must be at least maintained for the merger to be acceptable, we have:

$$P_{AV} \geqslant P_A \qquad (10.4)$$

Similarly, the wealth position of the victim company shareholders must be at least maintained, which gives us:

$$P_{AV} \geqslant P_V / ER \qquad (10.5)$$

Substituting (10.3) and (10.1) into the left- and right-hand sides, respectively, of (10.4), and using the equality relationship allows us to rearrange terms and solve for the *maximum* exchange ratio (ER_A) acceptable to the acquiring company shareholders (who will seek to negotiate lower exchange ratios), and so we have:

$$ER_A = \frac{PE_{AV} (E_A + E_V) - (PE_A \times E_A)}{PE_A \times E_A \times (1/S_A) \times S_V} \qquad (10.6)$$

The numerator in this expression represents the increased value of the combined business compared to A on its own, whilst the denominator gives us the ratio of the share price of A relative to the share price of V. We can similarly obtain an expression for the *minimum* exchange ratio acceptable to the victim company shareholders (who will try to negotiate higher exchange ratios), by substituting (10.3) and (10.2) into the left- and right-hand sides of the equality relationship in (10.5), which gives:

$$ER_V = \frac{PE_V \times EPS_V \times S_A}{PE_{AV} (E_A + E_V) - (PE_V \times E_V)} \qquad (10.7)\text{-}$$

In this case, the numerator is the price of a share in V multiplied by the number of shares in A, whilst the denominator is the increased value of the combined business less the original value of V. When using these formulae, it is important to ensure that the prices used for victim and acquiring companies are 'cleaned' to ensure that they are free of any bid rumours (see Chapter 3, page 31 for an explanation of how to achieve this). If we plot these exchange ratios on a graph as a function of the post-combination PE ratio[3] (see Figure 10.1), we can see that the rational bargaining area is that lying to the right of both the ER_A and ER_B curves (shown by quadrant I); all values of PE_{AV} to the right of $PE\star$ result in positive gains from the merger overall. Quadrant II covers the area where the victim shareholders gain but the acquirer loses, quadrant IV where the acquirer gains but the victim loses and quadrant III where both parties lose as a result of the combination.

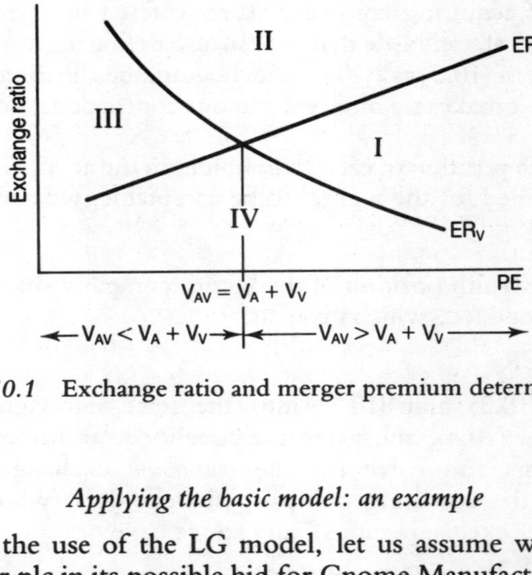

Figure 10.1 Exchange ratio and merger premium determination.

Applying the basic model: an example

To illustrate the use of the LG model, let us assume we are advising Megapredator plc in its possible bid for Gnome Manufacturing plc★, the world's largest producer of garden gnomes. The position of both parties can be summarised as:

	Megapredator	Gnome Manufacturing
Number of ordinary shares	250 million	250 million
Current price (ex-bid rumour effect)	£4.00	£2.00
Accounting earnings	£100 million	£62.5 million
Earnings per share	£0.4	£0.25
Price–earnings multiple	10	8
Market capitalisation	£1,000 million	£500 million

As Megapredator's advisers, we think that the current market capitalisation of Gnome is a fair indication of its 'ongoing' value, but that efficiency improvements could add another £50 million of value, and synergy effects a further £50 million; Gnome is therefore worth a maximum of £60 million to Megapredator. The maximum exchange ratio can be derived by realising that the market should rationally value the combined business at £1600 million (i.e. the sum of the two original market values plus the value of the efficiency and synergy gains); because the earnings immediately post-takeover will be the sum of the original earnings,[4] the PE ratio will be £1,600 million divided by £162.5 million, or 9.846. Our maximum exchange ratio is therefore:

$$ER_A = \frac{9.846(100 + 62.5) - (10 \times 100)}{10 \times 100 \times (1/250) \times 250} = 0.6$$

Similarly, the minimum offer acceptable to a shareholder in V is:

$$ER_V = \frac{8 \times 0.25 \times 250}{9.846(100 + 62.5) - (8 \times 62.5)} = 0.4545$$

This illustrates the point about share-for-share exchanges allowing victim shareholders to participate in post-merger gains; a naive analysis might have led us to believe that the minimum exchange ratio acceptable to Gnome shareholders would have been the ratio of the pre-bid share prices, or 0.5 (£2 ÷ £4). In fact, if the exchange ratio was only, say, 0.49 they would be better off as a result of the takeover, because post-combination the value of each Megapredator share should be £4.30 (there will be 250 million original shares in issue, plus 250 million old Gnome shares multiplied by the 0.49 exchange ratio, which gives a total of 372.5 million with a total market value of £1,600 million); as Gnome shareholders have 0.49 of these for every old share they held, their wealth position is £2.11 per old share.

The exchange ratio model with cash alternatives

The LG model, whilst of relevance to many UK takeovers, does not deal with the common UK situation where there is a cash alternative to the share-for-share offer. The UK City Code on Takeovers and Mergers (Rule 9) requires such an alternative where the acquiring company has purchased any of the intended victim company's shares for cash in the previous twelve months. Cooke and Gregory (1991) extends the LG model to cover this situation. If p is the proportion of V's shareholders who are expected to accept the share-for-share offer, and $(1 - p)$ are expected to accept the cash alternative offered per share, then (10.3) becomes:

$$P_{AV} = PE_{AV} \times (E_A + E_V) / [S_A + S_V(ER \times p)] \qquad (10.8)$$

Substituting (10.8) and (10.1) into the left- and right-hand sides of (10.4) and rearranging provides the equation for the maximum exchange ratio:

$$ER_A = \frac{PE_{AV}(E_A + E_V) - (PE_A \times E_A)}{PE_A \times E_A \times (1/S_A) \times S_V \times p} \qquad (10.9)$$

To analyse the position of a shareholder in the victim company, we assume that the cash alternative offered is no greater than the perceived value of his or her wealth if the share-for-share alternative is accepted, as given by (10.5). Note that if this was not the case, we would expect to see $p = 0$, and the takeover would be simply a cash deal.[5] As before, substituting (10.8) and (10.2) into the left- and right-hand sides of (10.5) and rearranging gives:

$$ER_V = \frac{PE_V \times EPS_V \times S_A}{PE_{AV}(E_A + E_V) - p(PE_V \times E_V)} \qquad (10.10)$$

However, at the *minimum* exchange ratio, this constraint on the value of the cash alternative amounts to saying that the cash offer must be no more than the current share price. In cases where the cash offer is greater than this, we can reformulate (10.5) as:

$$P_{AV} \times ER = c$$

Substituting (10.8) and (10.2) into this expression gives us the minimum exchange ratio when the cash offer is above the current share price (this will, of course, be the usual case in reality):

$$ER_V = \frac{c \times S_A}{PE_{AV}(E_A + E_V) - p(S_B \times c)} \qquad (10.10a)$$

To illustrate the effect of this, let us suppose that Megapredator decides to make a bid for Gnome Manufacturing and offers a cash alternative of £2.30 per share; assuming an acceptable share-for-share offer can be made, it is thought that some 20 per cent of Gnome's shareholders will opt for this alternative. The analysis can be carried out as before, but we shall assume the market value of the combination will be lower by the amount of cash paid out, which will be £250 million × 20 per cent × £2.30, or £115 million; this in turn suggests a post-combination PE ratio of (£1,600 million − £115 million) ÷ £162.5 million, which gives a PE of 9.14. Solving for the maximum exchange ratio gives us:

$$ER_A = \frac{9.14(100 + 62.5) - (10 \times 100)}{10 \times 100 \times (1/250) \times 250 \times 0.8} = 0.6063$$

As the cash alternative is above the current share price, the minimum exchange ratio is:

$$ER_V = \frac{2.30 \times 250}{9.14(100 + 62.5) - 0.8(250 \times 2.3)} = 0.561$$

Suppose the actual offer is 'three for five, or £2.30 cash', and 20 per cent of holders actually take the cash offer. We should then find that the ex-post market value of the firm is £1,485 million, which divided by the 370 million shares in issue (250 million plus the issue on takeover of 250 million × 80 per cent × 3/5) gives a post-takeover share price of £4.01, a marginal improvement for Megapredator's shareholders which has a value of £4.01 × 3/5 = £2.41 for Gnome's original shareholders.

The model with 'mixed' offers

The final form of offer for which we need to adapt the LG model is the 'mixed' offer where consideration involves a combination of shares plus cash. With these mixed offers, the ER_A constraint is unchanged but taking the equality relationship in (10.5) gives:

$$P_{AV} = (PV - K) / ER \qquad (10.11)$$

Where K is the cash portion of the offer per share in V (e.g. if an offer was made for V of '1 plus £1 for 5', ER = 0.2 and $K = £0.20$).

Substituting (10.3) and (10.2) into the left- and right-hand sides of (10.11) and rearranging gives:

$$ER_V = \frac{PE_V \times EPS_V \times (S_A - K) \times S_A}{PE_{AV}(E_A + E_V) - S_V([PE_V \times EPS_V] - K)} \qquad (10.12)$$

Back to Megapredator; suppose, immediately prior to the bid, we are advising on the alternative possibility of a mixed offer, the cash element of which is £1 per Gnome share. We have already calculated that the post-combination value should be £1,600 million and, as in the case of the cash alternative, this should fall by the amount of any cash paid out, which in this case is £250 million. We therefore should have a market value, post-takeover, of £1,350 million and an earnings multiple of 8.308 (1350/162.5). Plugging in the relevant numbers gives a maximum exchange ratio of:

$$ER_A = \frac{8.308(100 + 62.5) - (10 \times 100)}{10 \times 100 \times (1/250) \times 250} = 0.35$$

and a minimum exchange ratio of:

$$ER_V = \frac{(8 \times 0.25 \times 250) - (1 \times 250)}{8.308(100 + 62.5) - 250([8 \times 0.25] - 1)} = 0.2273$$

Thus the minimum offer Megapredator can make is '227 plus £1,000 for every 1,000 shares', whilst the maximum is '35 plus £100 for every 100 shares'.

Finally, it can similarly be shown that in the case where the mixed offer has an all-cash alternative attached, the maximum exchange ratio is given by (10.9), whilst the minimum exchange ratio is given by:

$$ER_V = \frac{PE_V \times EPS_V \times (S_A - K) \times S_A}{PE_{AV}(E_A + E_V) - S_V \times p[(PE_V \times EPS_V) - K]} \qquad (10.13)$$

Is the model empirically valid?

So far, we have models for determining the bargaining area that cover all simple share-for-share exchanges, cash alternatives and mixed offers. Whilst these models should rationally be useful, how well do they describe exchange ratios in reality? A US study by Conn and Nielsen (1977) finds some support for the original models; in the United Kingdom, Cooke and Gregory (1991) emphasise the importance of allowing for general market movements when calculating the exchange ratios and find that, when this is done, roughly half of a sample of ninety-five UK takeovers involving share exchanges falls into the 'rational' quadrant predicted by the LG model and its extensions; in a significant number of cases, it appears that the victim's shareholders gain at the expense of the acquiring companies. This appears to be compatible with other research findings on takeovers and mergers; there is virtually unanimous agreement on the fact that, on average, shareholders in the victim company gain (see Cooke (1986) for a discussion) but there is considerable debate about whether the acquiring company shareholders gain. Whilst Franks and Harris (1989) do not suggest that acquiring firms lose out, Limmack (1991) provides contradictory evidence that the average acquiring company shareholders *do* lose, and that most of this loss occurs 12 to 24 months after the bid announcement has been made. Interestingly, he notes that '[acquiring company] shareholders do appear. . . to suffer wealth losses with too high a price paid for the benefits obtained from the acquisition'. This appears to confirm the findings of other UK researchers (Firth, 1980). According to Limmack, the price paid is a premium, which may be as high as 37 per cent, depending upon the measurement criteria used. However, Franks *et al.* (1988) note that there is a considerable difference in this premium in cash and equity offers. They show premia of 30.5 per cent for cash, 18.2 per cent for equity, 28.2 per cent for cash or equity bids and 27.1 per cent for mixed offers; their analysis covers the period 1955 to 1985. This paper finds significant positive post-combination performance for *cash* acquirers, with results not significantly different from zero in the case of equity offers, but these results are sensitive to the research model used.

As a conclusion on the empirical research, we can partly agree with the observation of Franks *et al.* (1988) that, 'the issue that remains unresolved is whether postmerger performance in all-equity takeovers was less than zero';[6] we might add that there is at least some reason to suppose that this doubt be extended to cover the post-merger performance of *all* acquirers. However, it is interesting that the findings of this paper suggest that although the premium is higher in the case of cash offers, the post-combination performance is stronger. The authors suggest that this may be due to firms issuing equity when management believes their company to be over-valued; the market takes this as a signal and down-grades the valuation accordingly. By contrast, the issue of cash signals 'under-valuation'; furthermore, because any cash alternative offered is often underwritten, there exists an outside opinion to confirm this view. Whilst this may have some truth in it, Franks *et al.* (1988) do not examine how these cash offers are themselves financed. This is an important issue, because if financing comes either from the issue of debt or from retained earnings that were held as interest-bearing deposits, the question of debt tax shields arises (positive in both cases, because cash on interest-bearing deposit can have a negative tax shield value). It might therefore be the case that it is tax shield value that is the explanatory variable not market perceptions of over or under valuation of equity.[7]

Implications for acquirers

All this has implications for the acquiring company. There is at least some reason to believe that acquiring companies tend to pay too much for their victims. This might be because of 'hubris' on the part of management (Roll, 1986) or because managers pursue their own objectives other than shareholder wealth maximisation. A US study by Morck *et al.* (1990) finds that poor post-combination performance is associated with acquisitions intended as diversification ventures, the purchase of rapidly growing victims and where the acquiring company performed poorly prior to the acquisition. This is a particularly interesting analysis, because, whilst it is obvious why management might want to diversify, most of modern finance theory would suggest that it is not in the *shareholders'* interests. From their point of view, why have the company pay a 30 per cent premium to diversify when they can do the same themselves for stockbroker's commision plus bid–ask spread?

So far, we have discussed bargaining from a shareholder wealth perspective, and noted that in the acquisition of quoted companies, the victim company's shareholders appear to obtain the larger share of the gains in practice. How can the acquiring company ensure it gets a better deal? First, Newbould (1970) notes that a lower premium is paid in the case of agreed takeovers; this may be because the management of the acquired company recommends acceptance of a bid if its own interests are protected. It therefore appears that providing the acquirer has some faith in the management of the potential victim, a friendly approach is a sensible initial ploy. A key part of the bargaining process will then be getting management 'on-side' by guaranteeing their position (see Chapter 11). This raises regulatory questions in many countries; a detailed analysis can be found in Cooke (1986 and 1988), but it must be noted that, in the United Kingdom, the *City Code on Takeovers and Mergers* requires that any information provided to a friendly bidder must also be made available to any rival bidder, if requested. Furthermore, shareholders must be informed of all material facts concerning the proposed deal, and this would appear to require the disclosure of any managerial compensation, however structured. This clearly does not apply to the acquisition of unlisted companies, which is discussed below.

Second, a key point is to decide the upper bound of what the target is worth and not to pay more than that figure. There appear to be a considerable number of cases where the behavioural element has come into play, and the acquirer has been determined to win control at almost any price. This is a particular danger in the case of hotly contested bids where there is more than one bidder and there are some particularly interesting UK examples. This upper bound must be set on the basis of a rigourous valuation and analysis of synergistic gains. The *Financial Times* (27 September 1991) offers a useful warning here when it states that, 'The need for a more sceptical managerial attitude to acquisitions is evident.'

Private companies
In the case of private companies, a hostile takeover is difficult, if not impossible. It will certainly be the case that the major shareholders will need to be convinced of the desirability of the takeover. This may come about as a result of their being willing sellers anyway, in search of the best price, or by persuading them that their best long-term interests lie in selling out. Cases where the latter may arise are under-financed businesses and businesses where there is insufficient expertise to market or develop the product, or to enter larger markets, and so on. In such cases, the owners may well require a share in the acquiring company, and possibly a managerial role within it, with guarantees of tenure. Another key factor in private acquisitions is the importance of the target company's management (assuming some separation of management and control) being 'on-side', something more crucial in unquoted companies than quoted ones. The reason for this is that a recalcitrant management can easily wreck a potential deal, particularly if rival bidders are involved. In addition, management themselves can become bidders through the buyout route. A well-thought-out approach by the bidder will offer management appropriate incentives (job guarantees, bonuses and/or equity participation) to back the bid. However, it is important in all this not to assume that management is necessarily a cohesive group. A successful approach would attempt to assess the unity of the management team, and exploit any weaknesses. A reluctant group of senior managers might even be successfully usurped by a 'young turk' element.

Tax considerations
Another consideration is the tax position of the target's shareholders. This might be a major factor in the case of unquoted companies, where the payment of cash could result in a significant capital gains tax liability. On the other hand, an owner who is retiring may not want a large sum invested entirely in the equity of the acquiring company. One solution, depending on the credit rating of the acquirer, is the issue of fixed or floating rate loan notes which could be marketable in the case of very large acquisitions or redeemable at a series of dates in the case of smaller acquisitions. With the acquisition of quoted companies, pressure is

sometimes brought to bear on the acquirer to provide loan notes as an alternative to a cash offer, so that there is some flexibilty available to victim company shareholders; an example was the Unilever takeover of Brooke Bond.

Private versus public company bargaining areas
As a closing observation on the bargaining area, it may well be greater in the case of unquoted takeovers than quoted ones. In the case of quoted companies, the lower bound for any offer will be the current market price. Given that this does not exist in the case of unquoted firms, the lower bound is probably dictated by some average PE multiple observed from the stock market, less some sort of discount for non-marketability (alternatively, PE multiples can sometimes be observed on unquoted deals from the information given in publications such as *Acquisitions Monthly*, but quite often the terms of such offers are not disclosed).

FINANCING THE ACQUISITION

If the management team of potential bidders has been following the advice given in this book, it will already have formed an opinion of the true value of their own company. Although hubris needs to be guarded against (survey results invariably show that managers on average believe their company to be under-valued by the stock-market), the choice of financing must logically depend on an assessment of whether the shares are currently fairly valued; if the shares are perceived to be under-valued, a share-for-share deal would scarcely be a sensible option. Neither would a 'quasi-equity' deal; quasi-equity includes warrants, convertibles, a rights issue to existing shareholders to raise the necessary cash, vendor placing and vendor rights. The latter two involve the use of intermediaries (issuing houses or merchant banks) who effectively take up the issue to provide the victim company shareholders with cash. With a placing, the shares are issued to institutional buyers in exchange for cash, whilst with the rights issue the intermediary guarantees to buy back the 'rights' shares issued to the victim shareholders at a pre-specified price; these are then offered to the acquirer's shareholders as a rights issue.

We have already noted Franks *et al.*'s (1988) conclusion that although cash offers, on average, carry a higher premium, they also result in better post-combination performance. From a behavioural point of view, it may be that cash is perceived by victim company shareholders as a more 'serious' means of payment than shares; it is certainly less risky, in so far as there is no variation in payment between the offer and settlement dates as there is with an equity exchange. This is, of course, a negative factor from the bidder's point of view, as was grimly demonstrated to those bidders who had cash offers open during the stock market crash of October 1987.[8] Perhaps the difficulty lies with explaining why cash, which in all respects other than tax efficiency for some investors can be seen as the preferable means of remuneration, is associated with higher bid premia than share offers; this effect is also found in the United States. To some extent the solution might be that if bidders systematically offer too much for their targets, the effect on the share price on announcement of the bid will be negative. In turn, this will cause the *actual* premium, measured *ex post facto*, to be lower than the premium intended by the bidder's management at the time of the offer, assuming that management did not anticipate a negative market reaction. The empirical evidence here is not conclusive, but Limmack (1991) shows that the average return on all succesful bids on a value-weighted basis was 2.55 per cent negative over the whole bid period, whilst Franks *et al.* (1988) show a figure of −1.7 per cent in the month of bid on equity offers; unfortunately, neither figure is statistically significant at the 5 per cent level. Interestingly, Limmack (1991) shows that the return for bidders where the bid is abandoned is significantly negative, at −5.4 per cent. Another solution might be the signalling of intentions. Some companies, notably BTR and Hanson, finance their acquisitions with short-term finance; this might provide a signal to the market that the acquirer intends to dispose of some of the acquired businesses, because holding on to them all would require long-term financing. This would presumably have to come either from long-term debt or from equity. If the market perceives that the predator has a good record of disposing profitably of such acquired businesses, we might have another explanation of why cash bidders receive a more favourable share price response than equity bidders. Unfortunately, in the absence of further research in this area, all this remains conjecture. All we can conclude is that cash offers appear to be more favourably viewed than equity offers.

Equity or debt financing?

Clearly the bidder is going to take account of the relative cost of equity and debt. At this point, we need to be very careful indeed. Many corporate managers take the view that equity is cheap when stock market prices are high. In many cases such a view represents the confusion of historic dividend yield and cost of equity capital. In Chapter 6, we noted that the cost of equity capital was dependent upon the market risk premium, β, and the underlying risk-free rate. Note that the components of return are dividend *plus* capital gain; as we have already shown in previous chapters, if the market accepts lower dividend yields, it is presumably in exchange for higher growth in the future. If equity is *genuinely* inexpensive, it will be because of one of the following reasons:

1. The current share price is over-valued, relative to the market.
2. The market as a whole is over-valued.
3. The market risk premium is falling, or has fallen.
4. The risk-free rate of return has fallen.

Note that we have excluded the effect of what is sometimes called 'the PE game' (see below), which should be seen through quickly by informed market participants. Taking each of the above reasons for the perceived cheapness of equity in turn, if the firm is over-valued relative to the market as a whole, a smart market will realise this as soon as the firm tries to issue more equity (this is part of the basis of Myers' (1984) 'Pecking Order' theory of capital structure); the dilemma is that in attempting to exploit the cheapness of equity, management signal this fact to the market. If the market as a whole is 'over-valued',[9] presumably the mass actions of other corporate managers who realise this, and an attempt to exploit the position by share-for-share takeovers and rights issues, will provide an over-valuation signal to the market in a similar fashion, although the firms who are fastest off the mark may obtain some advantage. A falling market risk premium indicates a relative change in the cost of equity compared to debt, although in the long run we might expect a supply and demand equilibrium effect to occur. However, when 'cheapness' is attributable to a fall in the risk-free rate, we should also see a reduction in the cost of borrowing, and therefore equity is neither relatively cheap nor dear compared to debt.

For the largest UK companies, access to the international bond markets means that similar arguments apply to the cost of debt finance, with risk pricing effectively being based upon credit rating. However, such financing is not always suitable for funding acquisitions because of the size requirement (the scale is such that the market is available only to the largest acquirers who wish to fund large acquisitions), and also because of the minimum maturity of the issue, which would have to be five years or more. The majority of cash acquisitions would therefore be funded by bank borrowing, usually on a syndicated basis. The cost of such borrowing changes according to market perceptions and regulatory changes; for example, the 1988 Basle Accord requiring banks to back corporate loans by a full 8 per cent capital may have forced up lending margins. The *Financial Times* (27 September 1991) notes that BTR's £1 billion facility arranged in 1987 was priced at LIBOR plus 0.075 per cent, whereas its financing cost for the 1991 Rockware bid is expected to be LIBOR plus 0.3 per cent, a considerable increase in relative terms, especially when the increase in bank commitment fees (more than 0.1 per cent in this case) is considered. Smaller public companies would end up paying considerably more than this to finance an acquisition. The final cost of such debt finance will also depend upon the gearing level of the acquirer, after taking account of the change in gearing levels imposed by the acquisition of debt obligations of the victim.

Warrants and takeover financing

Finally, we need to consider the use of financing involving the use of warrants. This category includes convertible loan stock, convertible preference shares (preference dividends, whilst not tax deductible in the same way that debt interest is, can offer non-UK investors a tax-advantageous return because of the recoverable tax credit, which is reflected in a lower dividend rate for the issuing company) and straight warrants; a recent example of the latter was Hanson's cash plus warrants offer for Beazer. Provided the bidding company's management are fully aware of the true cost of such finance (see Chapter 6), such forms of financing have their place in certain situations. However, an important point is that the investors need to understand how to value the offer being made to them. Faced with an offering of 3 per cent convertible loan stock with complex conversion terms in Megapredator plc, it is far more likely that the group of elderly investors controlling the family property company of Snodgrass & Co Ltd★ will be frightened off by the deal than convinced by it.

Warrants are one method of giving the victim company investors a share in any 'upside' following an acquisition, whilst limiting their downside loss to the amount they have effectively paid for the warrant when surrendering the control of their company. From their point of view, the offer is similar to an acquisition for cash plus shares, but with an added element of gearing. To illustrate this point, imagine that Megapredator is considering the following two alternative offers for Victim plc★:

Offer 1

£1 cash plus one share (current price £2) for every four shares in Victim.

Offer 2

£1 cash plus one warrant (exercise price £2 in three years time) for every share in Victim.

Immediately prior to the bid rumours starting, Victim's shares were valued at £1.20 each by the market. We can now see what happens to the position of a Victim shareholder if he or she accepts either of these deals when the share price of Megapredator stays at £2, increases to £3.50 or falls to £1.50 in three years from now:

Megapredator share price	Wealth of original holder of 1000 shares in Victim in three years	
	Offer 1	*Offer 2*
£1.50	£1 + (0.25 × £1.50) = £1.375	£1 (warrant not exercised)
£2	£1 + (0.25 × £2) = £1.50	£1 (warrant not exercised)
£3.50	£1 + (0.25 × £3.50) = £1.875	£1 + (£3.50 − £2) = £2.50

his simple example ignores both the time value of money and dividends, but illustrates the type of company where warrants are likely to have most value; basically, those with low dividend payout, profitable reinvestment opportunities (and hence high share price growth) and those with volatile share prices.

If we combine the warrants with a loan stock with detachable or non-detachable warrants (in other words, a convertible), we can obtain a cash flow advantage because of the lower coupon rate attaching to the loan stock element. Such financing can be useful to those acquirers who believe that their newly purchased subsidiary will take some time to generate substantial cash flows, or where a considerable initial investment programme is necessary.

FINANCING: SOME ACCOUNTING CONSIDERATIONS

In theory, the accounting treatment of an acquisition should have absolutely no influence upon either the acquisition itself, or its financing. The reason for this is that informed analysts, fund managers and other market participants should be capable of seeing through any accounting treatment and its implications. However, many corporate managers obviously do not believe this is the case in reality; they may or may not be correct. The evidence from the US Efficient Markets literature suggests that markets are not fooled but, in the United Kingdom, Lee and Tweedie (1981) provide evidence that investors do not appear to have a particularly good understanding of accounting matters. Whether or not the market can be misled by the different presentation of accounting numbers and if so, to what extent, is an interesting but unresolved empirical question.

The PE effect of a takeover

The most obvious (and well known) accounting distortion is that occurring when a victim company with a lower price–earnings multiple than the acquirer is purchased via a share-for-share exchange. This is sometimes referred to as the 'PE effect', and it can be illustrated by a simple example. Take two companies, Cat plc* and Mouse plc*; by way of introducing a total surprise, let us assume that Mouse takes over Cat. Details of both firms, immediately prior to the takeover are as follows:

Item	Mouse plc	Cat plc
Number of shares	100 m	100 m
Market price (per share)	£2	£0.80
EPS	£0.20	£0.20
Accounting profit	£20m	£20m
PE ratio	10×	4×
Market capitalisation	£200m	£80m
Net asset value	£100m	£90m

Mouse now takes over Cat by a one- for two-share exchange, thereby valuing Cat at £1 per share, or £100 million. If we assume that Mouse makes no improvement to Cat's performance, post-acquisition, then the EPS will be the combined earnings (£40 million) divided by the number of shares now in issue (150 million), which gives a figure of 26.7 pence per share. If the market is totally naive, and still applies a PE of 10 to Mouse, we shall see the share price jump to £2.67. Now this would be reasonable if Mouse's management manages to turn round Cat's performance, but otherwise it fails to recognise that Cat presumably had a lower PE ratio either because it had a higher level of systematic risk, or poorer growth prospects, or both. Some managers appear to believe that the PE effect implies that they should never buy a company for an earnings multiple that exceeds their own; this is, of course, a mistaken belief. Companies can be bought for lower PE ratios and still be too expensive, whilst companies bought for higher multiples can still be bargains. The real issue is whether the price paid is less than the value to the acquiring company, not the relative earnings multiple of acquirer and victim. In fact, there is evidence to suggest that in practice acquirers are not concerned about the PE effect; Cooke and Gregory's 1991 study of exchange ratios studied ninety-five UK takeovers in the period between January 1984 and December 1988 and found that the median PE value paid for victim companies was actually slightly higher than the median PE value of the acquiring companies.

Goodwill

A second accounting consideration is goodwill, which is the difference between the price paid for the acquisition, and the fair value of the assets acquired (would-be creative accountants will doubtless notice the potential flexibility allowed by the term 'fair value'). Once again, the accounting treatment of this should be an irrelevance, but some company accountants clearly do not perceive it to be so. There are two broad alternatives permissible under current accounting standards. The first is that goodwill may be capitalised on the balance sheet, and written off, like any tangible asset, over the period of its 'useful life'. The alternative, which can be executed in a number of different ways, [10] involves writing-off the goodwill immediately to reserves; this means that the goodwill write-off never passes through the profit and loss account, and this method is the one used almost invariably by UK companies. SSAP 22 requires that purchased goodwill, 'should normally be eliminated from the accounts by immediate write-off', but also, 'allows a company to carry positive goodwill as an asset and to amortise it through the profit and loss account over its useful life';[11] the maximum useful life is not specified. The normal UK treatment is not a permitted method in many other countries, including the United States. In the United States, the goodwill figure has to be capitalised and then written off over a maximum period of forty years (APB017), and this would appear to be the method preferred by the recently formed UK Accounting Standards Board (ASB),[12] although it should be noted that the ASB has not assumed responsibility for previously issued exposure drafts concerning goodwill and acquisition accounting. The key reason why companies do not like this amortisation treatment is that it causes earnings dilution, which a write-off to reserves does not.

The reason that goodwill is discussed in the context of financing alternatives is that an equity issue provides more scope for the immediate write-off of goodwill than does a cash acquisition financed by debt. Using the 'merger relief' provisions of the 1985 Companies Act (Section 131), it appears that goodwill can be written off against the share premium arising on the acquisition, providing that the acquirer has captured at least a 90 per cent stake in the victim; this treatment has been used in several cases, for example by Tesco in accounting for its acquisition of Hillards. Broadly, this approach records the issue of shares at par value only, and creates a 'merger reserve' which captures the difference between the historic cost of the assets acquired and the par value of the shares issued. To illustrate this approach, let us assume that the par value of Mouse's shares is 25 pence. Clearly, 'goodwill' defined in textbook fashion would be £100 million less the £90 million assets acquired. The balance sheet impact would be:

Assets acquired	£90 million
Shares issued (50 m × 25 pence)	£12.5 million
'Merger reserve' (or similar)	£77.5 million

It is also possible for firms to adopt the merger accounting alternative allowed by SSAP 23, and some firms have extended this to cover vendor placings (Cooke 1986, Chapter 12). The key point about both merger accounting and merger relief is that they are only available to companies who acquire victims for equity.

It may well be that, in practice, firms are influenced in their choice of financing by the accounting implications of that choice. In theory, this should not be the case, but anecdotal evidence appears to suggest that company accountants pay a great deal of attention to the so-called 'bottom line' impact of the decision, in other words the effect on the reported EPS figure. To what degree the accounting alternatives actually play a role in the determination of financing methods is an interesting empirical question.

CHAPTER 11

ISSUES RELATING TO
MANAGEMENT

The company's management is an important consideration in any valuation, from at least three perspectives. First, the quality of the management team is one of the key factors that determine company value. Second, in any purchase of the business, having manangement 'on side' (i.e. supporting the buyer) is undoubtedly helpful and absolutely essential in the case of an agreed sale. Finally, in several situations a third party (which could be a buyer, major shareholder or provider of new finance) may want to protect the value of his or her position in some way through 'incentivising' management. We look at all three of these aspects in this chapter.

QUALITY OF MANAGEMENT

A study of the comments made in brokers' circulars suggests that analysts pay great attention to what they describe as 'quality of management'. Given the importance that analysts and fund managers appear to attach to meeting executive directors of the company, this is not surprising. Such meetings fulfil at least two key roles: (i) it puts the analyst in a position to form a judgement on the management team and (ii) it also allows the analyst to question management on their future plans and strategies (furthermore, it confers a potential advantage on those priveleged to attend such meetings, a point that has given cause for concern of late in some circles).

However, as we noted in Chapter 5, the understanding exhibited by some analysts of the companies' business activities and the relevant accounting data is sometimes less than ideal; whether these same analysts are able to make informed judgements about managerial ability would also appear to be open to question. There is certainly abundant anecdotal evidence suggesting that analysts and fund managers in the UK market have perhaps tended to follow individual personalities too much and company fundamentals not enough.

This should not be taken as suggesting that managerial ability is an unimportant factor in determining company value, but rather as a warning that managerial ability can easily be confused with the cult of personality. Except for followers of 'fad' or 'fashion' value, the latter should be an irrelevance, whilst the former should be of considerable importance. Managerial ability partly shows in track record, but only when measured over an entire business cycle. It is relatively easy to make good profits in an economic boom, simply by adopting high-risk strategies, particularly with regard to financing; it is quite another matter to generate sustainable value for the shareholders and other stakeholders.

An able management team should also be capable of communicating with the investment community. It should be able to demonstrate that it understands the state of the industry(ies) in which it operates, has a plan of where it wishes to go, has strategies in place to achieve that plan and understands the opportunities and threats that face both the company and the industry. It should also be prepared to be open in its reporting of results so that existing and potential investors can obtain a fair view of the business and each of its principal activities. Unfortunately, little else can be offered in terms of 'hard' guidance on judging the management of a company, except perhaps for suggesting caution in the case of companies that provide sparse information to their shareholders. Given some notable cases over the past year or so, many investors in the City may well have come to this conclusion for themselves. Arguably, concerns about overly-powerful chief executives may account for the apparent trend to appoint non-executive directors, presumably as a form of external monitoring of managerial decisions.

THE POSITION OF MANAGEMENT IN A TAKEOVER OR PURCHASE

Except in the case of a hostile takeover, which is often associated with the subsequent replacement of the victim company's most senior managers, the aim of most would-be purchasers is to have the co-operation of the incumbent managerial team, a process commonly referred to as having management 'on-side'. In takeovers of public companies Newbould (1970) found that the premium paid on acquisition is lower in the case of an agreed bid than that paid in a hostile takeover. Besides this 'cost' incentive, the importance of having management on-side in a friendly purchase cannot be over-stated, because it is easy for an unhappy management team to wreck negotiations. In the case of a privately owned company (or family-controlled public company) this can leave the vendor in the weak position of having to sell to either the managers themselves or to a buyer not favoured by the vendor him- or herself. Furthermore, post-acquisition, a well-motivated management team is a key factor in the subsequent success and profitability of the acquired enterprise.

It is therefore important to keep the management team informed of the position from the outset. Furthermore, where possible, management themselves should be given the opportunity to consider a buyout if they wish to and are in a position so to do, although in certain cases (for example, in a forced sale) this may not be possible. Furthermore, it is by no means the case that all management teams wish to stage a buyout; many may not relish the risk or other implications of the process. Throughout negotiations, it must be borne in mind that at some stage managers and purchaser will meet, so that failing to provide managers with information on what is going on may therefore waste a great deal of time and effort if the consequence is a negative reaction from the managers themselves. In fact, it is highly likely that the purchaser will meet the management team at a fairly early stage in the process, given the need to acquire the information described in detail in Chapter 4 and the desire of any purchaser to assess the managers.

Assuming for the moment that management are not intending to stage a buyout, some thought needs to be given to protecting the position of both the managers themselves and that of the prospective purchaser. A certain commonality of interest can be achieved here through the use of appropriate incentives; we examine such schemes below. The aim from the purchaser's point of view will presumably be both to protect the value of the company acquired and, assocaited with this, to ensure the truthful provision of information at the negotiation stage of the proceedings. For this reason 'earn-outs' are sometimes used; an 'earn-out' is a mechanism that ties the final purchase price of the business to its post-acquisition performance. We discuss earn-outs and their merits below.

In many cases, once it is known that the current owner (be this an individual or a company) wishes to sell, the question of management buyouts will arise. These can also occur when the management of a listed company wish to buy the firm back from the existing shareholders, or can arise at the instigation of management rather than as a result of reaction to a desire to sell on the part of the current owner(s).

Management buyouts

Although from most points of view valuation for the purpose of a management buyouts is no different from valuation for any other purpose, there is one crucial difference, which is the information assymmetry associated with buyouts. Although this position is regulated in the case of listed companies (because an offer by management constitutes a take-over bid, it is covered by *The City Code on Takeovers and Mergers*), the reality is that the incumbent management team have access to inside information that other parties do not have. This poses something of a problem for the seller; whilst he or she can have reasonable stab at estimating the 'ongoing' value of the business, establishing the value in a changed state can be a difficult task without the specialist knowledge of the management. The only light that can be shed on the problem is by looking at possible break-up alternatives or by looking at the value achieved by 'proxy' or 'analogue' companies. Given this information assymetry, we might expect that current owners will demand (and receive) a higher premium from management than from some other buyer. There is some evidence from the US that the premia paid by management teams that buy their companies back from the stock market are indeed higher in practice, with a median premium of 51 per cent being found on one US study (DeAngelo *et al.*, 1984).

Generally there will be at least three parties interested in valuing any buyout candidate, namely management, the vendor (or the shareholders in the case of diversely held firms) and the providers of finance. The latter are important because very few management buyouts are financed from the managers' own personal wealth; most rely heavily upon outside capital provision. This capital typically consists of equity, 'senior' (i.e. secured) debt, and various categories of subordinated debt or debt/equity hybrids, which are generically termed 'mezzanine finance'. As all these forms of finance can be categorised as either debt, equity or options, it should be apparent that we can value any of them using the approaches discussed in Chapters 6 and 7.

Whilst valuation from a vendor and management standpoint is a matter of applying the principles described elsewhere in this book, the provider(s) of finance is typically concerned with determining an *exit value*, or price at which the business can be sold either by way of a trade sale or subsequent flotation of the company. A common approach taken by capital providers is to estimate the value of the company on exit at some assumed PE multiple and then look for a high internal rate of return (frequently in excess of 30 per cent pa) on the capital provided. The problem is, of course, how to determine the exit PE multiple.

Not surprisingly, we would suggest that a better way is to apply the usual free cash flow valuation model described in Chapter 8, which has the advantage of considering the actual WACC with the financing structure that the company has at the time of 'exit' (note that if the structure changes after this date, using WACC may give misleading answers and an APV approach may be preferrable). Given that the exit point and the occurence of a 'steady-state' situation may well not coincide, it is important to realise that in such a case the specific forecast horizon needed will not be the same as this exit point. As such, following our discussion of horizon (or terminal) values in Chapter 8, we can see that the application of an earnings multiple to the exit year earnings figure is fraught with problems. However, if a steady-state assumption at the point of exit is reasonable, we can be more optimistic about the validity of applying a PE multiple to the exit year earnings.[1] The main point here is that we should not assume that the exit point and the forecast horizon year are the same, despite the fact that such an assumption is frequently made (often incorrectly) in venture capital valuations.

PROTECTING THE VALUE OF THE INVESTMENT

The most obvious need for ensuring that the value ascribed to a business is a fair one arises in the event of a takeover or purchase. However, there are other occasions when such considerations apply; the most obvious is the purchase of a major stake in a business by a new investor, whether this stake be an equity share or the provision of debt or 'mezzanine' financing. Less obvious is the position of ordinary shareholders, and indeed the position of central management who are stakeholders in the various different business activities (PLBs) of the company. In general, schemes for providing such valuations can be subdivided into those that actually relate the purchase consideration to the post-purchase performance of the company and those that provide management with performance incentives.

The usual example of the former is the 'earn-out'; however, there are variations on this, such as in the case of management buyouts where management's final stake in the company, post-exit of the venture capitalist, is decided according to some measure of performance. This can be brought about via so-called 'sweat capital' provisions, whereby management's equity share increases if certain performance targets are achieved. However, management's final stake is also influenced by the presence of 'equity kickers', which can give the providers of mezzanine finance an equity stake in the business dependent upon its actual performance.

The earn-out

In an earn-out, a proportion of the agreed price is paid at the time of acquisition, with the balance being paid over a period of time; in the case of acquisition by a listed company, payment often takes the form of shares in the acquirer. The advantage of the earn-out to the acquirer is, first, that it provides a check on the forecasts made in agreeing on the purchase price (and as earn-outs are invariably associated with friendly acquisitions these forecasts will normally have taken into account the vendor or acquiree's inputs), and second that it should motivate the managers of the acquired company. There is also a timing advantage, although this will presumably be reflected in the price finally agreed.

The disadvantages are that the terms of many earn-outs, concentrating as they do on profits in the immediate post-acquisition years, encourage short-term profit-boosting behaviour on the part of managers. Unfortunately, lengthening this period imposes other, possibly unacceptable, risks on the vendor, because the acquirer can run into difficulties. If the payment is arranged on a shares basis, the earn-out payments are typically made on some average of quoted prices; when the acquirer experiences a large fall in its share price, this can lead to the acquired company's owners having a far greater stake in the acquirer than was ever envisaged at the time of the deal being made, a recent example being supplied by Saatchi and Saatchi's acquisition programme. Other difficulties can also arise in the definition of profit, if intra-group service charges and transfer prices are involved.

Other incentive schemes

Before discussing such schemes, we should note that the objective here is rather different from that of the earn-out, in that no attempt is being made to tie the purchase consideration to post-acquisition performance. Indeed, there is no requirement for any purchase to have taken place at all, because the objective of such schemes should, rationally, be to maximise the long-term value of the firm to its shareholders. We are only concerned here with reward schemes for the company's senior management and the senior management of the firm's principal lines of business (PLBs).

Broadly, these incentive schemes can be subdivided into profit-related, share-price-related and other schemes. In the case of profit-related schemes, managers are paid some form of bonus depending upon the company's (PLB's) earnings. Whilst such schemes possess some advantages and are used in practice (for example, see Luther, 1992), a key disadvantage is the tendency of such schemes to encourage a focusing upon the short-term 'bottom line' implications of decisions regarding investment expenditure. As we have seen elsewhere in this book, the emphasis should really be on adding to the long-term wealth of stakeholders, and this can best be operationalised in decision-making by application of the NPV rule. Profit incentive schemes are particularly prevalent in schemes used to reward the performance of PLB (divisional) managers within the firm. The need is to find a scheme that rewards managers according to the additional value that they have created for the shareholders, which existing reward schemes for these managers typically fail to do (see Gregory (1988) for a full discussion and explanation). Whilst at *company* level schemes that tie corporate management rewards to long-term share performance are generally to be preferred, especially given the ability of senior management to adopt creative accounting practices, this is not a viable alternative at PLB level. At this level, divisional managers need to receive rewards related to the NPV of projects which they have adopted.

One practically applicable way of achieving this objective is to calculate divisional or PLB income after allowing for a notional lease payment on the assets (this replaces the accounting depreciation number and any allowance for cost of capital) charged by head office. The lease charge on each asset for any year is calculated with reference to the cash flow estimates supplied at the time the PLB managers proposed the project in the first place, and can be stated as:

$$\text{Lease charge}_{\text{Year } n} = \text{Planned cash flow}_{\text{Year } n} \times \frac{\text{asset cost}}{\text{Planned gross present value}}$$

'Profit', for incentive purposes, is then calculated by deducting cash expenses (fixed and variable), the sum of all the asset lease charges and interest on working capital from revenues; a full explanation of this model and why it is compatible with the NPV rule can be found in Gregory (1987).

Turning to the reward of managers at company level, the most obvious manifestation of such schemes is found in the share option schemes granted to many senior executives. Whilst these schemes have the advantage of relating reward to the shareholders' position, they suffer from several problems. The first of these is that general market movements may well have a greater influence on the share price than the actions of the managers themselves. Second, and somewhat ironically, the presence of option-based schemes provides incentives for the management team to limit dividend payout, because capital growth and retention of earnings are positively correlated. Furthermore, as we have seen in Chapter 7, since the option captures this growth but not the dividends, an option on a dividend paying share is always worth less than one on the same share with no dividends.

One way of solving these problems whilst retaining the positive aspects of share-price-related schemes is to use a 'quasi-option' reward system based upon the excess returns achieved by the company (Egginton et al., 1990). Excess returns are defined as the actual return achieved by the firm less the benchmark return derived from the CAPM or market models.[2]

Finally, and more generally associated with the reward of PLB or divisional managers, several authors (most notably Parker, 1979) have argued the case for a more broadly based view of performance extending beyond accounting profit numbers. Whilst any measure of profit used as the basis for incentive schemes should be compatible with the NPV rule (see above), it seems hard to deny that a focus upon broader measures might help to overcome some of the incentives that exist for short-termist behaviour in firms. Such broader measures might include the initiation of new R&D programmes, change in market share, the introduction of new products and various measures of quality, such as customer satisfaction, defect rates in production and number of faulty items returned by customers.

CHAPTER 12

CONCLUDING COMMENTS

The approach taken throughout this book has been to present a rational economic framework for the valuation process. That process consisted of valuing each principal line of business by forecasting the cash flows and discounting those cash flows using an appropriate cost of capital. We concluded that this value could be arrived at for differing strategies and that the optimal strategies should be put in place to maximise this value. We also noted the importance of examining the divestment, spin-off and shut-down alternatives.

Whilst this methodology, properly and accurately applied, should give us the 'rational' value of the company, it does not follow that in the case of a takeover such a figure is necessarily the price that a buyer would be prepared to pay or that a seller would accept. A full explanation of why this is so would be quite capable of filling a book by itself. For example, it is perfectly possible that the business has a special strategic value to one or more potential buyers, often for reasons connected with market entry or geographical location. If this is far above the value of the business to the current owners, the scope for bargaining may be enormous. Because of this, prices bid and asked may be related far more to bargaining strategies than any notion of economic worth. In addition, behavioural and other factors have a role to play. In the case of contested acquisitions, there have been notable examples where logic appears to have been discarded in favour of egotistical factors. With acquisitions of private companies, the offer accepted by a vendor may not be the highest one available if he or she likes a particular purchaser or feels that that purchaser's objectives are closer to his/her own.

In the case of listed companies, it is not necessarily the case that market price automatically equates to the 'value' perceived by management. This may simply reflect the fact that management are too optimistic about the company's worth. However, it may reflect a lack of communication between management and the investment community; if so, this situation needs to be addressed, preferably by management providing sufficiently detailed annual reports and explaining its strategies and plans, as far as commercial considerations allow.

In acquisitions, the particular circumstances of the purchaser and vendor are also important in determining the actual price paid for any business. For example, the seller may be in a forced sale situation; private companies may be sold because of the death, illness or retirement plans of the existing owner, or because of a shortage of funds. This latter reason has also motivated the sale of many subsidiaries of public companies, particularly over the past couple of years. In such cases, when the number of potential buyers is limited for reasons connected with the economic outlook, lack of specialist skills or knowledge, or some other reason, the seller may have to accept a figure lower than the 'true' value of the business.

Turning to the methodologies employed in this book, throughout we have tried to analyse the company in question in a manner compatible with current finance and economic theory. The recommended process might be summarised thus:

1. Identify each principal line of business (PLB).
2. Estimate a cost of capital for each PLB using (where possible) proxy or analogue companies, making due allowance for gearing and any differences in operating cost structure.
3. For current strategies in place, prepare a specific period (minimum five years) cash flow forecast and discount these at the rate set from step 2.
4. Select an appropriate horizon valuation model; this should be one that reflects the growth and return environment in which the business operates. Consideration should also be given to the use of a transition period model.
5. Forecast the necessary parameters in the horizon valuation model, estimate this horizon value and discount that figure back to today's value at the discount rate set in step 2. An alternative methodology is that of adjusted present value, in which case tax shield values need to be established and the rate set in step 2 will be the 'all-equity' cost of capital.
6. The value of the company is the sum of the PLB values, less the present value of head office and other support costs.
7. Check valuation for accuracy; conduct sensitivity analysis and/or scenario modelling to see how value changes with forecast parameters and assumptions.
8. Repeat steps 3–7 above (and, where necessary, step 2) for alternative strategies; the potential value of the company is the maximum of the values of these strategies.
9. In the case of acquisitions, ensure that synergies and merger gains are rationally valued. Examine the impact of alternative acquisition financing and managerial incentives on the value added for the acquiring company shareholders.

This process may be very different from that employed by practicing valuers at the moment. This does not necessarily mean that current valuation practice is in error, or that it is any less valid. For example, whilst our prescription has been to make a detailed estimate of the cash flows for a specific forecast period, calculate a horizon value based upon projected long-term growth rates, and discount these figures at the estimated cost of capital, the practitioner may well arrive at a similar figure by calculating a 'maintainable' earnings figure and applying a capitalisation multiple based upon 'feel'. Whilst the end result may be similar (or, of course, may be altogether different), one advantage of the detailed step-by-step approach is that it forces the valuer to be explicit about the assumptions that he or she has made in the valuation.

However, as we noted in earlier chapters, the critical variables in the valuation will generally be the sales and margin forecasts. In the end, the accuracy of these will typically have a greater impact than the purity of the valuation mechanism chosen. It is also important that what might be termed 'reality checks' are built into the process. Such checks include performing a secondary valuation based upon an alternative methodology (if the recommended DCF valuation has been used, what is the value arrived at by using an earnings multiple approach?), looking at the relationship between turnover (sales) and value, and cross-checking (where possible) against the values ascribed to other proxy or analogue companies. Unfortunately, following all these safeguards does not always result in a rational valuation. A salutary warning can be found in the level of earnings multiples being paid for estate agencies in the late 1980s; with hindsight, many buyers paid considerably too much for their acquisitions. This is a particularly difficult problem, because when everyone is over-bidding for companies, looking at any data connected with multiples paid does not help. Furthermore, in a non-acquisition context there is at least some evidence to suggest that markets may follow 'fads' and over-value some companies. Perhaps one lesson from research studies and individual case histories is that it pays not to get carried away in valuing fashionable or unfashionable companies and sectors; standing back and taking a detached view of rational economic growth expectations may save both the cash of the shareholders and the jobs of many employees. Furthermore, such an approach should encourage managers to take a long term view of the worth of their business, and to set in place strategies which increase this value.

APPENDICES

APPENDIX A

Compound sum of £1: $(1 + r)^n$ (Table A)

Period	1%	2%	3%	4%	5%	6%	7%	8%	9%	10%	12%	14%	15%	16%	18%	20%	24%	28%	32%	36%
1	1.0100	1.0200	1.0300	1.0400	1.0500	1.0600	1.0700	1.0800	1.0900	1.1000	1.1200	1.1400	1.1500	1.1600	1.1800	1.2000	1.2400	1.2800	1.3200	1.3600
2	1.0201	1.0404	1.0609	1.0816	1.1025	1.1236	1.1449	1.1664	1.1881	1.2100	1.2544	1.2996	1.3225	1.3456	1.3924	1.4400	1.5376	1.6384	1.7424	1.8496
3	1.0303	1.0612	1.0927	1.1249	1.1576	1.1910	1.2250	1.2597	1.2950	1.3310	1.4049	1.4815	1.5209	1.5609	1.6430	1.7280	1.9066	2.0972	2.3000	2.5155
4	1.0406	1.0824	1.1255	1.1699	1.2155	1.2625	1.3108	1.3605	1.4116	1.4641	1.5735	1.6890	1.7490	1.8106	1.9388	2.0736	2.3642	2.6844	3.0360	3.4210
5	1.0510	1.1041	1.1593	1.2167	1.2763	1.3382	1.4026	1.4693	1.5386	1.6105	1.7623	1.9254	2.0114	2.1003	2.2878	2.4883	2.9316	3.4360	4.0075	4.6526
6	1.0615	1.1262	1.1941	1.2653	1.3401	1.4185	1.5007	1.5869	1.6771	1.7716	1.9738	2.1950	2.3131	2.4364	2.6996	2.9860	3.6352	4.3980	5.2899	6.3275
7	1.0721	1.1487	1.2299	1.3159	1.4071	1.5036	1.6058	1.7138	1.8280	1.9487	2.2107	2.5023	2.6600	2.8262	3.1855	3.5832	4.5077	5.6295	6.9826	8.6054
8	1.0829	1.1717	1.2668	1.3686	1.4775	1.5938	1.7182	1.8509	1.9926	2.1436	2.4760	2.8526	3.0590	3.2784	3.7589	4.2998	5.5895	7.2058	9.2170	11.703
9	1.0937	1.1951	1.3048	1.4233	1.5513	1.6895	1.8385	1.9990	2.1719	2.3579	2.7731	3.2519	3.5179	3.8030	4.4355	5.1598	6.9310	9.2234	12.166	15.916
10	1.1046	1.2190	1.3439	1.4802	1.6289	1.7908	1.9672	2.1589	2.3674	2.5937	3.1058	3.7072	4.0456	4.4114	5.2338	6.1917	8.5944	11.805	16.059	21.646
11	1.1157	1.2434	1.3842	1.5395	1.7103	1.8983	2.1049	2.3316	2.5804	2.8531	3.4785	4.2262	4.6524	5.1173	6.1759	7.4301	10.657	15.111	21.198	29.439
12	1.1268	1.2682	1.4258	1.6010	1.7959	2.0122	2.2522	2.5182	2.8127	3.1384	3.8960	4.8179	5.3502	5.9360	7.2876	8.9161	13.214	19.342	27.982	40.037
13	1.1381	1.2936	1.4685	1.6651	1.8856	2.1329	2.4098	2.7196	3.0658	3.4523	4.3635	5.4924	6.1528	6.8858	8.5994	10.699	16.386	24.758	36.937	54.451
14	1.1495	1.3195	1.5126	1.7317	1.9799	2.2609	2.5785	2.9372	3.3417	3.7975	4.8871	6.2613	7.0757	7.9875	10.147	12.839	20.319	31.691	48.756	74.031
15	1.1610	1.3459	1.5580	1.8009	2.0789	2.3966	2.7590	3.1722	3.6425	4.1772	5.4736	7.1379	8.1371	9.2655	11.973	15.407	25.195	40.564	64.358	100.71
16	1.1726	1.3728	1.6047	1.8730	2.1829	2.5404	2.9522	3.4259	3.9703	4.5950	6.1304	8.1372	9.3576	10.478	14.129	18.488	31.242	51.923	84.953	136.96
17	1.1843	1.4002	1.6528	1.9479	2.2920	2.6928	3.1588	3.7000	4.3276	5.0545	6.8660	9.2765	10.761	12.467	16.672	22.186	38.740	66.461	112.13	186.27
18	1.1961	1.4282	1.7024	2.0258	2.4066	2.8543	3.3799	3.9960	4.7171	5.5599	7.6900	10.575	12.375	14.462	19.673	26.623	48.038	85.070	148.02	253.33
19	1.2081	1.4568	1.7535	2.1068	2.5270	3.0256	3.6165	4.3157	5.1417	6.1159	8.6128	12.055	14.231	16.776	23.214	31.948	59.567	108.89	195.39	344.53
20	1.2202	1.4859	1.8061	2.1911	2.6533	3.2071	3.8697	4.6610	5.6044	6.7275	9.6463	13.743	16.366	19.460	27.393	38.337	73.864	139.37	257.91	468.57
21	1.2324	1.5157	1.8603	2.2788	2.7860	3.3996	4.1406	5.0338	6.1088	7.4002	10.803	15.667	18.821	22.574	32.323	46.005	91.591	178.40	340.44	637.26
22	1.2447	1.5460	1.9161	2.3699	2.9253	3.6035	4.4304	5.4365	6.6586	8.1403	12.100	17.861	21.644	26.186	38.142	55.206	113.57	228.35	449.39	866.67
23	1.2572	1.5769	1.9736	2.4647	3.0715	3.8197	4.7405	5.8715	7.2579	8.9543	13.552	20.361	24.891	30.376	45.007	66.247	140.83	292.30	593.19	1178.6
24	1.2697	1.6084	2.0328	2.5633	3.2251	4.0489	5.0724	6.3412	7.9111	9.8497	15.178	23.212	28.625	35.236	53.108	79.496	174.63	374.14	783.02	1602.9
25	1.2824	1.6406	2.0938	2.6658	3.3864	4.2919	5.4274	6.8485	8.6231	10.834	17.000	26.461	32.918	40.874	62.668	95.396	216.54	478.90	1033.5	2180.0
26	1.2953	1.6734	2.1566	2.7725	3.5557	4.5494	5.8074	7.3964	9.3992	11.918	19.040	30.166	37.856	47.414	73.948	114.47	268.51	612.99	1364.3	2964.9
27	1.3082	1.7069	2.2213	2.8834	3.7335	4.8223	6.2139	7.9881	10.245	13.110	21.324	34.389	43.535	55.000	87.259	137.37	332.95	784.63	1800.9	4032.2
28	1.3213	1.7410	2.2879	2.9987	3.9201	5.1117	6.6488	8.6271	11.167	14.421	23.883	39.304	50.065	63.800	102.96	164.84	412.86	1004.3	2377.2	5483.8
29	1.3345	1.7758	2.3566	3.1187	4.1161	5.4184	7.1143	9.3173	12.172	15.863	26.749	44.693	57.575	74.008	121.50	197.81	511.95	1285.5	3137.9	7458.0
30	1.3478	1.8114	2.4273	3.2434	4.3219	5.7435	7.6123	10.062	13.267	17.449	29.959	50.950	66.211	85.849	143.37	237.37	634.81	1645.5	4142.0	10143.
40	1.4889	2.2080	3.2620	4.8010	7.0400	10.285	14.974	21.724	31.409	45.259	93.050	188.88	267.86	378.72	750.37	1469.7	5455.9	19426.	66520.	*
50	1.6446	2.6916	4.3839	7.1067	11.467	18.420	29.457	46.901	74.357	117.39	289.00	700.23	1083.6	1670.7	3927.3	9100.4	46890.	*	*	*
60	1.8167	3.2810	5.8916	10.519	18.679	32.987	57.946	101.25	176.03	304.48	897.59	2595.9	4383.9	7370.1	20555.	56347.	*	*	*	*

*FVIF > 99,999.

Present value of £1: $\dfrac{1}{(1+r)^n}$ (Table B)

Period	1%	3%	5%	6%	7%	8%	9%	10%	11%	12%	13%	14%	15%	16%	17%	18%	19%	20%	24%	28%
1	0.9901	0.9709	0.9524	0.9434	0.9346	0.9259	0.9174	0.9091	0.9009	0.8929	0.8850	0.8772	0.8696	0.8621	0.8547	0.8475	0.8403	0.8333	0.8065	0.7813
2	0.9803	0.9426	0.9070	0.8900	0.8734	0.8573	0.8417	0.8264	0.8116	0.7972	0.7831	0.7695	0.7561	0.7432	0.7305	0.7182	0.7062	0.6944	0.6504	0.6104
3	0.9706	0.9151	0.8638	0.8396	0.8163	0.7938	0.7722	0.7513	0.7312	0.7118	0.6930	0.6750	0.6575	0.6407	0.6244	0.6086	0.5934	0.5787	0.5245	0.4768
4	0.9610	0.8885	0.8227	0.7921	0.7629	0.7350	0.7084	0.6830	0.6587	0.6355	0.6133	0.5921	0.5718	0.5523	0.5336	0.5158	0.4987	0.4823	0.4230	0.3725
5	0.9515	0.8626	0.7835	0.7473	0.7130	0.6806	0.6499	0.6209	0.5934	0.5674	0.5428	0.5194	0.4972	0.4761	0.4561	0.4371	0.4190	0.4019	0.3411	0.2910
6	0.9420	0.8375	0.7462	0.7050	0.6663	0.6302	0.5963	0.5645	0.5346	0.5066	0.4803	0.4556	0.4323	0.4104	0.3898	0.3704	0.3521	0.3349	0.2751	0.2274
7	0.9327	0.8131	0.7107	0.6651	0.6227	0.5835	0.5470	0.5132	0.4817	0.4523	0.4251	0.3996	0.3759	0.3538	0.3332	0.3139	0.2959	0.2791	0.2218	0.1776
8	0.9235	0.7894	0.6768	0.6274	0.5820	0.5403	0.5019	0.4665	0.4339	0.4039	0.3762	0.3506	0.3269	0.3050	0.2848	0.2660	0.2487	0.2326	0.1789	0.1388
9	0.9143	0.7664	0.6446	0.5919	0.5439	0.5002	0.4604	0.4241	0.3909	0.3606	0.3329	0.3075	0.2843	0.2630	0.2434	0.2255	0.2090	0.1938	0.1443	0.1084
10	0.9053	0.7441	0.6139	0.5584	0.5083	0.4632	0.4224	0.3855	0.3522	0.3220	0.2946	0.2697	0.2472	0.2267	0.2080	0.1911	0.1756	0.1615	0.1164	0.0847
11	0.8963	0.7224	0.5847	0.5268	0.4751	0.4289	0.3875	0.3505	0.3173	0.2875	0.2607	0.2366	0.2149	0.1954	0.1778	0.1619	0.1476	0.1346	0.0938	0.0662
12	0.8874	0.7014	0.5568	0.4970	0.4440	0.3971	0.3555	0.3186	0.2858	0.2567	0.2307	0.2076	0.1869	0.1685	0.1520	0.1372	0.1240	0.1122	0.0757	0.0517
13	0.8787	0.6810	0.5303	0.4688	0.4150	0.3677	0.3262	0.2897	0.2575	0.2292	0.2042	0.1821	0.1625	0.1452	0.1299	0.1163	0.1042	0.0935	0.0610	0.0404
14	0.8700	0.6611	0.5051	0.4423	0.3878	0.3405	0.2992	0.2633	0.2320	0.2046	0.1807	0.1597	0.1413	0.1252	0.1110	0.0985	0.0876	0.0779	0.0492	0.0316
15	0.8613	0.6419	0.4810	0.4173	0.3624	0.3152	0.2745	0.2394	0.2090	0.1827	0.1599	0.1401	0.1229	0.1079	0.0949	0.0835	0.0736	0.0649	0.0397	0.0247
16	0.8528	0.6232	0.4581	0.3936	0.3387	0.2919	0.2519	0.2176	0.1883	0.1631	0.1415	0.1229	0.1069	0.0930	0.0811	0.0708	0.0618	0.0541	0.0320	0.0193
17	0.8444	0.6050	0.4363	0.3714	0.3166	0.2703	0.2311	0.1978	0.1696	0.1456	0.1252	0.1078	0.0929	0.0802	0.0693	0.0600	0.0520	0.0451	0.0258	0.0150
18	0.8360	0.5874	0.4155	0.3503	0.2959	0.2502	0.2120	0.1799	0.1528	0.1300	0.1108	0.0946	0.0808	0.0691	0.0592	0.0508	0.0437	0.0376	0.0208	0.0118
19	0.8277	0.5703	0.3957	0.3305	0.2765	0.2317	0.1945	0.1635	0.1377	0.1161	0.0981	0.0829	0.0703	0.0596	0.0506	0.0431	0.0367	0.0313	0.0168	0.0092
20	0.8195	0.5537	0.3769	0.3118	0.2584	0.2145	0.1784	0.1486	0.1240	0.1037	0.0868	0.0728	0.0611	0.0514	0.0433	0.0365	0.0308	0.0261	0.0135	0.0072
25	0.7798	0.4776	0.2953	0.2330	0.1842	0.1460	0.1160	0.0923	0.0736	0.0588	0.0471	0.0378	0.0304	0.0245	0.0197	0.0160	0.0129	0.0105	0.0046	0.0021
30	0.7419	0.4120	0.2314	0.1741	0.1314	0.0994	0.0754	0.0573	0.0437	0.0334	0.0256	0.0196	0.0151	0.0116	0.0090	0.0070	0.0054	0.0042	0.0016	0.0006
40	0.6717	0.3066	0.1420	0.0972	0.0668	0.0460	0.0318	0.0221	0.0154	0.0107	0.0075	0.0053	0.0037	0.0026	0.0019	0.0013	0.0010	0.0007	0.0002	0.0001
50	0.6080	0.2281	0.0872	0.0543	0.0339	0.0213	0.0134	0.0085	0.0054	0.0035	0.0022	0.0014	0.0009	0.0006	0.0004	0.0003	0.0002	0.0001	*	*
60	0.5504	0.1697	0.0535	0.0303	0.0173	0.0099	0.0057	0.0033	0.0019	0.0011	0.0007	0.0004	0.0002	0.0001	0.0001	*	*	*	*	*

*The factor is zero to four decimal places.

Sum of an annuity of £1 for n periods:

$$A - 1 \qquad \sum_{t=0} (1+r)^t$$

(Table C)

No. of Periods	1%	2%	3%	4%	5%	6%	7%	8%	9%	10%	12%	14%	15%	16%	18%	20%	24%	28%	32%	36%
1	1.0000	1.0000	1.0000	1.0000	1.0000	1.0000	1.0000	1.0000	1.0000	1.0000	1.0000	1.0000	1.0000	1.0000	1.0000	1.0000	1.0000	1.0000	1.0000	1.0000
2	2.0100	2.0200	2.0300	2.0400	2.0500	2.0600	2.0700	2.0800	2.0900	2.1000	2.1200	2.1400	2.1500	2.1600	2.1800	2.2000	2.2400	2.2800	2.3200	2.3600
3	3.0301	3.0604	3.0909	3.1216	3.1525	3.1836	3.2149	3.2464	3.2781	3.3100	3.3744	3.4396	3.4725	3.5056	3.5724	3.6400	3.7776	3.9184	4.0624	4.2096
4	4.0604	4.1216	4.1836	4.2465	4.3101	4.3746	4.4399	4.5061	4.5731	4.6410	4.7793	4.9211	4.9934	5.0665	5.2154	5.3680	5.6842	6.0156	6.3624	6.7251
5	5.1010	5.2040	5.3091	5.4163	5.5256	5.6371	5.7507	5.8666	5.9847	6.1051	6.3528	6.6101	6.7424	6.8771	7.1542	7.4416	8.0484	8.6999	9.3983	10.146
6	6.1520	6.3081	6.4684	6.6330	6.8019	6.9753	7.1533	7.3359	7.5233	7.7156	8.1152	8.5355	8.7537	8.9775	9.4420	9.9299	10.980	12.135	13.405	14.798
7	7.2135	7.4343	7.6625	7.8983	8.1420	8.3938	8.6540	8.9228	9.2004	9.4872	10.089	10.730	11.066	11.413	12.141	12.915	14.615	16.533	18.695	21.126
8	8.2857	8.5830	8.8923	9.2142	9.5491	9.8975	10.259	10.636	11.028	11.435	12.299	13.232	13.726	14.240	15.327	16.499	19.122	22.163	25.678	29.731
9	9.3685	9.7546	10.159	10.582	11.026	11.491	11.978	12.487	13.021	13.579	14.775	16.085	16.785	17.518	19.085	20.798	24.712	29.369	34.895	41.435
10	10.462	10.949	11.463	12.006	12.577	13.180	13.816	14.486	15.192	15.937	17.548	19.337	20.303	21.321	23.521	25.958	31.643	38.592	47.061	57.351
11	11.566	12.168	12.807	13.486	14.206	14.971	15.783	16.645	17.560	18.531	20.654	23.044	24.349	25.732	28.755	32.150	40.237	50.398	63.121	78.998
12	12.682	13.412	14.192	15.025	15.917	16.869	17.888	18.977	20.140	21.384	24.133	27.270	29.001	30.850	34.931	39.580	50.894	65.510	84.320	108.43
13	13.809	14.680	15.617	16.626	17.713	18.882	20.140	21.495	22.953	24.522	28.029	32.088	34.351	36.786	42.218	48.496	64.109	84.852	112.30	148.47
14	14.947	15.973	17.086	18.291	19.598	21.015	22.550	24.214	26.019	27.975	32.392	37.581	40.504	43.672	50.818	59.195	80.496	109.61	149.23	202.92
15	16.096	17.293	18.598	20.023	21.578	23.276	25.129	27.152	29.360	31.772	37.279	43.842	47.580	51.659	60.965	72.035	100.81	141.30	197.99	276.97
16	17.257	18.639	20.156	21.824	23.657	25.672	27.888	30.324	33.003	35.949	42.753	50.980	55.717	60.925	72.939	87.442	126.01	181.86	262.35	377.69
17	18.430	20.012	21.761	23.697	25.840	28.212	30.840	33.750	36.973	40.544	48.883	59.117	65.075	71.673	87.068	105.93	157.25	233.79	347.30	514.66
18	19.614	21.412	23.414	25.645	28.132	30.905	33.999	37.450	41.301	45.599	55.749	68.394	75.836	84.140	103.74	128.11	195.99	300.25	459.44	700.93
19	20.810	22.840	25.116	27.671	30.539	33.760	37.379	41.446	46.018	51.159	63.439	78.969	88.211	98.603	123.41	154.74	244.03	385.32	607.47	954.27
20	22.019	24.297	26.870	29.778	33.066	36.785	40.995	45.762	51.160	57.275	72.052	91.024	102.44	115.37	146.62	186.68	303.60	494.21	802.86	1298.8
21	23.239	25.783	28.676	31.969	35.719	39.992	44.865	50.422	56.764	64.002	81.698	104.76	118.81	134.84	174.02	225.02	377.46	633.59	1060.7	1767.3
22	24.471	27.299	30.536	34.248	38.505	43.392	49.005	55.456	62.873	71.402	92.502	120.43	137.63	157.41	206.34	271.03	469.05	811.99	1401.2	2404.6
23	25.716	28.845	32.452	36.617	41.430	46.995	53.436	60.893	69.531	79.543	104.60	138.29	159.27	183.60	244.48	326.23	582.62	1040.3	1850.6	3271.3
24	26.973	30.421	34.426	39.082	44.502	50.815	58.176	66.764	76.789	88.497	118.15	158.65	184.16	213.97	289.49	392.48	723.46	1332.6	2443.8	4449.9
25	28.243	32.030	36.459	41.645	47.727	54.864	63.249	73.105	84.700	98.347	133.33	181.87	212.79	249.21	342.60	471.98	898.09	1706.8	3226.8	6052.9
26	29.525	33.670	38.553	44.311	51.113	59.156	68.676	79.954	93.323	109.18	150.33	208.33	245.71	290.08	405.27	567.37	1114.6	2185.7	4260.4	8233.0
27	30.820	35.344	40.709	47.084	54.669	63.705	74.483	87.350	102.72	121.09	169.37	238.49	283.56	337.50	479.22	681.85	1383.1	2798.7	5624.7	11197.9
28	32.129	37.051	42.930	49.967	58.402	68.528	80.697	95.338	112.96	134.20	190.69	272.88	327.10	392.50	566.48	819.22	1716.0	3583.3	7425.6	15230.2
29	33.450	38.792	45.218	52.966	62.322	73.639	87.346	103.96	124.13	148.63	214.58	312.09	377.16	456.30	669.44	984.06	2128.9	4587.6	9802.9	20714.1
30	34.784	40.568	47.575	56.084	66.438	79.058	94.460	113.28	136.30	164.49	241.33	356.78	434.74	530.31	790.94	1181.8	2640.9	5873.2	12940.	28172.2
40	48.886	60.402	75.401	95.025	120.79	154.76	199.63	259.05	337.88	442.59	767.09	1342.0	1779.0	2360.7	4163.2	7343.8	22728.	69337.	*	*
50	64.463	84.579	112.79	152.66	209.34	290.33	406.52	573.76	815.08	1163.9	2400.0	4994.5	7217.7	10435.	21813.	45497.	*	*	*	*
60	81.669	114.05	163.05	237.99	353.58	533.12	813.52	1253.2	1944.7	3034.8	7471.6	18535.	29219.	46057.	*	*	*	*	*	*

*FVIFA > 99,999

Present value of an annuity of £1 for n periods: $\displaystyle\sum_{t=1}^{n} \frac{1}{(1+k)^t}$ (Table D)

No. of payments	1%	3%	5%	6%	7%	8%	9%	10%	11%	12%	13%	14%	15%	16%	17%	18%	19%	20%	24%
1	0.9901	0.9709	0.9524	0.9434	0.9346	0.9259	0.9174	0.9091	0.9009	0.8929	0.8850	0.8772	0.8696	0.8621	0.8547	0.8475	0.8403	0.8333	0.8065
2	1.9704	1.9135	1.8594	1.8334	1.8080	1.7833	1.7591	1.7355	1.7125	1.6901	1.6681	1.6467	1.6257	1.6052	1.5852	1.5656	1.5465	1.5278	1.4568
3	2.9410	2.8286	2.7232	2.6730	2.6243	2.5771	2.5313	2.4869	2.4437	2.4018	2.3612	2.3216	2.2832	2.2459	2.2096	2.1743	2.1399	2.1065	1.9813
4	3.9020	3.7171	3.5460	3.4651	3.3872	3.3121	3.2397	3.1699	3.1024	3.0373	2.9745	2.9137	2.8550	2.7982	2.7432	2.6901	2.6386	2.5887	2.4043
5	4.8534	4.5797	4.3295	4.2124	4.1002	3.9927	3.8897	3.7908	3.6959	3.6048	3.5172	3.4331	3.3522	3.2743	3.1993	3.1272	3.0576	2.9906	2.7454
6	5.7955	5.4172	5.0757	4.9173	4.7665	4.6229	4.4859	4.3553	4.2305	4.1114	3.9976	3.8887	3.7845	3.6847	3.5892	3.4976	3.4098	3.3255	3.0205
7	6.7282	6.2303	5.7864	5.5824	5.3893	5.2064	5.0330	4.8684	4.7122	4.5638	4.4226	4.2883	4.1604	4.0386	3.9224	3.8115	3.7057	3.6046	3.2423
8	7.6517	7.0197	6.4632	6.2098	5.9713	5.7466	5.5348	5.3349	5.1461	4.9676	4.7988	4.6389	4.4873	4.3436	4.2072	4.0776	3.9544	3.8372	3.4212
9	8.5660	7.7861	7.1078	6.8017	6.5152	6.2469	5.9952	5.7590	5.5370	5.3282	5.1317	4.9464	4.7716	4.6065	4.4506	4.3030	4.1633	4.0310	3.5655
10	9.4713	8.5302	7.7217	7.3601	7.0236	6.7101	6.4177	6.1446	5.8892	5.6502	5.4262	5.2161	5.0188	4.8332	4.6586	4.4941	4.3389	4.1925	3.6819
11	10.3676	9.2526	8.3064	7.8869	7.4987	7.1390	6.8052	6.4951	6.2065	5.9377	5.6869	5.4527	5.2337	5.0286	4.8364	4.6560	4.4865	4.3271	3.7757
12	11.2551	9.9540	8.8633	8.3838	7.9427	7.5361	7.1607	6.8137	6.4924	6.1944	5.9176	5.6603	5.4206	5.1971	4.9884	4.7932	4.6105	4.4392	3.8514
13	12.1337	10.6350	9.3936	8.8527	8.3577	7.9038	7.4869	7.1034	6.7499	6.4235	6.1218	5.8424	5.5831	5.3423	5.1183	4.9095	4.7147	4.5327	3.9124
14	13.0037	11.2961	9.8986	9.2950	8.7455	8.2442	7.7862	7.3667	6.9819	6.6282	6.3025	6.0021	5.7245	5.4675	5.2293	5.0081	4.8023	4.6106	3.9616
15	13.8651	11.9379	10.3797	9.7122	9.1079	8.5595	8.0607	7.6061	7.1909	6.8109	6.4624	6.1422	5.8474	5.5755	5.3242	5.0916	4.8759	4.6755	4.0013
16	14.7179	12.5611	10.8378	10.1059	9.4466	8.8514	8.3126	7.8237	7.3792	6.9740	6.6039	6.2651	5.9542	5.6685	5.4053	5.1624	4.9377	4.7296	4.0333
17	15.5623	13.1661	11.2741	10.4773	9.7632	9.1216	8.5436	8.0216	7.5488	7.1196	6.7291	6.3729	6.0472	5.7487	5.4746	5.2223	4.9897	4.7746	4.0591
18	16.3983	13.7535	11.6896	10.8276	10.0591	9.3719	8.7556	8.2014	7.7016	7.2497	6.8399	6.4674	6.1280	5.8178	5.5339	5.2732	5.0333	4.8122	4.0799
19	17.2260	14.3238	12.0853	11.1581	10.3356	9.6036	8.9501	8.3649	7.8393	7.3658	6.9380	6.5504	6.1982	5.8775	5.5845	5.3162	5.0700	4.8435	4.0967
20	18.0456	14.8775	12.4622	11.4699	10.5940	9.8181	9.1285	8.5136	7.9633	7.4694	7.0248	6.6231	6.2593	5.9288	5.6278	5.3527	5.1009	4.8696	4.1103
25	22.0232	17.4131	14.0939	12.7834	11.6536	10.6748	9.8226	9.0770	8.4217	7.8431	7.3300	6.8729	6.4641	6.0971	5.7662	5.4669	5.1951	4.9476	4.1474
30	25.8077	19.6004	15.3725	13.7648	12.4090	11.2578	10.2737	9.4269	8.6938	8.0552	7.4957	7.0027	6.5660	6.1772	5.8294	5.5168	5.2347	4.9789	4.1601
40	32.8347	23.1148	17.1591	15.0463	13.3317	11.9246	10.7574	9.7791	8.9511	8.2438	7.6344	7.1050	6.6418	6.2335	5.8713	5.5482	5.2582	4.9966	4.1659
50	39.1961	25.7298	18.2559	15.7619	13.8007	12.2335	10.9617	9.9148	9.0417	8.3045	7.6752	7.1327	6.6605	6.2463	5.8801	5.5541	5.2623	4.9995	4.1666
60	44.9550	27.6756	18.9293	16.1614	14.0392	12.3766	11.0480	9.9672	9.0892	8.3240	7.6873	7.1401	6.6651	6.2492	5.8819	5.5553	5.2630	4.9999	4.1667

APPENDIX B

Standard normal distribution function

$d_{(n)}$	0	1	2	3	4	5	6	7	8	9
−3.0	0.0013									
−2.9	0.0019	0.0018	0.0018	0.0017	0.0017	0.0016	0.0015	0.0015	0.0014	0.0014
−2.8	0.0026	0.0025	0.0024	0.0023	0.0023	0.0022	0.0021	0.0021	0.0020	0.0019
−2.7	0.0035	0.0034	0.0033	0.0032	0.0031	0.0030	0.0029	0.0028	0.0027	0.0026
−2.6	0.0047	0.0045	0.0044	0.0043	0.0041	0.0040	0.0039	0.0038	0.0037	0.0036
−2.5	0.0062	0.0060	0.0059	0.0057	0.0055	0.0054	0.0052	0.0051	0.0049	0.0048
−2.4	0.0082	0.0080	0.0078	0.0075	0.0073	0.0071	0.0069	0.0068	0.0066	0.0064
−2.3	0.0107	0.0104	0.0102	0.0099	0.0096	0.0094	0.0091	0.0089	0.0087	0.0084
−2.2	0.0139	0.0136	0.0132	0.0129	0.0125	0.0122	0.0119	0.0116	0.0113	0.0110
−2.1	0.0179	0.0174	0.0170	0.0166	0.0162	0.0158	0.0154	0.0150	0.0146	0.0143
−2.0	0.0228	0.0222	0.0217	0.0212	0.0207	0.0202	0.0197	0.0192	0.0188	0.0183
−1.9	0.0287	0.0281	0.0275	0.0268	0.0262	0.0256	0.0250	0.0244	0.0239	0.0233
−1.8	0.0359	0.0351	0.0344	0.0336	0.0329	0.0322	0.0314	0.0307	0.0300	0.0294
−1.7	0.0446	0.0436	0.0427	0.0418	0.0409	0.0401	0.0392	0.0384	0.0375	0.0367
−1.6	0.0548	0.0537	0.0526	0.0516	0.0505	0.0495	0.0485	0.0475	0.0465	0.0455
−1.5	0.0668	0.0655	0.0643	0.0630	0.0618	0.0606	0.0594	0.0582	0.0571	0.0560
−1.4	0.0808	0.0793	0.0778	0.0764	0.0750	0.0735	0.0721	0.0708	0.0694	0.0681
−1.3	0.0968	0.0951	0.0934	0.0918	0.0901	0.0885	0.0869	0.0853	0.0838	0.0823
−1.2	0.1151	0.1131	0.1112	0.1093	0.1075	0.1056	0.1038	0.1020	0.1003	0.0985
−1.1	0.1357	0.1335	0.1314	0.1292	0.1271	0.1251	0.1230	0.1210	0.1190	0.1170
−1.0	0.1587	0.1562	0.1539	0.1515	0.1492	0.1469	0.1446	0.1423	0.1401	0.1379
−0.9	0.1841	0.1814	0.1788	0.1762	0.1736	0.1711	0.1685	0.1660	0.1635	0.1611
−0.8	0.2119	0.2090	0.2061	0.2033	0.2005	0.1977	0.1949	0.1921	0.1894	0.1867
−0.7	0.2420	0.2389	0.2358	0.2327	0.2296	0.2266	0.2236	0.2206	0.2177	0.2148
−0.6	0.2743	0.2709	0.2676	0.2643	0.2611	0.2578	0.2546	0.2514	0.2483	0.2451
−0.5	0.3085	0.3050	0.3015	0.2981	0.2946	0.2912	0.2877	0.2843	0.2810	0.2776
−0.4	0.3446	0.3400	0.3372	0.3336	0.3300	0.3264	0.3228	0.3192	0.3156	0.3121
−0.3	0.3821	0.3783	0.3745	0.3707	0.3669	0.3632	0.3594	0.3557	0.3520	0.3483
−0.2	0.4207	0.4168	0.4129	0.4090	0.4052	0.4013	0.3974	0.3936	0.3897	0.3859
−0.1	0.4602	0.4562	0.4522	0.4483	0.4443	0.4404	0.4364	0.4325	0.4286	0.4247
−0.0	0.5000	0.4960	0.4920	0.4880	0.4840	0.4801	0.4761	0.4721	0.4681	0.4641
0.00	0.5000	0.5040	0.5080	0.5120	0.5160	0.5199	0.5239	0.5279	0.5319	0.5359
0.1	0.5398	0.5438	0.5478	0.5517	0.5557	0.5596	0.5636	0.5675	0.5714	0.5753
0.2	0.5793	0.5832	0.5871	0.5910	0.5948	0.5987	0.6026	0.6064	0.6103	0.6141
0.3	0.6179	0.6217	0.6255	0.6293	0.6331	0.6368	0.6406	0.6443	0.6480	0.6517
0.4	0.6554	0.6592	0.6628	0.6664	0.6700	0.6736	0.6772	0.6808	0.6844	0.6880
0.5	0.6915	0.6950	0.6985	0.7019	0.7054	0.7088	0.7123	0.7157	0.7190	0.7224
0.6	0.7257	0.7291	0.7324	0.7357	0.7389	0.7422	0.7454	0.7486	0.7517	0.7549
0.7	0.7580	0.7611	0.7642	0.7673	0.7704	0.7734	0.7764	0.7794	0.7823	0.7852
0.8	0.7881	0.7910	0.7939	0.7967	0.7995	0.8023	0.8051	0.8078	0.8106	0.8133
0.9	0.8159	0.8186	0.8212	0.8238	0.8264	0.8289	0.8315	0.8340	0.8365	0.8389
1.0	0.8413	0.8438	0.8461	0.8485	0.8508	0.8531	0.8554	0.8577	0.8599	0.8621
1.1	0.8643	0.8665	0.8686	0.8708	0.8729	0.8749	0.8770	0.8790	0.8810	0.8830
1.2	0.8849	0.8870	0.8888	0.8907	0.8925	0.8944	0.8962	0.8980	0.8997	0.9015
1.3	0.9032	0.9049	0.9066	0.9082	0.9099	0.9115	0.9131	0.9147	0.9162	0.9177

Appendix B (*continued*)

$d_{(n)}$	0	1	2	3	4	5	6	7	8	9
1.4	0.9192	0.9207	0.9222	0.9236	0.9251	0.9265	0.9279	0.9292	0.9306	0.9319
1.5	0.9332	0.9345	0.9357	0.9370	0.9382	0.9394	0.9406	0.9418	0.9429	0.9441
1.6	0.9452	0.9463	0.9474	0.9484	0.9495	0.9505	0.9515	0.9525	0.9535	0.9545
1.7	0.9554	0.9564	0.9573	0.9582	0.9591	0.9599	0.9608	0.9616	0.9625	0.9633
1.8	0.9641	0.9649	0.9656	0.9664	0.9671	0.9678	0.9686	0.9693	0.9700	0.9706
1.9	0.9713	0.9719	0.9726	0.9732	0.9738	0.9744	0.9750	0.9756	0.9761	0.9767
2.0	0.9772	0.9778	0.9783	0.9788	0.9793	0.9798	0.9803	0.9808	0.9812	0.9817
2.1	0.9821	0.9826	0.9830	0.9834	0.9838	0.9842	0.9846	0.9850	0.9854	0.9857
2.2	0.9861	0.9864	0.9868	0.9871	0.9875	0.9878	0.9881	0.9884	0.9887	0.9890
2.3	0.9893	0.9896	0.9898	0.9901	0.9904	0.9906	0.9909	0.9911	0.9913	0.9916
2.4	0.9918	0.9920	0.9922	0.9925	0.9927	0.9929	0.9931	0.9932	0.9934	0.9936
2.5	0.9938	0.9940	0.9941	0.9943	0.9945	0.9946	0.9948	0.9949	0.9951	0.9952
2.6	0.9953	0.9955	0.9956	0.9957	0.9959	0.9960	0.9961	0.9962	0.9963	0.9964
2.7	0.9965	0.9966	0.9967	0.9968	0.9969	0.9970	0.9971	0.9972	0.9973	0.9974
2.8	0.9974	0.9975	0.9976	0.9977	0.9977	0.9978	0.9979	0.9979	0.9980	0.9981
2.9	0.9981	0.9982	0.9982	0.9983	0.9984	0.9984	0.9985	0.9985	0.9986	0.9987
3.0	0.9987									

Source: Bookstaber (1981).

NOTES

CHAPTER 1

1. This is by no means a rigorous list; in fact, we are talking about what an economist would call a 'perfect market'.
2. This does not imply that it is impossible to ever beat the market. You may just be lucky (compared to the mean, 50 per cent will be and 50 per cent will be 'unlucky'). Then again, you may have succesfully persuaded the Chancellor to tell you the date and size of the next interest rate changes (in which case you have what is known as 'insider information').
3. Although, as we shall see in Chapter 3, some researchers believe that the market is rather more volatile than it should be if prices are determined by 'fundamental factors'.
4. Note that in the case of large target companies, this may be unlikely, particularly when one considers the international nature of acquisitions. Perhaps more typical is the case where a particular company has a special strategic value to a few potential bidders, as in the case of Jaguar.
5. Modern finance theory usually assumes that the sole objective is to maximise shareholder wealth. However, many of the prescriptions made in this book should prove useful even if one assumes a less 'purist' objective such as producing a satisfactory rate of return for shareholders.
6. A spin-off is where the shares in a subsidiary are distributed directly to the shareholders of the parent, the spun-off subsidiary then having its own stock market quotation, as in the case of Argos from BAT. Divestment covers the actual sale of a subsidiary, either to its existing management (*a management buyout*) or to another buyer.
7. Although there is some US and UK evidence to suggest that buyers might, on average, pay too much for firms they acquire; see Chapters 8 and 9 for a discussion of this.
8. Note that throughout this book £1 billion refers to £1,000 million.
9. To the author's knowledge, there is no current empirical research that reports on valuation methods used by any groups other than investment analysts. As regards the latter, Arnold and Moizer (1984) reports that PE valuation models are the most commonly used.

CHAPTER 2

1. This is also known as the *economic value*.
2. In fact, they should be the same. The company would be unwilling to sell the patent for less than its economic value, and no rational buyer (assuming he or she could not improve on the cash flow prospects arising from the patent) would pay more than the economic value for it.
3. The general formula for an annuity factor is given by:

$$[1 - (1 + r)^{-n}]/r$$

4. For an informal derivation of this, we take the annuity formula in note 3, and ask what happens when n becomes very large? The answer is that $(1 + r)^{-n}$ becomes very small, so the annuity factor reduces to $1/r$. Multiplying this by the cash flow gives us the perpetuity formula.
5. This is discussed in detail in Chapter 6.
6. Although we perform the calculation in total only, in practice readers may find it helpful to present each component in real terms, as this may give a better 'feel' for the reasonableness of the assumptions. In this case, rentals are decreasing in real terms, other costs are constant, whilst labour costs and property prices are increasing in real terms
7. This should not be surprising, because a kind of 'economic Darwinism' is at work; if one forecasting agency was that much better than the competition, it would presumably have put everyone else out of business by now.
8. A detailed description of the calculation is beyond the scope of this book, but for a clear explanation see Rutterford (1982).
9. Some of these figures are taken directly from the BZW publication, whilst others have been calculated from their data tables.
10. For future use, the annual US data published by Ibbotson and Associates and the UK data published by BZW are very useful sources of information on real rates of return on equities, gilts and treasury bills.
11. A more precise solution would allow for changing expectations of real rates of return and the actual (semi-annual) timing of the coupon payments. For a full explanation of spot rate calculation and gilt valuation see Rutterford (1982).
12. In fact, we do not need to look to South America to encounter such required rates of return; venture capitalists in the UK have frequently sought returns in excess of 30 per cent, partly to cover risk, and partly to cover a perceived optimism in forecasts supplied by company managers.

CHAPTER 3

1. This ignores any effects associated with takeovers, such as market anticipation and synergistic benefits.
2. In general, the evidence on weak form efficiency suggests that markets are efficient in this respect. As this literature is not directly relevant to company valuation, which normally requires a long term view, it is not reviewed here but a useful summary can be found in Elton and Gruber (1991).
3. Note that if market rules prohibit or restrict short sales, it may be possible to create a 'synthetic' short by using options (buying a 'put' and selling a 'call'). A brief explanation of options is given in Chapter 7.
4. However, in the very recent past, smaller companies have tended to perform

less well than larger ones; the UK Hoare–Govett Smaller Companies Index under-performed the *FT* All Share Index in 1989 and 1990.

5. See Basu (1983).
6. For a UK analysis, see Bulkley and Tonks (1989).
7. One way of doing this is to apply the market model methodology (outlined above) to detect abnormal price behaviour. Research into bid premia indicates that such effects may start to occur up to eight months prior to the announcement of any bid.
8. Besides the research into analysts' forecasts outlined above, Ou and Penman (1989) provides some interesting evidence on accounting numbers, price earnings ratios and returns.
9. This issue is addressed in Chapters 9 and 10.
10. As BZW point out in their 1991 Equity–Gilt Study, if one assumed a continuation of historical growth rates for IBM, in the 1970s it was possible to forecast that the company would soon be larger than the United States.
11. For a discussion of the calculation of RONI, see Chapter 8.
12. For an example of the FCF calculation applied to a UK plc, see Chapter 8.
13. The caution reflects the debate over gearing and weighted average cost of capital, which we explore in Chapter 6.
14. This is an important point which is analysed in detail (with examples) in Chapter 8.

CHAPTER 4

1. Note that in theory a change in the cost structure would lead to a change in the discount rate. This issue is dealt with in Chapter 6.
2. Empirical research suggests that forward rates are unbiased predictors of future spot rates, but not very accurate ones.
3. As we shall see in Chapter 6, more detailed economic risk exposure models that price exposure separately from interest rate risk, inflation risk, GDP growth risk and so on can be used.
4. Note that this assumes that the economic equilibria referred to earlier do not hold.
5. For a detailed discussion of these issues see Cooke (1988) and Eitman and Stonehill (1989).
6. For a discussion of this issue, see Eckl and Robinson (1990).
7. By contrast, short-term certain streams (such as receipts from contract payments) can be hedged through the forward market for virtually no cost.
8. Most good accountants have long been aware of this, but seem to come under considerable pressure to provide 'true' full unit cost figures for management use; in a recent survey, Coates and Longden (1989) quote an accountant as observing people have difficulty in accepting there are some things we cannot know.
9. See Gregory and Wallace (1992) for a discussion of this issue.
10. As an example, it will be difficult to sell artificial Christmas trees at a decent margin in January.
11. A basis point is 0.01 of 1 per cent.
12. A complicating factor is the dividends receivable on the shares; we ignore these here for simplicity, but this point is covered in Chapter 6.

CHAPTER 5

1. Whilst in an international context this is the meaning attributed to GAAP, in the United Kingdom it is more usually taken as meaning generally accepted accounting *practice*.
2. For an explanation of deferred tax accounting, see Chapter 4, Appendix III (p. 80).
3. For a detailed discussion of the provisions of the act and changes from previous legislation, see Pimm (1990).
4. Or, indeed, to estimate cost of capital – see Chapter 6.
5. All this assumes that the market sees the reality which lies behind the historic cost accounting numbers.
6. It should be noted that, in the United States, both discounted cash flow and the capital asset pricing model have been used in the context of regulatory cases.
7. Whilst the derivation of such rates is the subject of Chapter 6, this figure of 14 per cent is compatible with the average long-term return being generated on new investment (15 per cent), and the PE ratio chosen (see Chapter 3, Appendix, for an explanation).
8. Except, of course, for the purposes of negotiation, be this with potential bid targets or the Inland Revenue.
9. A discussion of this issue is beyond the scope of this text, but it should be noted that it is *unlikely* that an optimal management accounting solution is to price goods and services at market price; see, for example, Emmanuel *et al.* (1990) for a discussion.
10. For example, when Hanson acquired Beazer in 1991, it was widely thought that the former would gain some advantage by being able to replace Beazer's borrowing with debt carrying lower rates of interest.
11. This issue is discussed further in Chapter 8.
12. Asking 20 accountants to produce a fair allocation of overhead probably guarantees more than 20 different answers.
13. The estimation of profits on long-term contracts is highly subjective and has real implications for the reliability of reported profit numbers; enthusiasts of the PE valuation method need to be aware of this problem when forecasting earnings and multiples.
14. The calculation of such values is dealt with in Chapter 6.
15. Note that this is not always the case. A well managed firm in a declining industry may well have a q ratio less than 1.0 if there is no intention of replacing the assets but the economic value of these assets is greater than their realisable value.

CHAPTER 6

1. The epithet 'modern' is now looking a little dated, unless we allow some idea of post-modernism to enter into finance theory. The central principles were established by Harry Markowitz in the late 1950s.
2. For an excellent and detailed explanation, see Elton and Gruber (1991).
3. For a good, rigorous explanation of the necessary assumptions and derivation see Elton and Gruber (1991); for a more intuitive approach, Brealey and Myers (1991) is useful. We do not go into details here because virtually all competent finance texts cover this at length.

4. Note that the CAPM is very similar to the market model discussed in Chapter 3. Essentially, the CAPM tells us what value σ should have for any given level of β, whereas it is merely an intercept in the market model.
5. This paper goes on to suggest that dividend yields are a relevant factor in determining required returns in the United States; at the time of writing, there is no unambiguous evidence on whether or not this is true of the United Kingdom.
6. Academically inclined readers should see Roll (1977).
7. Papers worthy of further reading are Black and Scholes (1974), Fama and MacBeth (1973, 1974) and Stambaugh (1982); and also see Roll (1977) for a critique of such tests.
8. There are also other plausible versions of the CAPM (such as Merton's (1973) continuous time model), which are capable of explaining the empirical data; see Copeland and Weston (1988) for an explanation.
9. Note that market risk and specific risk cannot be simply added to give the total risk (variability) of BT's shares. In fact, the formula is:

$$\text{Variability}_{BT} = [(\beta^2_{BT} \times \text{Variability}^2_{Market}) + (\text{Specific risk}^2)]^{1/2}$$

10. Note that the practical use of the CAPM is not limited to calculating just discount rates. It has been used in US regulatory cases and recently (July 1991) The Office of Water Services (Ofwat) discussed the model extensively in their consultation paper on cost of capital (but concluded that a dividend discount model should be used), whilst the Water Services Association's reply relies entirely on the CAPM to arrive at a cost of capital for the industry.
11. A particular advantage of the APT is that it can be extended to a multi-period setting with less restrictive assumptions than the CAPM.
12. Duration is a measure of exposure to interest rate risk and is the weighted average maturity of the gilt (or equity); in other words the average time it takes to receive the cash flows of the gilt. For a zero coupon bond, duration is the maturity; for a coupon-bearing bond duration must be less than maturity (see Blake (1990) for a full explanation). Strictly speaking, equities do not have a 'duration' because income from them goes on (hopefully) for ever; however, the mechanics of the discounting process mean that future cash flows carry less and less weight so that duration can be approximated.
13. The BZW figures used here use a twenty-year gilt from 1962, and undated gilts before that.
14. Note that there is some dispute over whether geometric or arithmetic mean rates of return should be used. The view taken here is that because, in valuation, we are interested in long-term returns, a geometric mean is more appropriate. For a detailed explanation of why the geometric mean is the better of the alternatives, see Copeland et al. (1990) pp. 193–6. It should also be noted that whilst the weighted arithmetic mean is preferred for calculating cross-sectional averages (i.e. returns made across companies on any day/month/year), the analogy does not hold for calculating average returns through time, when the geometric mean is preferred.
15. Useful references here are Brealey and Myers (1991) and Copeland and Weston (1988).
16. Finance theory (if not its practice) is still something of a cottage industry.
17. Note also that our analysis assumes that gearing levels are not re-adjusted each period to take account of actually realised market values of debt and equity. See Strong and Appleyard (1992) for a discussion.

18. The alternative is to enter into the realms of general equilibrium models (see Ashton 1989b), or develop a UK version of the after tax CAPM following Brennan (1970) or Elton and Gruber (1991).

19. This situation is analysed in Dempsey (1991), where he calculates that given a corporation tax rate of 35 per cent, an after tax cost of debt of 10 per cent and no dividend payout, the effective corporation tax rate falls to 32 per cent. Note that while this is critical to a WACC calculation, with the APV approach the *actual* timing of the cash flows is modelled and therefore no adjustment is necessary.

20. Note that in a survey of seventy-nine top UK companies, conducted by Chris Higson of the London Business School, forty-two reported surplus ACT at the end of 1990 (*Financial Times*, 19 November 1991).

21. For example, at the end of June 1991, the 100 companies which constitute the FTSE index accounted for 72.4 per cent of the market capitalisation of the entire FTA Index (664 companies).

22. In fact, the effect in terms of returns appears to be a sharp upward shift for the lowest two deciles, experienced mainly in January, which suggests an association between the so-called January effect and the small companies effect.

23. Note that the PE methodology is no alternative, since we face exactly the same difficulty in finding an analogue earnings multiple.

CHAPTER 7

1. Actually, it turns out that even straight debt has option-like properties due to the concept of limited liability. These need not worry us unduly, but for an interesting analysis see Hsia (1981).

2. For a more detailed explanation see Brealey and Myers (1991) for a basic analysis and Bookstaber (1981) for a thorough explanation of the topic.

3. Readers who find continuous compounding and discounting difficult can probably get away with using the more familiar $1/(1 + r)^t$ without serious loss of accuracy (see note 4).

4. For those struggling with continuous compounding:

$$e^{-0.1 \times 78/365} = 1/e^{0.1 \times 78/365} = 0.9789$$

Note that the result of this calculation is not much different from the result obtained by using a discount factor based upon the daily equivalent rate of interest at 10 per cent pa $\{1/[1 + (0.1 \div 365)^{78}]\}$; however, the loss of accuracy from such an approximation increases through time and with increases in the rate of interest.

5. Copeland and Weston (1988).

6. Strictly speaking, we need the standard deviation of the log price relative – see Blake (1990) for a detailed explanation.

7. Strictly, the value of such a call option is the higher of the value assuming exercise immediately before the share goes ex-dividend, and the value of the option (allowing for the present value of dividends receivable) assuming exercise at maturity (see Elton and Gruber, 1991, pp. 595–6).

8. Readers requiring a more accurate analysis are referred to Ingersoll (1977).

9. Note that this implies: (i) that new debt is issued when conversion takes place; and (ii) that debt is issued throughout the life of the company so that target levels of gearing are maintained.

10. The version of the Black–Scholes model we are using here assumes that the dividend payments are known with certainty.

11. This borrowing margin seems in line with the average of those reported for other large UK firms in the recent 'Ofwat' report on cost of capital in the water industry (1991). There, an analysis of the borrowing margin over and above the relevant gilt rates was presented, with the premium ranging between 0.41 per cent for Unilever's AAA rated debt, to 2.01 per cent for Associated British Port's 'unrated' debt issue. In general, *Datastream* is a useful source for such data.

CHAPTER 8

1. Note that the British Vita accounts have been used because they form the base example in Parker (1979), to which readers unfamiliar with financial accounting were referred in the Preface.

2. See Chapter 3 (Appendix) for an explanation.

3. Overseas PLBs should be valued separately; issues relating to cost of capital for such operations are discussed in Chapter 6, whilst those relating to cash flow estimation are covered in Chapter 9.

4. For a detailed discussion of the area, together with an investigation of how accounting can be made to generate economically useful information Edwards *et al.* (1987) offers an excellent analysis.

5. The internal rate of return (IRR) is the discount rate that gives an NPV of zero; in general the IRR should not be used for investment decisions (see Brealey and Myers (1991) or any other competent finance text for an explanation of the problems of the IRR). The reason that RONI $\neq$ IRR is that the latter assumes that retained cash can be reinvested at the IRR (in this case 11.4 per cent), whereas the assumption made in our valuation is that in the interim surplus cash is reinvested at the company's opportunity cost of capital (this can either be achieved by the company or by the shareholders if all FCF is paid as dividends and a new capital issue is made at the time of asset replacement). For this reason, RONI is in fact a function of the opportunity cost of capital used.

6. It is always possible to find an implied PE ratio (in this case 14.6) but only once we already know the theoretical value of the firm. In other words, we cannot rationally determine *ex ante* what the PE multiple should be.

7. Note that this requirement is particularly onerous in the case of long life assets. In our example, if the asset life had been ten years we would have needed to project cash flows and earnings out to year 17 before we could reasonably have used a PE ratio dependent upon a steady-state.

8. See Chapter 5 for a discussion of this topic.

9. Preference shares are valued in a manner identical to that used to value debt. Preference dividends are not allowable against corporation tax.

CHAPTER 9

1. The *Independent on Sunday* (10 November 1991) quotes Rick Greenbury, the M&S chairman as admitting to shareholders 'The stores hadn't had a lick of paint for 30 years' (readers of this book, having read the comments on fixed asset inspection in chapter 4, will not, of course, be unaware of the state of what they are buying) and, 'You were right, we paid too much.'

2. See Cooke (1986) for a detailed description.
3. Note that this will not benefit most of the employees, as they remain exposed to the economics of the sector in which they work. In fact, given the performance record of many conglomerates, one might argue that they lose out as a result of such mergers.
4. For a discussion of this literature, see Dorward (1987).
5. As we shall see in Chapter 10, there are significant premia differences between cash and paper bids.
6. Note that this standard deviation is that of the present value of the project over the next five years; if most of the uncertainty is resolved by then, the standard deviation of the project's cash flows at the time of any decision to go ahead (i.e. in five years time) would be much lower than this.
7. See Brealey and Myers (1991, Chapter 21) for an explanation and detailed examples.
8. Forecasters sometimes find it difficult to elicit probability estimates from others (who typically may be the company managers). A useful device in such circumstances is for the forecaster to assign an arbitrary probability of equal likelihood to each scenario; this sometimes produces a horrified response from the recalcitrant party, who finds that he or she can provide a better estimate.
9. For a detailed discussion, see the *Venture Capital Supplement* (*Financial Times*, 6 November 1991).

CHAPTER 10

1. As we shall see, in many cases the real victims turn out to be the acquiring company's shareholders.
2. By this we mean the share prices before any takeover rumours have started to affect the market.
3. Note that as $\delta ER_A / \delta PE_{AV} > 0$ and $\delta'' ER_A / \delta PE_{AV} = 0$, ER_A is a linear function of PE_{AV} and, provided the expected value of the combined entity is greater than the value of the victim company (clearly a necessary condition for the takeover or merger to go ahead), $\delta ER_B / \delta PE_{AV} < 0$ and $\delta'' ER_B / \delta PE_{AV} > 0$, implying that the minimum exchange ratio will be a decreasing concave function of the expected price–earnings ratio.
4. Note that the earnings figure that actually appears in the first year's post-combination accounts will depend upon the timing of the takeover and whether any efficiency and synergy gains are realised in the period between takeover and the accounting year end.
5. This is only strictly true if we ignore tax effects. The point of this condition is to ensure that the share-for-share exchange (or indeed the cash alternative) is not a cosmetic offer, and that on average rational investors would not clearly prefer one to the other.
6. 'Zero' refers to abnormal performance; see the explanation of the market model in Chapter 3.
7. Note that the Franks *et al.* (1988) view contradicts the efficient markets hypothesis, whilst the latter view does not.
8. A similar fate befell underwriters and some small investors in the Government sale of BP shares.
9. Such a notion would appear to contradict the efficient markets hypothesis; however, in the case of the UK market, Bulkley and Tonks (1989) show that

an exploitable trading rule can be formulated, which appears to be capable of exploiting 'over-' and 'under-valuations' relative to treasury bills.

10. See Cooke (1986) for a discussion.

11. The cynical might wonder about the point of an accounting standard that essentially allows companies to do more or less what they like.

12. However, the ASB has tightened up on the treatment of goodwill when acquired subsidiaries are subsequently sold (FRED 1). The basic rule is that any profit or loss on disposal must be calculated after taking into account any goodwill on acquisition that has not been amortised through the profit and loss account.

CHAPTER 11

1. To be precise, the PE multiple arrived at by using the principles discussed in Chapter 8 is one that should be applied to the *prospective* earnings for the year following exit.

2. See Chapters 3 and 6 for an explanation.

REFERENCES

Abeysekera, S. P. and A. Mahajan (1987) 'A test of the APT in pricing UK stocks', *Journal of Business Finance and Accounting*, vol. 14, no. 3.

Altman, E. (1984) 'A further empirical investigation of the bankruptcy cost question', *Journal of Finance*, (September), pp. 1067–89.

Arnold, J. and P. Moizer (1984) 'A survey of the methods used by UK investment analysts to appraise investments in ordinary shares', *Accounting and Business Research*, (Summer).

Ashton, D. J. (1989a) 'Textbook formulae and UK taxation: Modigliani and Miller revisited', *Accounting and Business Research* (Summer), pp. 207–12.

Ashton, D. J. (1989b) 'The cost of capital and the UK imputation tax system', *Journal of Business Finance and Accounting*, vol. 16, no. 1.

Asquith, P. (1983) 'Merger bids, uncertainty and stockholder returns', *Journal of Financial Economics*, no. 11, pp. 51–83.

Asquith, P., R. F. Brunner and D. W. Mullins, Jr (1983) 'The gains to bidding firms from merger', *Journal of Financial Economics*, no. 11, pp. 121–39.

Auerbach, A. J. and D. Reishus (1987) 'The effects of taxation on the merger decision', *National Bureau of Economic Research, Inc*, Working Paper No. 2192.

Ball, R. and J. Bowers (1986) 'Distortions created by taxes which are options on value creation – the case of windfall profits taxes', *Paper presented to the BAA Conference, Aberystwyth* (March).

Barclays de Zoete Wedd Research (1991) *Equity–Gilt Study (January)*. Barclays de Zoete Wedd Research Ltd, London.

Bartley, J. W. and C. M. Boardman (1984) 'The replacement cost adjusted valuation ratio as a discriminator among target and nontarget firms', *University of Utah*, Working paper.

Basu, S. (1983) 'The relationship between earnings yield, market value and return for NYSE stocks: Further evidence', *Journal of Financial Economics*, vol. 12, June, pp. 129–56.

Beaver, W. H. and J. Manegold (1975) 'The association between market-determined and accounting-determined measures of systematic risk: Some further evidence', *Journal of Financial and Quantitative Analysis*, June, pp. 231–84.

Black, F. and M. Scholes (1974) 'The effects of dividend yield and dividend policy on common stock prices and returns', *Journal of Financial Economics*, vol. 1, pp. 1–22.

Blake, D. (1980) *Financial Market Analysis*, McGraw-Hill, London.

Bonbright, J. C. (1937) *Valuation of Property*, McGraw-Hill, New York.

Bookstaber, R. M. (1981) *Option Pricing and Strategies in Investing*, Addison-Wesley, Reading, MA.

Bookstaber, R. M. (1991) *Option Pricing and Investment Strategies*, 5th edn, Probus, Chicago.

Brealey, R. A. and S. C. Myers (1991) *Principles of Corporate Finance*, McGraw-Hill, New York.

Brennan, M. J. (1970) 'Taxes, market valuation, and corporate financial policy', *National Tax Journal*, vol. 25, pp. 417–27.

Buckley, A. (1981) 'Beta geared and ungeared', *Accounting and Business Research*, Spring.

Bulkley, G. and I. Tonks (1989) 'Are UK stock prices excessively volatile? Trading rules and variance bound tests', *Economic Journal*, December, pp. 1083–98.

Burmeister, E. and M. McElroy (1987), *'APT and Multifactor Asset Pricing Models with Measured and Unobserved Factors: Theoretical and Econometric Issues'*, Discussion Paper, Department of Economics, University of West Virginia and Duke University.

Burmeister, E. and M. McElroy (1988) 'Joint estimation of factor sensitivities and risk premia for the arbitrage pricing theory', *Journal of Finance*, vol. 43, July, pp. 721–33.

CAM-i (1988) *Management Accounting in Advanced Manufacturing Environments: A Survey* (CAM-i, London).

Canning, J. B. (1929) *The Economics of Accountancy: A Critical Analysis of Accounting Theory*, Ronald Press, New York.

Chappell, H. W. and D. C. Cheng (1984) 'Firms' acquisition decisions and Tobin's q ratio', *Journal of Economics and Business*, pp. 29–42.

Chen, N. R. Roll and S. Ross (1986) 'Economic forces and the stock market', *Journal of Business*, July, pp. 386–403.

Clark, J. J. (1985) *Business Merger and Acquisition Strategies*, Prentice Hall, Englewood Cliffs, NJ.

Coase, R. H. (1937) 'The nature of the firm', *Economica*, reprinted in 'Readings in Price Theory', American Economic Association, Irwin, New York, 1952.

Coates, J. B. and S. G. Longden (1989) *Management Accounting: The Challenge of Technological Innovation, 1*, Chartered Institute of Cost and Management Accountants, London.

Constantinides, G. (1980) 'Admissible uncertainty in the intertemporal asset pricing model', *Journal of Financial Economics*, March, pp. 71–86.

Cooke, T. E. (1986) *Mergers and Acquisitions*, Blackwell, Oxford.

Cooke, T. E. (1988) *International Mergers and Acquisitions*, Blackwell, Oxford.

Cooke, T. E. (1991) 'Price–earnings ratios and corporate financial reporting in Japan', paper presented to the *Conference on International Trends in Financial Reporting*, University of Exeter, March.

Cooke, T. E. and A. Gregory (1991) 'A UK empirical test of the Larson–Gonedes exchange ratio model', *International Accounting and Finance Research Group Discussion Paper*, No. 9011 University of Exeter.

Conn, R. L. and J. F. Nielsen (1977) 'An empirical test of the Larson–Gonedes exchange ratio determination model', *Journal of Finance*, vol. 32, No. 3, June.

Copeland, T. E. and J. F. Weston (1988) *Financial Theory and Corporate Policy*, Addison-Wesley, Reading, MA.

Copeland, T. E., T. Koller and J. Murrin (1990) *Valuation: Measuring and Managing the Value of Companies*, Wiley, New York.

Coulthurst, N. (1989) 'The new factory', *Management Accounting*, April, pp. 26–8.

Day, J. F. S. (1986) 'The use of annual reports by UK investment analysts', *Accounting and Business Research*, Autumn, pp. 295–307.

DeAngelo, H., L. DeAngelo and E. M. Rice (1984) 'Going private: the effects of a change in corporate ownership structure', *Midland Corporate Finance Journal*, Summer, pp. 35–43.

De Bondt, W. F. M. and R. Thaler (1985) 'Does the stock market overreact?', *Journal of Finance*, July, pp. 557–81.

Dempsey, M. J. (1991) 'Modigliani and Miller again revisited: The cost of capital under the assumption of unequal borrowing and lending rates', *Accounting and Business Research*, Summer, pp. 221–6.

Dimson, E. and P. Marsh (1984) 'An Analysis of brokers' and analysts' unpublished forecasts of UK stock returns', *Journal of Finance*, vol. 36, no. 5, December, pp. 1257–92.

Dimson, E. and P. Marsh (1989) 'The smaller companies puzzle', *Investment Analyst*, January.

Dimson, E. and P. Marsh (1991) *The Hoare Govett Smaller Companies Index 1991* (Hoare Govett Investment Research Ltd, London.

Dorward, N. (1987) *The Pricing Decision*, Harper and Row, London.

Eckbo, E. and H. Langohr (1986) '*Disclosure Regulations and Determinants of Takeover Premiums*', University of California working paper.

Eckl, S. and J. N. Robinson (1990) 'Some issues in corporate hedging policy', *Accounting and Business Research*, Summer.

Edwards, J., J. Kay and C. Mayer (1987) *The Economic Analysis of Accounting Profitability*, Clarendon Press, Oxford.

Eggington, D., J. Forker and M. Tippett (1989) 'Share option rewards and managerial performance: An abnormal performance index model', *Accounting and Business Research*, Summer, pp. 255–66.

Eitman, D. K. and A. I. Stonehill (1989) *Multinational Business Finance*, Addison-Wesley, Reading, MA.

Elton, E. J. and M. J. Gruber (1991) *Modern Portfolio Theory and Investment Analysis*, John Wiley, New York.

Emmanuel, C., D. Otley and K. Merchant (1991) *Accounting for Organizational Control*, Chapman & Hall, London.

Fama, E. F. (1970) 'Efficient capital markets: A review of theory and empirical work', *Journal of Finance*, May, pp. 383–417.

Fama, E. F. (1977) 'Risk-adjusted discount rates and capital budgeting under uncertainty', *Journal of Financial Economics*, August, pp. 3–24.

Fama, E. F. and J. MacBeth (1973) 'Risk, return and equilibrium: empirical tests', *Journal of Political Economy*, May/June, pp. 607–36.

Fama, E. F. and J. MacBeth (1974) 'Tests of the multi-period two-parameter model', *Journal of Financial Economics*, vol. 1, May. pp. 43–66.

Finnerty, J. E. (1976) 'Insiders and market efficiency', *Journal of Finance*, vol. 31, pp. 1141–8.

Firth, M. (1980) 'Takeovers, shareholders' return and the theory of the firm', *Quarterly Journal of Economics*, March, pp. 235–60.

Franks, J. R. and R. S. Harris (1989) 'Shareholders' wealth effects of corporate takeovers; the UK experience 1955–1985', *Journal of Financial Economics*, vol. 23, pp. 225–49.

Franks, J. R., R. S. Harris and C. Mayer (1988) 'Means of payment in takeovers: Results for the United Kingdom and the United States', in A. J. Auerbach (ed.) *Corporate Takeovers: Causes and Consequences*, University of Chicago Press, Chicago.

Galai, D. and R. W. Masulis (1976) 'The option pricing model and the risk factor of stock', *Journal of Financial Economics*, Jan–Mar, pp. 53–82.

Glosten, L. R. and P. R. Milgrom (1985) 'Bid, ask and transaction prices in a specialist market with heterogenously informed traders', *Journal of Financial Economics*, vol. 14, pp. 71–100.

Gregory, A. (1987) 'Divisional performance measurement with divisions as lessees of head office assets', *Accouting and Business Research*, Summer, pp. 241–6.

Gregory, A. (1988) 'A review of divisional manager performance evaluation', *Management Accounting*, January, pp. 38–43.

Gregory, A. (1991) 'Management accounting and information technology', in Williams B. C. and B. Spaul (eds) *I.T. and Accounting*, Chapman & Hall, London.

Gregory, A. and Wallace, R. S. O. (1992) 'A note on a role for cost allocation in decisions concerning central service provision', *Journal of Business Finance and Accounting*, vol. 19, no. 1, pp. 73–86.

Gregory, A., J. Matatko, I. Tonks and R. Purkiss (1992) *'UK Directors' Trading: A closer look'*, International Accounting and Finance Research Group Discussion Paper, University of Exeter, Exeter.

Grossman, S. J. and J. Stiglitz (1980) 'The impossibility of informationally efficient markets', *American Economic Review*, June, pp. 393–408.

Harris R. S. and D. Ravenscraft (1991) 'The role of acquisitions in foreign direct investment: Evidence from the US stock market', *Journal of Finance*, July, pp. 825–44.

Ibbotson, R. G. and R. Sinquefield (1986) *Stocks, Bonds, Bills and Inflation: 1986 Yearbook*, Ibbotson Associates Inc, Chicago.

Ingersoll, J. E. (1977) 'A contingent claims valuation of convertible securities', *Journal of Financial Economics*, vol. 4, May, pp. 289–322.

Jaffe, J. F. (1974) 'Special information and insider trading', *Journal of Business*, vol. 47, pp. 410–28.

Jensen, M. C. and R. S. Ruback (1983) 'The market for corporate control: The scientific evidence', *Journal of Financial Economics*, vol. 11, April, pp. 5–50.

Jensen M. C. et al. (1978) 'Symposium on some anomolous evidence regarding market efficiency', *Journal of Financial Economics*, vol. 6, June/September, pp. 93–330.

Kaplan, R. S. and A. A. Atkinson (1989) *Advanced Management Accounting*, Prentice Hall, Englewood Cliffs, NJ.

Kelly, G. and M. Tippett (1991) 'Economic and accounting rates of return: A statistical model', *Accounting and Business Research*, vol. 21, no. 84, pp. 321–30.

Krinsky, I., W. D. Rotenberg and D. B. Thornton, (1988) 'Takeovers – A synthesis', *Journal of Accounting Literature*, vol. 7, pp. 243–79.

Larson, K. D., and N. J. Gonedes (1969) 'Business combination: An exchange ratio determination model', *The Accounting Review*, October, pp. 720–8.

Lee, J. Y. (1987) *Managerial Accounting Changes for the 1990s*, Addison-Wesley, Reading, MA.

Lee, T. A. and D. P. Tweedie (1981) *The Institutional Investor and Financial Information*, ICAEW, London.

Limmack, R. J. (1991) 'Corporate mergers and shareholder wealth effects: 1977–1986', *Accounting and Business Research*, Summer, pp. 239–52.

Litzenberger, R. H. and K. Ramaswamy (1979) 'The effect of personal taxes and dividends on capital asset prices: Theory and empirical evidence', *Journal of Financial Economics*, vol. 7, pp. 163–96.

Luther, R. (1992) 'A review of Inland Revenue approved profit-related pay schemes', ICAEW, London.

Merton, R. C. (1973) 'An intertemporal capital asset pricing model', *Econometrica*, vol. 41, pp. 867–87.

Morck, R., A. Shleifer and R. W. Vishny (1990) 'Do managerial objectives drive bad acquisitions?', *Journal of Finance*, March, pp. 31–48.

Myers, S. C. (1984) 'The capital structure puzzle', *Journal of Finance*, July, pp. 581–2.

Newbould, G. D. (1970) *Management and Merger Activity*, Guthshead, Liverpool.

Nobes, C. and R. Parker (1991) *Comparative International Accounting*, Prentice Hall, Hemel Hempstead.

Ou, J. A. and S. H. Penman (1989) 'Accounting measurement, price–earnings ratio, and the information content of security prices', *Journal of Accounting Research*, vol. 27, Supplement, pp. 111–44.

Parker, L. D. (1979) 'Divisional performance measurement: Beyond an exclusive profit test', *Accounting and Business Research*, Autumn, pp. 309–19.

Pimm, D. (1990) 'Off balance sheet vehicles survive redefinition', *Accountancy*, June.

Pope, P. F., R. C. Morris and D. A. Peel (1990) 'Insider trading: Some evidence on market efficiency and directors' share dealings in Great Britain', *Journal of Business Finance and Accounting*, vol. 17, No. 3, pp. 359–80.

Pound, J. K., K. Lehn and G. Jarrell (1986) 'Are takeovers hostile to economic performance?', *Regulation*, September/October, pp. 25–56.

Roberts, K. and M. Weitzman, (1981) 'Funding criteria for research, development and exploration projects', *Econometrica*, September, pp. 1261–88.

Roll, R. (1977) 'A critique of the asset pricing theory's tests', *Journal of Financial Economics*, vol. 4, May, pp. 129–76.

Roll, R. (1986) 'The Hubris hypothesis of corporate takeovers', *Journal of Business*, April, 197–216.

Rubenstein, M. E. (1973) 'A mean–variance synthesis of corporate financial theory', *Journal of Finance*, March, pp. 167–81.

Rutterford, J. (1982) *Introduction to Stock Exchange Investment*, MacMillan, London.

Schiller, R. J. (1981) 'Do stock prices move too much to be justified by subsequent changes in dividends?', *American Economic Review*, June, pp. 421–36.

Schnabel, J. A. (1983) 'Beta geared and ungeared: An extension', *Accounting and Business Research*, Spring, pp. 128–30.

Scholes, M. and M. Wolfson (1990) 'The effects of changes in tax laws on corporate reorganisation activity', *Journal of Business*, No. 63, pp. S141–64.

Seyhun, H. N. (1986) 'Insiders' profits, costs of trading and market efficiency', *Journal of Financial Economics*, vol. 16, pp. 169–80.

Shapiro, A. C. (1989) *Mulinational Financial Management*, Allyn and Bacon, Needam Heights, MA.

Stamburgh, R. F. (1982) 'On the exclusion of assets from tests of the two-parameter model: A sensitivity analysis', *Journal of Financial Economics*, vol. 10, November, pp. 237–68.

Stark, A. W. (1990) 'Irreversibility and the capital budgeting process', *Management Accounting Research*, vol. 1 no. 3, pp. 167–80.

Strong, N. C. and T. R. Appleyard (1992) 'Investment appraisal, taxes and the security market line', *Journal of Business Finance and Accounting*, vol. 19, no. 1, pp. 1–24.

Warner, J. B. (1977) 'Bankruptcy costs: Some evidence', *Journal of Finance*, vol. 26, May, pp. 337–48.

Weetman, P. and S. J. Gray (1991) 'A comparative analysis of the impact of accounting principles on profits: The USA versus the UK, Sweden and the Netherlands', *Accounting and Business Research*, vol. 21, No 84, pp. 363–80.

Wheatley, S. (1988) 'Some tests of international equity integration', *Journal of Financial Economics*, vol. 21, pp. 177–212.

INDEX